Crime and Power

Pamela Davies · Tanya Wyatt

Crime and Power

palgrave
macmillan

Pamela Davies
Department of Social Sciences
Northumbria University
Newcastle upon Tyne, UK

Tanya Wyatt
Department of Social Sciences
Northumbria University
Newcastle upon Tyne, UK

ISBN 978-3-030-57313-3   ISBN 978-3-030-57314-0   (eBook)
https://doi.org/10.1007/978-3-030-57314-0

This Palgrave Macmillan imprint is published by the registered company Springer Nature Switzerland AG.
The registered company address is: Gewerbestrasse 11, 6330 Cham, Switzerland

Acknowledgements

We would like to thank Frank Pearce for his inspirational text *Crimes of the Powerful*. It has been the foundation of our undergraduate module of the same name and greatly influenced our research. Thanks as well to Steve Tombs for his inspirational work in this area and to Peter Francis for his collaboration on *Invisible Crimes and Social Harms*, another influential text.

Contents

About the Authors

Pamela Davies is a Professor of Criminology at Northumbria University, Newcastle, UK. She is a criminologist whose research focuses on gender, harm, crime and victimisation. Pam has published widely on the subject of victimisation and social harm and on how gender connects to matters of community safety. Pam is the series editor of the Palgrave Macmillan 'Victims and Victimology' book series (with Professor Matthew Hall). She is vice president of the British Society of Criminology (BSC) and the chair and founder of the BSC Victims Network.

Tanya Wyatt is a Professor of Criminology at Northumbria University, Newcastle, UK. She is a green criminologist specialising in wildlife crime, wildlife trafficking and non-human animal abuse and the intersections of organised crime, corporate crime and corruption. Her publications include *Wildlife Criminology* with Dr. Angus Nurse and numerous journal articles, book chapters and commissioned reports on wildlife and green crimes.

List of Figures

List of Tables

List of Boxes

Crime and Power: Introduction

1

Crime and Power

Welcome to *Crime and Power*. This is a unique textbook merging numerous criminological theories and concepts into an applied case-study-based learning and teaching guide. *Crime and Power* explores some of the central tenets essential to studying criminology at undergraduate level. These include:

- the processes of criminalisation and victimisation;
- causes and organisation of crime at individual, group, family, community, institutional and state levels;
- the intersectionalities of crime, offending, harm and victimisation;
- official and unofficial responses to crime, deviance, social and environmental harm; and
- social and cultural constructions and representations of crime, offending and victims

Although, like most textbooks, we investigate these central tenets, the scope of our textbook encompasses a wider conceptualisation of criminology than conventional mainstream books. A vast majority of textbooks (and scholarship) in criminology are solely focused on visible street crimes, for example. Our critical and victimological perspectives allow for a more far-reaching exploration and examination of explanations of a more expanded notion of harm and crime and approaches to their control. All of this is situated within a framework of power. Here, too,

© The Author(s) 2021
P. Davies, T. Wyatt, *Crime and Power*,
https://doi.org/10.1007/978-3-030-57314-0_1

our perspective is unique and again allows for a more far-reaching exploration of the relationships and dynamics between offenders and victims. As we will detail in depth in Chap. 2, we propose power is multifaceted and specific; hidden and visible; individual and collective. It underpins many harms and crimes and is essential to understand in order to prevent victimisation as well as deter offending.

Woven into the framework of power are numerous other perspectives and theoretical underpinnings. An important recurring perspective is that the activities, behaviours, acts and omissions of powerful 'elites' are not widely regarded as 'crime' (Croall 2011). In these instances, we draw on the key contributors who have challenged conventional notions of crime to be too narrow by mostly ignoring corporate crime in particular. These theorists include Croall (2011), Shover (2001), Levi (2014) and Nelken (2012) on white-collar crime and fraud and Slapper and Tombs (1999) and Tombs and Whyte (2003, 2007) on corporate criminality and health and safety crimes. Their research supports the notion that will be evident in this textbook's cases studies that 'non-conventional crime' rarely features as 'crime' or 'victimisation' in popular discourse, in political debates and in criminal justice processes.

Interlinked with power is theorising about the significance of patriarchal structures in society with reference to second-wave feminism and the authors who explored the implications of this criminologically (see, e.g., Gelsthorpe 2002; Heidensohn 2006; Heidensohn and Silvestri 2012, Smart 1977). We draw on feminist scholars in particular who have made important contributions such as Dobash and Dobash (1979, 1998, 2008) and, more recently, Groves and Thomas (2013) and Mooney (2000). Further structural components to power are explored when examining race and ethnicity. The questions of urban unrest and racial inequality, racial discrimination and violence and hate crime are investigated with a focus on contemporary examples and illustrations (Ray 2011; Ray and Smith 2001, 2004; Ray et al. 2003, 2004; Bowling 1990, 1993, 1999; Webster 2007, 2012).

Culture criminology informs our discussion around contemporary concerns regarding the culture of control, risk society and security threats to understand some forms of crime and victimisation in the twenty-first century. We draw on the seminal work of Sen (2005) and Siddiqui (2005) as well as the contemporary work of A. Hall (2014). We also investigate crime and power through the age-power dynamic, which can be an illuminating lens through which to conduct criminological and victimological inquiry (see Hall 2015, Muncie 2014). We address the conundrums associated with young people and children as victims and offenders, patterns and risks to offending and victimisation and theoretical explanations that have been postulated to account for the enduring age/crime curve to offending as well as the lack of attention given to the enduring age/victimisation curve to much victimisation.

The above perspectives and theoretical underpinnings by and large are applied to power in interpersonal more individual relationships. We utilise other perspectives and theories to support our discussion of power in relation to groups. For instance, we rely on the research of Pearce and Tombs (1998) and Croall (2001, 2007) when documenting the criminogenic nature of corporations. Corporate crime is an extensive and significant category of offending, so we also draw upon theorists contributing to the scholarship around green, health and safety and financial crimes in the case studies explored (Beirne and South 2007; Levi 2014; Tombs 2014; White, 2008, 2009; White and Heckenberg 2014). Also in investigating group power, we analyse historical and contemporary stereotypes of organised crime and test the utility of criminological theorising (Abadinsky 2007; Rawlinson 2009 and others) that ignores the often invisible nature of organised criminality and victimisation as well as the power dynamics that contribute to its emergence and persistence.

Corporations are not the only groups theorised to be criminogenic. The state, with its many facets, is responsible for a range of crimes and victimisations. Green and Ward (2004), Doig (2010) and Rothe (2009) propose in different ways what states are as well as conceptualisations of organisational deviance linked to why states can be criminogenic. States' criminogenic nature is expressed in state corruption, state-corporate crime, natural disaster response, police crime, state terror, torture, war crime and genocide (Green and Ward 2004; Short 2016). Other powerful groups committing crimes are seen in contemporary examples, such as Boko Haram and the Lord's Resistance Army. In these instances, we interrogate the power relationship between the groups, the victims and the state, which, as with other examples, links back to the intersectionalities of individual characteristics that are linked to victimisation.

Why Power Is Important

We are not the first to propose that power is essential in the commission of crime or in the omission of certain acts from consideration as crimes. Much of our inspiration regarding power comes from Pearce's (1976) *Crimes of the Powerful*, a ground-breaking text exposing the role of power in capitalist societies, particularly the United States. In capitalist countries, the control systems in place favour the ruling class by and large because it is the ruling class who have control over the legal system and therefore what is and is not defined in the law as crime. This results in criminalisation and visibility of working-class activities and not the harm brought about by the elite. In addition, the power of the elite maintains and reinforces their own domination and their values throughout larger society (Pearce 1976). They are able to deflect attention from their own acts and class conflict through their power over institutions like the media (we reserve a fuller discussion of the media for Chap. 3). Pearce (1976) argues there are paradoxes and contradictions between the ruling class' rhetoric and their actions in that they speak of integrity, for instance, but are unable to adhere to their own rules and regulations.

Pearce's description of how and where power existed was in contradiction to other scholars' perceptions of 1970s pluralism. Proponents of pluralism argued that there were no power elites and that power was actually widely distributed throughout communities in society. Power was always observable and directly applied, and only official people and political organisations should be the subjects of research into power (Pearce 1976). Yet, Pearce gave examples of clear power differentials in society. Different people in different groups dependent on their age, class, ethnicity, gender and so forth did not have the same ability to make rules or to apply them to other people. This was not isolated to the legal sphere, but to informal rules as well. Group social position, in part tied to these characteristics, imparts weapons and power to enforce their rules to different degrees.

Pearce criticised that attention was only given to those people who had broken the rules as defined by the powerful capitalist groups. So, only those labelled as 'deviant' by the ruling class were the focus of study. People who manipulated laws, violated ethical and moral standards, harmed people and were able to hide their actions and/or deflect the label and punishment went untouched. To reiterate, Pearce argued power was an essential aspect of perpetrating harm and that power enabled the elite to define crime, to enforce their dominant values, to keep the harm they committed hidden and to deflect scrutiny.

Pearce concentrated on this power dynamic in capitalist societies and advocated power was largely related to class. We, in contrast, propose power is not confined to the ruling class of capitalist economies. Power is a key component of harms and crimes in relation to capitalism, but also of other harms and crimes. We will provide evidence that power is also expressed in social, cultural and political ways that occur both inside and outside of capitalist societies and contexts. With respect to the latter—power imbalances in non-capitalist states—the pitfalls may not be the same in socialist states, but hierarchies have an uncanny prevalence across political systems. To understand fully global power relations, the nuanced elements of the class strata and potential for heightened internal class struggles in non-capitalist countries cannot be overlooked. Thus, we extend Pearce's analysis and expand upon the Marxist ideas of the sociological domination of the working class (see

Chap. 4). We are signalling here that our approach to the dynamics of power captures political processes and how democratic transformation attending to social and cultural features in societies is important.

In Part I, we provide proof that power also exists and is expressed differently in different individuals. The characteristics of a person—their class, gender, race, religion and/or age (in addition to others)—and the complex interplay of these and our diverse identities result in each of us potentially having power or being powerless and equally important result in the potential for us to be the focus of power from another individual or from a group. These ideas are further examined in the introduction to the series of chapters that form Part I of the book. In additional, power exists and manifests differently in different groups depending upon their structure and function. For instance, corporations and states are both powerful, but in different ways. This dual expression of power at the individual and group level is our unique approach to power that we hope will help you to understand and conceptualise why and how some crimes and harms happen.

As harms and crimes committed by the powerful, both individuals and groups, often remain hidden, research into them can be particularly challenging. With that in mind, the text utilises a case study approach that allows for examination of incidents and examples of crime and power, which are hard to gather information on. The reason for this approach is outlined below. First, however, a number of key words are foregrounded here as they recur throughout the chapters. Providing short uncontested definitions of these words/terms is not straightforward given the topic of this text features the conjoined dynamics of 'crime' *and* 'power'. Take the first word in the title of this book—perhaps the most common and key word in criminology—'crime' as an example. Definitional issues abound and what constitutes crime is vehemently contested across time, space and place. Who constructs dominant definitions of crime is, we contend, of huge significance. Notwithstanding the caveats of doing so however, we attempt to lay down some direction for the readers' understanding of several keywords. The reader will find these terms defined in context in the relevant chapters.

Useful Terminology

Power—for criminologists and readers of this textbook, the word power ought to conjure up synonyms such as 'control', 'dominance', 'rule' and' supremacy'. However, with your criminological imagination in full swing, you will appreciate there are many facets to the concept of power, and this textbook helps you unpack some of the key power dynamics at work in society that produce and reproduce crime, harm and injustice. See Chap. 2 'What Is Power and Who Are the Powerful?' for a fuller discussion.

Invisible crime—criminal acts that are not visible. Different crimes have different degrees of visibility and invisibility. Many criminology texts refer to the so-called dark figure of crime, which refers to unreported and unrecorded crime, and these factors have a bearing on what crime is transparent, what crimes are relatively visible and what crime is hidden. The factors giving rise to the different degrees of visibility and invisibility of crime are further discussed in Chap. 3 'The Invisibility of Crimes of the Powerful'.

Gender—a cultural concept relating to the social classification of 'masculine' and feminine'. Gender is part of our identity and alludes to the differences between men and women that are socially constructed and sustained. For further discussion, see the introduction to Part I of the book *Individual Characteristics and Power Dynamics* and Chap. 7 'Gender and Power'.

Environmental crime and green crime—the former is mostly used as a legal term for crimes against the environment. The crime element involves the application of state sanctions for illegal activity (acts and omissions determined to be criminally harmful under the law). See Chap. 9 'Corporations' for an extended discussion of environmental crime and power. The latter may also be used to discuss environmental crime but is also used to refer to environmental *harms* that may incorporate wider definitions of crime than are provided by strictly legal definitions. Examples of green harm include animal rights abuses and state-corporate land grabs, through to the victimisation of indigenous peoples, environmental injustices and the consequences wrought by extractive industries. The study of green crime covers environmental harms, environmental laws, and environmental regulation and crime prevention.

Corporate crime—sometimes also called organisational crime, corporate crime can take on many forms, the common feature is the making use of the workplace and legitimate employment to maximise rewards for illegal profit. The illegality might include illegal acts or omissions, punishable by the state under administrative, civil or criminal law. In Chap. 9, 'Corporations', the criminogency of corporations is examined using case studies to illustrate the uses and abuse of power in the commission of corporate crime.

State—a much disputed and contested term in general and for criminologists likewise. A definition of *the* state is often synonymous with the government or a kingdom/country. Chapter 11 begins by exploring what a state is and what state crimes are in a fuller exposition—through case study examples—of various dimensions of state power. See also war crime below.

Genocide—genocide is often thought to be the extermination of a whole group of peoples. In Chap. 11, 'State Crime', a section on 'Genocide' explains that though this may be the end goal, genocides are more complex than this and may also include cultural genocide and ecocide.

Victim—can be considered a label or identity. As such, 'victim' is a social artefact, constructed by different actors in different contexts. However, it is usually associated with crime and relates to someone suffering some kind of misfortune. See our caveats with regard to the term victimisation below.

Victimisation—whilst a typical dictionary definition is likely to refer to the action of singling someone out for cruel, ill or unjust treatment, context is important as is the *who* and *what*. Criminal victimisation narrows the definition of victimisation to human individuals as criminally victimised. In this text, we adopt a broader and more expansive understanding of the term victimisation such that humans, non-human species and environments can experience persecution, degradation and harm that constitutes victimisation. For a follow-up discussion, see Chap. 3 'The Invisibility of Crimes of the Powerful'.

War crime—a war crime has 'official' definitions. As criminologists, we ask questions about from where and whom do such definitions come. One such example is that adopted by the United Nations, which defines war crimes as violations of international humanitarian law. In Chap. 11, 'State Crime', a section on 'War Crime' considers the military arm of the state and its use of force in armed conflict and war.

Militias and insurgents—small groups of non-state actors that are challenging the state. Other terms used to refer to militias and insurgents are rebels, guerrillas and terrorists. In Chap. 12, the subtle distinctions between militias and insurgents are examined through case studies that tap into the particular power dynamics at work.

The Case Study Approach

The case study is a unique, versatile and, we argue, necessary approach to studying and uncovering crimes of the powerful. This is because traditional sources of data around crime, such as police statistics and victims surveys, are not available or appropriate to this avenue of inquiry. In addition, research into powerful people and entities may not be research that would receive funding, so other more costly methods of research may not be possible. A case study—an in-depth use of a single incident to critically explore theoretical and conceptual frameworks—is therefore essential to bring to light the range of powerful offenders and invisible victims.

Case study designs have been used across a number of disciplines, but particularly in the social sciences (Schwandt and Gates 2018). Their use in social sciences has a long and varied history, with a growing reputation as an effective methodology to investigate and understand complex issues in real-world settings. Case study research is a complex and far-reaching approach to doing criminological research, and there is not one way to deliver it. Case studies can be assembled utilising a range of methods and types of data collection (interviews, observations, focus groups, artefact and document review, questionnaires and/or surveys) and analysis (methods of analysis vary and depend on data collection methods and cases) to bring depth and breadth to the topic area under review. With a background in the emerging Chicago school of criminology, utilising a range of data, methods of investigation and approaches to analysis and interpretation, sociological and criminological case study research usually focuses on a detailed case or cases. The case is the object of the case study, the entity of interest or unit of analysis. The case might be an initiative or programme, an individual, a group, a social situation, organisation, event, phenomena or process. Sometimes the case or cases are deliberately selected as studies of deviant individuals, groups or *cause celebre* inspired through activist interest groups as part of the pressure to generate maximum impact for the cause. Other case studies might be very personal and sobering and based on oneself or the impact on communities. See, for example, Davies' (2011) case study of the impact of a child protection investigation and her more recent case study examination (2014) of the closure of an aluminium plant in the north-east of England serving to illustrate the contemporary tensions around social and environmental justices and victimisations. Case studies may focus on life-changing experiences of individuals. For example, Alice Sebold, a victim of rape, laid out the core of her experience in *Lucky* (1999), and Susan Brison was a victim of rape and attempted murder. *Aftermath: Violence and the Remaking of the Self* (2002) is the book in which Susan draws on her experience of rape and living through the consequences. She also invokes the testimonies of other survivors of violence, rape, genocide and the Holocaust.

Kathleen Daly (2018) has recently examined the use of case study methods in criminological research. By way of contextualisation, her discussion refers to three authors and their use of the case study method in education (Yazan 2015). The first, Yin, is an oft-cited author of the case study with his text on this topic having moved into its sixth edition in 2018 (1984/2018). This approach to case study research is positivist; he recommends a well-prepared design at the start of the research, which focuses on testing a theory or hypothesis. This deductive approach to case study research is well-suited for programme or policy evaluation. Daly goes on to explain that, by comparison, texts by Merriam (1998) and Stake (1995) view knowledge as constructed or interpreted rather than discovered. Thus, case study researchers have different assumptions about how best to study the social world and build knowledge. Nevertheless, despite variation in the approaches of the different exponents of a case study, there are characteristics common to most of them. Case study research is consistently and, as illustrated in this section, aptly described as a versatile form of qualitative inquiry most suitable for a comprehensive, holistic and in-depth investigation of a complex issue (a phenomena, event, situation, organisation, programme, individual or group) in context.

What Is a Case Study?

Above, we state what a case study is understood to be in the context of studying crime and power. A recent definition of a case study appears in a textbook on doing criminological research. In that text, such a study is described as an approach that uses in-depth investigation of a single 'case' or several 'cases'. Data may derive from individuals, social activities, groups or organisations (Davies and Francis 2018). An even shorter definition suggests a case study is 'the detailed examination of a single example of a class of phenomena' (Abercrombie et al. 1984: 34). Abercrombie et al. (1984) propose that such studies are useful in the early stages of research to generate hypotheses, and whilst such studies cannot provide reliable data that can be applied to the broader category or phenomena under study, they can be tested by gathering many more cases. The point about reliability signals there are limitations. Flyvbjerg (2006) offers a detailed assessment of case studies arguing they have very particular strengths whilst acknowledging that they do indeed have limitations. Before exploring what these are however, we have some further justifications for adopting the case study throughout the pages of this book. In this section, so far we have begun to stress that *context* is important to understanding the case in the study. A common feature to the case study method is studying the case/s in context, in its real-life setting or natural environment. Contextual variables include political, economic, social, cultural, historical and/or organisational factors. Let us now consider how these contextual factors are captured by the case study approach by further exploring the merits of the case study given that application of the case study method is a major feature of this book.

The Case for the Case Study in Criminological Research

Case study research 'has gained a spotlight within social science' (Yin 1984/2018: xv). However, as Flyvbjerg (2011) has noted, the case study has not always been held in high regard within the academy. Flyvbjerg uses this as a spur to counter the criticisms and misunderstandings about the case study method and to build the case for its wider use and acceptance. He commences his dismantling of the paradox of the case study method by confronting head on what counts as knowledge. General theoretical knowledge (context-independent theory) has been valued more than concrete practical knowledge (context-dependent) (Flyvbjerg (2006). Social science research may be considered less valuable because it has not generated context-independent theory. A context-independent theory would be a theory that explained a phenomenon regardless of the specific circumstances. This is true of criminology as well. No single theory exists to explain all the causes of crime. There is not even a theory that is absolutely 100% accurate in a small number of cases. This should not be taken as a criticism or as a weakness of the social sciences or of criminology. The lack of context-independent theory is more a reflection that human behaviour is not bound by simple rules (Flyvbjerg 2006). We need research techniques that enable us to unpick reality in nuanced complex ways. The strength of social sciences and of the case study approach in criminological research is to develop concrete, context-*dependent* knowledge, which can strive to make sense of the nuance and the complexity. Flyvbjerg (2006, 2011) argues this is the very heart of becoming an expert. We are not saying that quantitative, rule-based or context-independent knowledge is not valuable (nor is Flyvbjerg), but that for research into areas such as those explored in this textbook, the case study provides the best method.

We have already alluded to the problem that case studies cannot provide reliable data that can be applied to the broader category or phenomena under study (Abercrombie et al. 1984). This speaks to the problem not only of reliability, but also generalisability. The lack of generalisability means that case studies alone do not contribute to scientific knowledge (Flyvbjerg 2006). Yet, it is possible to generalise in some instances from one example. More important perhaps is that the ability to generalise is over-valued and the knowledge of specific examples may be equally valuable (Flyvbjerg 2006, 2011). Furthermore, as we have also mentioned above, the case study is useful to generate hypotheses and to test hypotheses as well as perform other research functions such as comparative analysis and primary data collection.

Perhaps the biggest misunderstanding of case studies is that they are biased towards the researcher's preconceived beliefs about the topic under examination. Flyvbjerg (2006, 2011) argues that there is no evidence that case studies are any more biased than other forms of research. In fact, they may be more prone to rejection of preconceptions rather than verification of them. Finally, case studies can be difficult to summarise. Flyvbjerg (2006) counters this too, arguing that summarising is not always warranted, but many phenomena should be captured in their entirety.

And so, to cement our case for the case study in criminological research, we briefly return to the useful chapter by Kathleen Daly (2018) that we drew on earlier. Within this chapter, Daly reminds us of some evocative examples of classic case studies including: Erving Goffman's *Asylums* (1961), which examined 'the inmate's situation' from different vantage points; Carol Stack's (1974) *All Our Kin: Strategies for Survival in a Black Community*—a case study of poor black families in a US Midwest city in the late 1960s; and Stanley Cohen's (1972) *Folk Devils and Moral Panics*—a case study of the emergence and decline of the Mods and Rockers as a social phenomenon in 1960s England. Daly also provides a rich variety of examples of contemporary case studies on topics linked to crime, disorder and justice, and readers are directed to this resource for further inspiration.

Our Case Studies

As indicated, for our purposes, a case study is the study of a discrete harm or crime or group of harms or crimes. The harm or crime is usually large scale in nature. This may be that it has caused a significant financial loss or resulted in a large number of victims. These victims may be consumers, employees and/or local residents. It is likely that the harm or crime may have some symbolic, political or popular effect. For instance, from the late 1950s through the 1960s, the birth defects stemming from proscribing Thalidomide to pregnant women could be used as a case study; from the 1970s, the poor design of the Ford Pinto petrol tank; from the 1980s, the explosion of the Union Carbide factory in Bhopal, India; from the 1990s, the Rwandan genocide and from 2010, the Deepwater Horizon oil spill caused by British Petroleum in the Gulf of Mexico.

When compiling a case study, it is beyond just stating the facts of the chosen research area. Case study designs address a wide range of questions that ask why, what and how of an issue allowing criminological researchers to explore, explain, describe, evaluate and theorise about complex issues in context. It may be helpful to think of it as a social science reconstruction of events and processes (Flyvbjerg

2006) surrounding a particular harm/crime or group of harms/crimes. Within the reconstruction, the case studies presented within this textbook focus on the power dynamics between the ranges of actors who were involved. We analyse the relationships and structures that enable the harm or crime to take place as well as to remain hidden. As there is more often than not a lack of official data and statistics to support research into crimes of the powerful, often the information used is based on intimate accounts of witnesses, whistle blowers or journalists (thus, many of our sources are not from academia). The result is a detailed case history that enables the understanding of the process by which harms and crimes emerge, occur and are responded to and how power is critical to that process. The collective outcome of the case studies is that they lead to a critically informed in-depth understanding of behaviours, processes, practices and relationships.

The Layout

The textbook has three sections. This introduction, Chaps. 2 and 3 make up the first section that provides the rationale for the content and structure of the textbook as well as all of the background information that underpins the analyses in the remaining chapters. There are then Parts I and II, which explore individual and group power, respectively. Each chapter explores case study or case examples and contains a reference list as well as suggestions for further reading. In addition, there are boxes and tables of highlighted information to make them easy to refer to. There are also summaries and study questions at the end of each chapter. An overview of these parts and the individual chapters are as follows.

This first substantive chapter—'What Is Power and Who Are the Powerful?'—begins to unpick the core theoretical and conceptual frameworks, which the book is based upon. It focuses on power and its relationships to crime, offending, criminalisation, crime control and the regulation and responses to crime, harm and offending. After reading Chap. 2, we want you to be able understand

- what power is (the ability to influence and/or control);
- who has power (individuals such as men, the upper class and so forth as well as corporations and other groups);
- where power is concentrated (behind closed doors, historically embedded in some groups, North vs. South, etc.);
- why power is located in certain places (historical and institutional explanations) and;

- how power manifests (what crimes do the police focus on and record, and as further discussed in Chap. 3, what does the media cover, etc.).

Then in Chap. 3, 'Invisibility', we present one of the core theoretical underpinnings of our perspective on power. We explain that the enabling potential of power is expressed in the seven features of invisibility (Jupp et al. 1999). These seven features make it possible for powerful individuals and groups to avoid detection, prosecution, punishment and accountability. In this chapter, first, we draw on this framework (Jupp et al. 1999), which proposes that the relative absence of knowledge, statistics, research, theory, control, politics and panic (as compared with more traditional crime types and offenders) enables powerful entities to remain hidden. The broader role of the media is further examined in relation to the seventh feature alongside Cohen's conceptualisation of moral panics. Second, invisible crimes can be categorised into typologies with similar characteristics (Davies et al. 2014). These spatial typologies are as follows: the body, home, street, environment, suite, state and virtual space. Together, these conceptualisations of the features of invisibility and spatial typologies provide a framework for the investigation of the range of crimes of the powerful in the individual chapters belonging to Parts I and II.

Reflecting our unique perspective on power being expressed by both individuals and groups, our textbook is broken down into two parts exploring specific examples of this. Part I—'Individual Characteristics and Their Power Dynamics'—investigates the existence of power in interpersonal relationships. The personal characteristics of an individual can play a role in their offending and victimisation, and the visibility of both. The preamble to this part of the book also expands on the important sociological concept of intersectionality and the theoretical construct class-race-gender and the significance of these formulations in the context of criminology.

We discuss the following individual personal characteristics though there are others as well:

- class and status (Chap. 4),
- race and ethnicity (Chap. 5),
- religion (Chap. 6),
- gender (Chap. 7) and
- age (Chap. 8).

We investigate each of these characteristics in relation to power and the resulting crime and victimisation through theoretical and conceptual exploration as well as in-depth case study examination through contemporary examples.

In Part II—'The Power of Groups and the Doing of Crime'—we explore crime and victimisation that are not carried out by individuals upon other individuals, though, as we have mentioned, this is often the focus of conventional criminology. We argue that much crime—and a significant amount of it that is hidden—is perpetrated by four main groups and/or institutions that injure numerous people (though other groupings may be feasible, we propose these four categories account for the majority of hidden victimisations). As we explore, this is possible because of the power of these groups to remain outside of the law, to construct and influence what crime is, and to distract and deflect attempts to hold them accountable. Those that they victimise may be targeted for their individual characteristics, thus linking the intersectionalities of Part I to the discussion of victimisation in Part II. The groups that we will investigate are as follows:

- corporations (Chap. 9),
- organised crime (Chap. 10),
- the state (Chap. 11) and
- militias and insurgents (Chap. 12).

The final chapter is a summary of the key themes that underpin the case study examples and illustrations that we have explored in Chaps. 4–12. We summarise these in the context of power, the powerful and in connections with our 'invisibility' thesis as well as our newer conceptualisations surrounding spatial typologies of victimisation and harm (Davies et al. 1999, 2014). In concluding this text, we take a glimpse into the future and consider the terrain of the crimes of the powerful in the local, regional, national, international and global contexts of the twenty-first-century world.

References

Abadinsky, H. (2007). *Organized Crime* (8th ed.). Belmont, CA: Wadsworth/Thomson Learning.

Abercrombie, N., Hill, S., & Turner, B. (1984). *The Penguin Dictionary of Sociology*. London: Penguin.

Beirne, P., & South, N. (Eds.). (2007). *Issues in Green Criminology*. Cullompton: Willan.

Bowling, B. (1990). Conceptual and Methodological Problems in Measuring 'Race' Differences in Delinquency. *British Journal of Criminology, 30*(4), 483–493.

Bowling, B. (1993). Racial Harassment and the Process of Victimisation: Conceptual and Methodological Implications for the Local Crime Survey. *British Journal of Criminology, 33*(1), 231–250.

Bowling, B. (1999). *Violent Racism: Victimisation, Policing and Social Context*. Oxford: Clarendon Press.

Brison, S. J. (2002). *Aftermath: Violence and the Remaking of the Self*. Princeton: Princeton University Press.

Cohen, S. (1972). *Folk Devils and Moral Panics*. London: Granada Publishing Limited.

Croall, H. (2001). *Understanding White-collar Crime*. Buckingham, UK: Open University Press.

Croall, H. (2007). Victims of White-Collar and Corporate Crime. In P. Davies, P. Francis, & C. Greer (Eds.), *Victims, Crime and Society*. London: Sage.

Croall, H. (2011). *Crime and Society in Britain* (2nd ed.). London: Longman.

Daly, K. (2018). Using Case Study Methods in Criminological Research. In P. Davies & P. Francis (Eds.), *Doing Criminological Research* (3rd ed., pp. 475–498). London: Sage.

Davies, P. (2011). The Impact of a Child Protection Investigation: A Personal Reflective Account. *Child & Family Social Work, 16*, 201–209.

Davies, P. (2014). Green Crime and Victimisation: Tensions between Social and Environmental Justice. *Theoretical Criminology, 18*(3), 300–316.

Davies, P., & Francis, P. (Eds.). (2018). *Doing Criminological Research* (3rd ed.). London: Sage.

Davies, P., Francis, P., & Jupp, V. (Eds.). (1999). *Invisible Crimes, Their Victims and Their Regulation*. Basingstoke, UK: Macmillan.

Davies, P., Francis, P., & Wyatt, T. (Eds.). (2014). *Invisible Crimes and Social Harms*. Basingstoke, UK: Palgrave Macmillan.

Dobash, R. E., & Dobash, R. P. (1979). *Violence Against Wives: A Case Against Patriarchy*. Shepton Mallet: Open Books.

Dobash, R. P., & Dobash, R. E. (1998). *Rethinking Violence Against Women*. London: Sage.

Dobash, R. P., & Dobash, R. E. (2008). Women's Violence to Men in Intimate Relationships: Working on the Puzzle. In K. Evans & J. Jamieson (Eds.), *Gender and Crime: A Reader*. Maidenhead: Open University Press.

Doig, A. (2010). *State Crime*. Cullompton: Willan.

Flyvbjerg, B. (2006). Five Misunderstandings about Case Study Research. *Qualitative Inquiry, 12*(2), 219–245.

Flyvbjerg, B. (2011). Case Study. In N. K. Denzin & Y. S. Lincoln (Eds.), *The Sagehandbook of Qualitative Research* (4th ed., pp. 301–316). Thousand Oaks, CA: Sage.

Gelsthorpe, L. (2002). Feminism and criminology. In M. Maguire, R. Morgan & R. Reiner (Eds), *The Oxford Handbook of Criminology* (3rd ed.). Oxford: Clarendon Press.

Goffman, E. (1961). *Asylums*. Garden City, NY: Anchor Books.

Green, P., & Ward, T. (2004). *State Crime: Governments, Violence and Corruption*. London: Pluto Press.

Groves, N., & Thomas, T. (2013). *Domestic Violence and Criminal Justice*. London: Routledge.

Hall, A. (2014). Honour Crimes. In P. Davies, P. Francis, & T. Wyatt (Eds.), *Invisible Crime and Social Harms* (pp. 81–101). Basingstoke, UK: Palgrave Macmillan.

Hall, M. (2015). Older People, Crime and Victimisation. In P. Davies, P. Francis, & C. Greer (Eds.), *Victims, Crime and Society* (2nd ed.). London: Sage.

Heidensohn, F. (2006). *Gender and Justice.* Cullompton: Willan.

Heidensohn, F., & Silvestri, M. (2012). Gender and Crime. In M. Maguire, R. Morgan, & R. Reiner (Eds.), *The Oxford Handbook of Criminology* (5th ed.). Oxford: Oxford University Press.

Jupp, V., Davies, P., & Francis, P. (1999). The Features of Invisible Crimes. In P. Davies, P. Francis, & V. Jupp (Eds.), *Invisible Crimes: Their Victims and their Regulation.* Basingstoke: Macmillan Publishers.

Levi, M. (2014). Regulating Fraud Revisited. In P. Davies, P. Francis, & T. Wyatt (Eds.), *Invisible Crime and Social Harms* (pp. 221–243). Basingstoke, UK: Palgrave Macmillan.

Merriam, S. B. (1998). *Qualitative Research and Case Study Applications in Education.* San Francisco: Jossey-Bass.

Mooney, J. (2000). *Gender, Violence and the Social Order.* London: Macmillan.

Muncie, J. (2014). *Youth & Crime* (4th ed.). London: Sage.

Nelken, D. (2012). Chapter 21 White Collar and Corporate Crime. In M. Maguire, R. Morgan, & R. Reiner (Eds.), *The Oxford Handbook of Criminology* (5th ed.). Oxford: Oxford University Press.

Pearce, F. (1976). *Crimes of the Powerful.* London: Pluto Press.

Pearce, F., & Tombs, S. (1998). *Toxic Capitalism: Corporate Crime and the Chemical Industry.* Aldershot: Ashgate.

Rawlinson, P. (2009). Understanding Organised Crime. In C. Hale, K. Hayward, A. Wahidin, & E. Wincup (Eds.), *Criminology Second Edition* (pp. 323–342). Oxford: Oxford University Press.

Ray, L. (2011). *Violence & Society.* London: Sage.

Ray, L., & Smith, D. (2001). Racist Offenders and the Politics of 'Hate Crime'. *Law and Critique, 12,* 203–221.

Ray, L., & Smith, D. (2004). Racist Offending, Policing and Community Conflict. *Sociology, 38*(4), 681–699.

Ray, L., Smith, D., & Wastell, L. (2003). Understanding Violent Racism. In B. Stanko (Ed.), *The Meanings of Violence.* London: Routledge.

Ray, L., Smith, D., & Wastell, L. (2004). Shame, Rage and Violent Racism. *British Journal of Criminology, 44*(3), 350–368.

Rothe, D. (2009). *State Criminality: The Crime of All Crimes.* Lanham: Lexington Books.

Schwandt, T. A., & Gates, E. F. (2018). Case Study Methodology. In N. K. Denzin & Y. S. Lincoln (Eds.), *The Sage Handbook of Qualitative Research* (5th ed., pp. 301–316). Thousand Oaks, CA: Sage.

Sebold, A. (1999). *Lucky.* New York: Scribner.

Sen, P. (2005). 'Crimes of Honour', Value and Meaning. In L. Welchman & S. Hossain (Eds.), *Honour: Crimes, Paradigms and Violence against Women* (pp. 42–63). London: Zed Books.

Short, D. (2016). *Redefining Genocide: Settler Colonialism, Social Death and Ecocide.* London: Zed Books.

Shover, N. (Ed.). (2001). *Crimes of Privilege: Readings in White-collar Crime.* Oxford: Oxford University Press.

Siddiqui, H. (2005). There is No 'Honour' in Domestic Violence, Only Shame! Women's Struggles against "Honour" Crimes in the UK. In L. Welchman & S. Hossain (Eds.), *Honour: Crimes, Paradigms and Violence against Women*. London: Zed Books.

Slapper, G., & Tombs, S. (1999). *Corporate Crime*. London: Longman Criminology Series.

Smart, C. (1977). *Women, Crime and Criminology: A Feminist Critique*. London: Routledge and Kegan Paul.

Stack, C. (1974). *All Our Kin: Strategies for Survival in a Black Community*. New York: Basic Books.

Stake, R. E. (1995). *The Art of Case Study Research*. Thousand Oaks: SAGE Publications.

Tombs, S. (2014). Health and Safety 'Crimes' in Britain: The Great Disappearing Act. In P. Davies, P. Francis, & T. Wyatt (Eds.), *Invisible Crime and Social Harms* (pp. 199–220). Basingstoke, UK: Palgrave Macmillan.

Tombs, S., & Whyte, D. (Eds.). (2003). *Unmasking the Crimes of the Powerful: Scrutinizing States and Corporations*. New York: Peter Lang.

Tombs, S., & Whyte, D. (Eds.). (2007). *Safety Crimes*. Cullompton: Willan.

Webster, C. (2007). *Understanding Race and Crime*. Maidenhead: Open University Press.

Webster, C. (2012). The Discourse on 'Race' in Criminological Theory. In S. Hall & S. Winlow (Eds.), *New Directions in Criminological Theory*. London: Routledge.

White, R. (2008). *Crimes Against Nature: Environmental Criminology and Ecological Justice*. Cullompton: Willan.

White, R. (Ed.). (2009). *Environmental Crime: A Reader*. Cullompton: Willan.

White, R., & Heckenberg, D. (2014). *Green Criminology: An Introduction to the Study of Environmental Harm*. London: Routledge.

Yazan, B. (2015). Three Approaches to Case Study Methods in Education: Yin, Merriam, and Stake. *The Qualitative Report, 20*(2), 134–152.

Yin, R. K. (1984/2018). *Case Study Research and Applications* (1st, 6th ed.). London: Sage.

What Is Power and Who Are the Powerful?

2

Introduction

This first substantive chapter begins to unpick the core theoretical and conceptual frameworks, which the book is based upon. The aim of the chapter is to justify why a thorough understanding of power in its many variations is essential to the study of criminology. To do this, power and its relationships to harm and crime (criminalisation, offending, crime control and victimisation) must be clarified and unpacked. Therefore, this chapter begins with a full explanation of what power is. We then go on to discuss who wields power, where power is concentrated, why power is located in certain places, and how it manifests. We end with a summary of the relationship between power, harm and crime. (How power is maintained is the topic of Chap. 3 about invisibility.) Throughout the book, but particularly evident in our discussion of power in this chapter, our conceptualisation and discussion of power, harm and crime are set within the critical and radical traditions of criminology. In relation to power, particularly, we draw on the pioneering work of Pearce (1976) and his argument that powerful entities are those who define crime, so are able to insulate themselves from the legal system. In order to appreciate fully how this happens, we start with a discussion of definitions of power.

© The Author(s) 2021
P. Davies, T. Wyatt, *Crime and Power*,
https://doi.org/10.1007/978-3-030-57314-0_2

What Is Power?

Giddens (1984) suggests that power must be recognised as a primary concept in sociological analysis. Yet even though power is central to the understanding of relationships (both between people and between people and institutions), decision-making, agency, economics, resources and social structures, there is a surprising lack of a concrete definition of power. Those who have defined power have done so in rather straightforward ways. Giddens (1984: 257) defines power as 'the capacity to achieve outcomes' and Parsons (1963) as a capacity to achieve ends, though the latter was focused more on systems rather than people. Hobbes, too, viewed power in a generalised way, where it simply means to attain ends or goals in social relations regardless of how or the person's authority (Parsons 1963). To Parsons (1963), this means that influence, sometimes money and coercion are all power, which makes it impossible to debate power as a specific mechanism bringing about change. Whilst we agree that Hobbes' view, as well as Giddens' and Parsons' is rather broad, we do not think that this inhibits a discussion of the many facets of power. Having a broad view of power has advantages and disadvantages, such as being applicable both to individuals and to groups, but also useful in describing skills a person may have. For instance, we have the capacity to write this book chapter (an outcome), but that is not really the 'power' that we mean when we are examining the actions detailed throughout this text. What is agreed upon is that power is a contested concept. It has and continues to be discussed in academic literature, including in the disciplines of criminology and sociology. Debates about the definition of power are often political (Lukes 2005) and ideological, because of the inclusion or exclusion of aspects of class, gender and socio-economic status and the multiple interlocking intersectionalities (which we discuss in more detail in Part I) of these and other social characteristics (class-race-age-gender-ability-sexuality) in its definitions and conceptualisations, which we will highlight below.

And whilst there is power, there is also *powerlessness*. People may have less or no power compared to other people wielding power. This, too, as we explore throughout Chaps. 4 through 8, often links to an individual's characteristics and how these intersect. Furthermore, powerlessness may be conceptualised as vulnerability or susceptibility to being harmed and/or victimised. There are times in the examples below, and throughout this book, where we refer to this dichotomy of power versus powerless.

Power Is Relational

For some, power is relational, an aspect of all relationships (Giddens 1984). Mills (1956) proposed power is a relationship in which one side prevails over the other. Lukes (2005) distinguishes that there is relational power, which is power 'over' someone, whereas there is also the power 'to', which indicates someone's capacity, facility or ability. For him, power is the capacity for individuals to realise their wills despite the resistance of others (Lukes 2005). That power is relational in nature is widely recognised. A relational conceptualisation is often articulated in the early sociological literature. Dahl (1957) proposed that power is: A has the power over B to the extent that he can get B to do something that B would not otherwise do. Weber conceptualised power similarly: 'a chance of man or men to realize their own will in a communal action even against the resistance of others who are participating in the action' (Gerth and Mills 1958: 180). Blau's (1964) conceptualisation of power is similar. He suggested that power arises from social associations and interactions. Like Weber and Giddens, Blau (1964) suggested power is legitimate, and fair, if it is used in ways that are within social norms. His exemplification focused on the exchange of goods and services. Supplying services people need is what made people or companies powerful. This was particularly the case if there was one or only a few sources of that service. Supplying electricity then, for example, would be a source of power because people need it and not many people or companies are able to offer it. The exchange of services, and goods, is part of what sets out the differences in power between people and groups.

There is agreement amongst some scholars that part of the conceptualisation of power is around relationships. Yet, relationships are structured around social norms, and there are disagreements as to how common-value systems or social norms are created. For Parsons (1963), power is in part a direct derivative of authority, which is agreed to/legitimised in Western democracies. It is important to note what a legitimate authority is or a definition of legitimacy. For Weber (1918), legitimacy is the acceptance of authority as well as the need to obey that authority. For Beetham (1991: 11), a 'power relationship is not legitimate because people believe in its legitimacy, but because it can be justified in terms of their [the public's] beliefs'. Thus, by electing officials and passing legislation, those societies have come to an agreed-upon set of social norms. Others argue that the common-value system is arrived at through force and constraint (Dahrendorf 1959). We would agree with Parsons (1963) that power and social norms are not so clear-cut. He addresses the debate about whether 'power is "essentially" a phenomenon of coercion or of consensus' by saying, 'It is both, precisely because it is a phenomenon which integrates a plurality of factors and outputs of political effectiveness and is not to be identified with any one of them' (Parsons 1963: 258). Weber (Gerth and Mills 1958) seems to agree when he suggested power exists in both legitimate (authoritative) and non-legitimate (coercive) ways. Authority, either which has been legitimately conferred or stolen, usurped or assumed, is clearly an element to power.

Power Is About Decision-Making

Access to authority and becoming or being made the authority are closely linked to decision-making. Authorities at all levels and in all organisations or structures are critical to decision-making. Decision-making, in turn, gives people power over numerous, if not all, aspects of society. Lukes (2005) proposed, based upon the scholarship around power, that the existing conceptualisations can be categorised into three dimensional views of power. He argued that decision-making is a core element of each of the three dimensions. First, the one-dimensional view of power indicates that decision-making is a concrete, observable behaviour. This rather simplistic view of power is often known as the pluralist view (Lukes 2005). In this view, power can be researched by the first-hand study of behaviour during decision-making or by analysing policies to reconstruct the actions that led to the writing of the document. Lukes (2005) disagrees with two aspects of the one-dimensional view of power. First, decision-making is not the only form or opportunity for power. There are other ways that power can be exhibited, so this is not a pluralist view at all; hence, why he calls it one-dimensional. Second, to claim that power is always observable first-hand or that actions and behaviours can be re-created by analysing documents ignores the fact that not all interactions are observable and people's influence over one another is difficult to see. Therefore, the way to study one-dimensional power is incomplete and unrealistic.

The two-dimensional view of power, according to Lukes (2005), is that conceptualised by Bachrach and Baratz (1970). They suggest 'to the extent that a person or group—consciously or unconsciously—creates or reinforces barriers to the public airing of policy conflicts, that person or group has power" (Bachrach and Baratz 1970: 8). This conceptualisation clearly is grounded in decision-making and also raises the interesting aspect of intention, or lack thereof by including consciously or unconsciously. Bachrach and Baratz (1970: 43–44) talk about the "the mobilisation of bias', where

> a set of predominant values, beliefs, rituals, and institutional procedures ('rules of the game') that operate systematically and consistently to the benefit of certain persons

and groups at the expense of others. Those who benefit are placed in a preferred position to defend and promote their vested interests.

Part of Foucault's (1975 [1977]) conceptualisation of power is similar. He proposed that an element of power (particularly sovereign power) is that the law can be made for a few and brought to bear on others.

Such two-dimensional power advances the concept of power by including the idea that control over the agenda of politics is part of power and, in the case of Bachrach and Baratz, also by including the ways in which potential issues are kept out of the political process (Lukes 2005). Lukes (2005) argues though this is still not enough for three reasons:

1. By focusing on the public aspect of decision-making, the conceptualisation is too committed to behaviourism, similar to the one-dimensional view where power is observable. Behaviourism is an approach to research that believes and relies on situations or conflicts being overt and concrete. What such an approach fails to take into account is not all behaviour derives from an individual's chosen actions. Individual behaviour is influenced by socially structured and culturally patterned behaviour of groups, which plays a part in the bias of systems (Lukes 2005). Therefore, collective action and the structure of organisations are also elements to Bachrach and Baratz's (1970) mobilisation of bias.
2. Bachrach and Baratz (1970) focus on the *public* airing of policy *conflict*. Again, Lukes (2005) points out that by focusing on what is observable, they ignore that power and conflict are not always visible and that conflict does not have to be present. Manipulation and authority both lack conflict and are not necessarily observable. Lukes (2005) suggests that the most effective and insidious form of power is where an individual or a group is able to keep conflict from occurring at all.
3. Which brings us to Lukes' (2005) third point, which is when there are no airings of public conflicts or grievances does not mean that there are no grievances. Again, perceptions and so forth could have been manipulated for there to be no grievances though people are being harmed (Lukes 2005) or people may be too frightened or apathetic to air their grievances.

To summarise, power does not have to be observable or involve conflict or grievances. Furthermore, it is not only grounded in individual acts, but also stems from complex social and cultural elements that influence people's behaviours. In addition, access to decision-making is complex and depends on many factors such as wealth (Parsons 1963), but also as others have pointed out on class or social status, which affects people's differential access to authority (Dahrendorf 1959).

Power Is About Having Agency

Agency is simply 'human action' (Sewell 1992: 2) or 'is the actor's capacity to reinterpret and mobilize an array of resources … other than those that initially constituted the array' (Sewell 1992: 19). This relates quite closely to the discussion above about power and decision-making as well as to the link between power and resources (see below). If someone is unable to act or they can be dominated, that person is powerless, at least in those situations.

Giddens (1987) suggested that domination should be one of the focal points of explorations of power. Autonomy or dependence, again both on the part of individuals or groups, can greatly influence agency as well as the capability to alter events and/or to be altered. To be an agent is, at least in part, to have dominion and thus to be able to make a difference to the world, and to be able to make a difference is to have power. To sociologists, like Giddens (1968) the domination of some and the subordination of others is the nature and source of power. This is one of the main points of contention between functionalist/integration theory and coercive/conflict theory. Functionalist theory, according to Dahrendorf (1959), is that social order is a general agreement of values, which outweighs the possible or actual differences of opinions or interests that many individuals may have. In contrast, coercive theory suggests society is based on force and constraint (Dahrendorf 1959).

Domination, then, and the lack of agency are central to conceptualisations of power. Domination can be economic, but also can be legal, charismatic or traditional factors (Mills 1956).

Power Is Economic

So far, the literature and authors drawn upon have placed power as a social concept, foregrounding power as relational in nature. However, Marx argued that social power came from economic power or wealth and that the social power stemming from wealth enables the powerful to build society to suit them (Calhoun et al. 2012). As such, Marxist sociologists focus on property and capital, and the resulting largely economic relationships as the basis for people's inequitable access to power (Calhoun et al. 2012). Nigam (1996) suggests that explicit application of power is absent from Marxist theory, but in discussing capitalism, power—specifically related to labour—is evident. In contrast, Chakravarty (1996) posits that in Marxist theory power is always political power. Political power cannot be disentangled from class inequality, and thus power in Marxist theory appears to also be relational as well as economic in nature. The economic element of power overlaps with other conceptualisations that include resources.

Power Is About Resources

As mentioned, Giddens (1987) raised dominion or domination as another important aspect of power. Primarily, this was in relation to resources and a person's control over them. Property and wealth referred to above are just two kinds of resources. Control over natural resources, human resources and technological resources also involves power and may or may not tie into the powerful's property and financial resources. Giddens' (1987) notion of power as being a transformative capacity is a useful one as it is clear and applicable to both individuals and groups. He further described power as the capability to intervene in a given set of events, so as in some way to alter them. As he rightly proposed, the agent, or the actor, must have the resources to be able to intervene and thus resources are related to power. Giddens (1987) divided resources into material capabilities (allocative) and the dominion over other humans (authoritative). Clearly, both physical resources (i.e. property, natural resources) and authority (human resources) play a role in whether an individual or a group has power.

Power Is Structural

A person's or a group's power is not completely dependent on their own capabilities, position, wealth or resources. Scholars have noted that social structure also plays a part in power (Foucault (1975 [1977]; Mills 1956). The connection between power and structure is evident because of the continuous nature of power (Mills 1956) for some individuals and groups over time and despite challenges to that power. Marxist theory as it pertains to power is arguably structural as well. Class, organised around labour, determines whether someone is powerful or powerless. Mostly, class is structural as one's class is largely based on socio-economic status or place of birth, although in some places a person can move between classes based on achievements, education, profession and so forth. To Foucault, at least in part, power is a structural expression of 'a complex strategic situation in a given social setting' (Gordon 1980). The role that structure has to play in terms of power will be discussed more in Chaps. 9 (Corporations) and 11 (States). In investigating these two groups, the institutional and structural mechanism that underpin power will be made much clearer.

Power Can Be Positive

Under several definitions of power, power is not always negative. Whilst it can be constraining, it can also be emancipating and can simply be the ability to make a difference (Giddens 1984). Again, such conceptualisation could entail power having a positive aspect (Giddens 1987). Grassroots social and environmental movements are good examples of this. The environmental activist group, Extinction Rebellion, for instance, in 2019 staged large disruptions to public transportation in London and around the world to draw attention to the climate crisis. The collective power of the group, at least in part, led to the UK government declaring a climate emergency. In this example, and there are many more, power is used as a positive force for improvement. Parsons (1963) proposed power is a relation from which both sides might gain. Like Giddens and Parsons, Blau (1964) outlined how power can be a positive force. It can benefit subordinates. Blau did, however, highlight that power can also lead to exploitation and oppression and proposed that those with coercive force are the most powerful.

Power Is Visible and Invisible

Foucault (1975 [1977]) may be the scholar who has most directly unpicked the (in) visible aspects of power. He highlights political ceremony as an expression of potency or power. This would seem to be the case for military parades, for example. Furthermore, Foucault suggested that the regular observation undertaken in certain spaces was a form of power. For instance, in hospitals and prisons, there is continual monitoring; in schools, there are perpetual examinations. Observations and examinations create hierarchies between the people within these spaces and also lead to differing levels of power between those doing the observations or giving the examinations and those being observed or examined. 'The examination transformed the economy of visibility unto the exercise of power' (Foucault 1975 [1977]: 187). Foucault[1] lays out how punishment, a specific aspect of power, historically

---

[1] In *Discipline and Punishment* and his larger body of work, Foucault spends a great deal of

was very public. Executions and flogging used to be public spectacles that were very visible. In the West, this has largely changed, with prisons being the predominant form of punishment. Therefore, whilst on one hand power is visible in the sense we as a society know that people are in prisons, on the other hand there is an element of invisibility because we do not physically see the punishment, in the form of bodily control. We will focus on the visibility and invisibility of power and powerful entities in Chap. 3.

Summary

Power may simply be defined as the ability or capacity to achieve an outcome. If that is what power is, this would mean it is likely every individual has some form of power at least at some point in time. This is not the sort of power that we will be exploring in the coming chapters. As Lukes (2005) points out, it is important in discussions of power to know and focus on what is being affected and in what way. Although it may be difficult to unpick if someone is behaving in a way that they otherwise would not have or if something happened that otherwise would not have (Lukes 2005), power does have some essence of magnitude that is important. For example, convincing someone to go to a particular lunch place in contrast to convincing that person not to disclose that they have been victimised are two very different levels of power.

Furthermore, power, in the forms of wealth and prestige in particular, is likely to be accumulative (Mills 1956). The more you have of either, the more likely it is that people will do what you ask them. According to Weber, power is distributed by social class (market position), status (social honour) and party (political power) (Gerth and Mills 1958). We suggest this falls under the categories of power being relational as well as related to decision-making and to agency. Social structure also affects a person's or a group's power as does their control over resources, both material and human. Relations, decision-making, agency, economics, resources and structures all intersect and interlock in complex ways to amplify or constrain power. Furthermore, depending upon the historical, socio-political, economic and/or cultural context where these types of power are expressed, that power may vary considerably. And an additional layer of complication stems from the powerful person's characteristics and intersectionalities of their age-class-gender with other elements of the situation. This is the case for positive power too. As we discuss in

time on unpacking power. See the power triangle, for instance, of discipline, sovereignty and governmentality, which focuses on similar aspects of power that we propose here.

the next chapter at length, power is both visible and invisible. This book focuses on instances where power is used as a negative, controlling, harmful force, but we do agree with several of the scholars cited here that power can be a positive force as well. Power, then, for us is an (in)visible capability to control and manipulate relationships and structures. Power varies with who wields it and where. That brings us to a discussion of who it is that has power.

Who Has Power?

As discussed in the first section 'What is Power?', both individuals and groups have the capability to achieve outcomes, and some, more than others, have the financial, human, natural and/or technical resources to do so. In this book, we differentiate between individuals and groups. We suggest that there are certain characteristics or demographics of individual people that lead to them having more power than others do. For instance, in most, if not all, Western countries, being a man will mean he will have power, at least to some degree. In the West, the same is likely true for white people, Christians and heterosexuals. This stems from complex historical and social contexts that privilege these characteristics over others. As alluded to in several places, the combination or intersectionality of a person's characteristics is also relevant to an individual's power. As we discuss in more detail in Part I and in the chapters therein, being a wealthy older white male in the West is a combination of characteristics that lends to being more powerful than others.

Furthermore, we suggest that certain groups have power and that they can use their power in harmful ways. Corporations, organised crime groups, states and insurgents wield power to maintain control and/or to maximise profit often causing suffering or using violence. We are not saying that, for example, a single individual will have the same power as a corporation. We agree with Blau (1964), and will make the case throughout the two sections of this book, that '[t]here are fundamental differences between the dynamics of power in a collective situation and the power of one individual over another'. Similarly, it is important whether it is only an individual or whether it is a group that approves and/or recognises power. Collective approval of power can legitimate that power, whereas collective disapproval of power can destabilise the position of that person or group (Blau 1964).

A key part of power outlined above in 'What Is Power?' is that power is linked to decision-making. Drawing extensively on the ground-breaking work of Pearce (1976), himself influenced by Marx, we, like he, suggest that power is linked to policy-making. It is worth describing in detail Pearce's view on who the powerful are, as this perspective underpins most of the discussions going forward.

Frank Pearce's (1976) *Crimes of the Powerful*

Pearce proposed that in Western systems, the United States in particular, the ruling class, who were the bourgeoisie in the capitalist economy, held power. The ruling class used their power to rig the system in their favour. This means that the legal, economic and criminal justice systems all were (are) biased towards the ruling class at the expense of the working class. Such bias and inequity of power resulted in the continuation and reinforcement of class domination and values. The ruling class are able to manipulate the system because they are able to deflect attention from the issue of class conflict and because they control what gets defined as deviant and/or criminal behaviour:

> It comes about because they concentrate their attention on those who have been *successfully labelled 'deviant'*, and not on those who break laws, fix laws, violate ethical and moral standards, harm individuals and groups, etc., but who either are able to hide their actions, or when known can deflect criticism, labelling, and punishment. (Liazos 1972: 109)

Crimes of the powerful are concealed by the system itself, which reinforces their interests, 'particularly the need to be legitimated through maintaining the appearance of respectability' (Box 1983: 6). The crimes of the powerless, on the other hand, are revealed and exaggerated, also serving the interests of the powerful because this criminality legitimises the control agencies (Box 1983). There are flaws in this assessment, however. For example, the relative lack of female crime contradicts the orthodox view that crime and powerlessness are connected (Box 1983).

Pearce also pointed out that the powerful entities, like corporations and states, were rife with paradoxes and contradictions. They will champion justice, equality and fairness, but there is a huge disparity between this rhetoric and their performance. He observed, in particular, that institutions of the state are unable to adhere to their own rules and regulations. Since apparently the powerful tend towards criminality, it is crucial for them to try to hide or to keep their own actions from being defined as criminal or deviant.

Clearly, this has links to the radical tradition emerging from pluralist sociological theories. Becker's (1963) 'labelling theory' proposed the so-called self-fulfilling prophecy, whereby those labelled as deviant become deviant due, at least in part, to the stigma of the label. Pearce reiterates that it is the powerful who do the labelling and thus their own actions are not labelled as deviant, though clearly at times their actions are more harmful. This is the case with the legal system where laws defining criminality do not include actions of powerful actors. As Foucault (1975 [1977]: 276) stated, 'law and justice do not hesitate to proclaim their necessary class dissymmetry'. The ruling class and the working class have different languages, and the law is inadequate as it must be one class to another and they do not have the same words or ideas (Foucault 1975 [1977]). The real-world consequence of this disparity is that prison focuses on one form of illegality and other criminality is left in the 'shade' and tolerated (Foucault 1975 [1977]: 277).

A further key aspect of labelling deviancy that is relevant to Pearce's conceptualisation of crimes of the powerful is the societal reaction of the audience or witness to the act of deviancy. As Lemert (1951) notes, the person labelled as deviant is shaped by the amount of deviancy engaged in, how visible the deviancy is, whether or not the deviant person sees the audience's reaction, and what exactly that reaction is. Crimes of the powerful are often hidden, so there is no audience and, therefore, no reaction. The media has a role to play in exposing crimes of the powerful and challenging these labels, and we return to this important aspect in Chap. 3 when discussing invisibility.

But for now, suffice it to say, power is central because the powerful may well control the dissemination of what that societal reaction is. For instance, in 2018, knife crime in the United Kingdom was receiving substantial media coverage, and there was vocal concern over the rise in violence. Some media coverage focused on the working-class neighbourhoods where the stabbings occurred and talked about the 'surge' in violent crime and Britain's crime 'epidemic' (Petkar and Rogers 2018). Knife crime, for years, has been a concern in the United Kingdom, but a rise of 16% in 2017–18 makes knife crime 6% of all violent incidents and it continues to be an unusual occurrence (Shaw 2018). There is a clear labelling of people carrying knives as deviant and association of these people with particular, working-class, areas. In contrast, the government officials who are trying to deport UK residents from Caribbean nations and other Commonwealth countries who immigrated to the UK post-World War II because of labour shortages (BBC News 2018) are not labelled as deviant or stigmatised. The Windrush Scandal is labelled as just that—a 'scandal'; not as a violation of these people's human rights when they are facing life-changing discrimination through disruption of their jobs, lives and citizenship status.

Furthermore, Pearce, like Lukes (2005), challenged traditional notions of power that argued power is always directly applied and observable. He, too, advocated for wider research into power rather than the status quo, which stated only decisions made by formal political bodies or persons should be studied. Pearce also argued against ideas that there are no power elites and that power is widely distributed throughout communities. Instead, Pearce called for community power to be investigated, including case studies of 'important decisions'. In addition to drawing on Becker's (1963) labelling theory, Pearce also expanded upon Becker's work on 'radical pluralism'. Becker (1963: 191) recognised, and Pearce agreed, that not all groups benefit from power equally:

> Differences in the ability to make rules and apply them to other people are essentially power differentials (either legal or extra-legal). Those groups whose social position gives them weapons and power are best able to enforce their rules. Distinctions of age, sex, ethnicity, and class are all related to differences in power, which accounts for differences in the degree to which groups so distinguished can make rules for others.

Pearce criticised Durkheim's suggestions on empiricism and interactionism, which proposed that crime, or at least its punishment, is necessary for society in that it helps define group norms and boundaries. Pearce's concern with this idea is that it assumes that there are shared interests and a unitary set of values. We know that this is not the case because citizens in democracies have the possibility to initiate laws or to pressure their politician to initiate laws that negatively affect the powerful (Pearce 1976). Thus, 'anti-social acts [are] hidden from public scrutiny, or, failing that, have them dealt with administratively, but sometimes their acts become liable to criminal action—e.g. offences against factory safety regulations, income tax evasion or involvement with corruption' (Pearce 1976: 63–4). This indicates that not only can power at times be challenged, but also that society is not homogenous with a universal set of norms on the part of individuals or of groups.

Individual and Group Power

As mentioned, power can be thought of as a relationship in which one side prevails over the other (Mills 1956). For Blau (1964), the powerful are those who are able to realise their will, even if others resist it. We suggest both of these conceptualisations clearly apply in the instances of individuals with power as well as groups with power. As mentioned above, in most Western societies, the individual power elite have typically been men. In addition to gender, characteristics that also typically are associated with power are age (not too young and not too old), race (white), sexuality (heterosexual) and religion (in the West, Christianity). Individual power may also be linked to owning property, membership in certain organisations (according to Pearce, historically trade unions), level of education and wealth amongst other factors. As Calhoun et al. (2012) detail, individual identities (i.e. gender, race, ethnicity, sexual orientation, etc.) have a critical role in social stratification. Social stratification is linked to power often in a complex interplay with sociological factors like class, status and political power (Calhoun et al. 2012).

Individual identities or characteristics in combination (intersectionalities) with social factors may contribute to the power of groups. For instance, a Board of Trustees that is made up of all white men has typically wielded more power than a Board with a diverse membership. The composition of the group is not the only reason that groups wield power. Blau (1964) suggested that organisations/groups have double the power. Not only do groups have power over their employees or members, but the group may well also have power over others externally—industries, markets, communities and so forth. If the group has control over institutions, this gives particularly strong power (Blau 1964). Whilst the individual members of the group may lend to this power, the collective nature of groups plays an important aspect in organisations and groups being particularly powerful, as we will demonstrate in Part II of this book.

As mentioned, in Part I of the book, we will explore in greater detail the role that individual characteristics have in creating and maintaining power and concealing the crimes and harms that such individual power permits. In Part II of the book, we will investigate the double power of groups. Not only do groups have levels of power amongst their membership, but the group as a unit also has power over other aspects of society and other people outside of the group. Here, too, we assess how groups are able to become powerful, how they keep their power, and how this enables them to hide the crimes and harms they commit.

Where Is the Power?

The discussion so far in this chapter has given some indication as to where scholars argue power exists and is situated. In particular, power is linked to places where decisions are made. This section will foreground discussion of places of power but also related elements of time and space. Giddens (1987) suggests in the modern era this is in places or sites like businesses, cities and universities amongst other similar places and locations. Furthermore, he proposes locales, which he includes time, space and place relations, can form 'power containers'. These are arenas for generation of administrative power. This raises an important aspect of power—that of time. An individual in one place over an extended period of time or a group that exists for a long time is more likely to have power. This is in part due to the accumulation of influence and resources that are often connected to longevity. For example, in the US Congress, Senators in the US Senate and members of the US House of Representatives are chosen to lead committees based upon their seniority in relation to other members. Therefore, those who have been in Congress the longest (in one place over an extended period of time) sit in leadership positions that control the agendas of committees, which then control which legislation or political appointees might make it to the full membership to be voted on. So, Senator Chuck Grassley, head of the US Senate Judiciary Committee because he was the senior Republican on the committee, had substantial power in how the confirmation of, now Supreme Court Justice, Brett Kavanaugh was handled. Senator Grassley needed to give approval for the FBI to investigate other allegations against Kavanaugh and decided, largely on his own, what would happen from the findings of that investigation (nothing) (Bolton 2018). Furthermore, he has tremendous power to sway the other Republicans on the committee because of his status in the Senate. Clearly, this has significant consequences for reproducing the status quo as well as further cementing power into the hands of the few who have the most.

In regard to resources, these, too, accumulate over time. Giddens (1987) highlighted a build-up of resources enables individuals and organisations to engage in various activities that further and maintain power. These are conducting surveillance (collecting and keeping information on people and conducting direct supervision), assembling, facilitating scope and intensity of sanctions (military) and creating conditions that influence the formation of ideology (Giddens 1987). These are similar to the three realms—financial, government, military—where Mills (1956) suggested power is located. He found that a few elite individuals move within and between these realms. This results in the centralisation of power as well as making power more and more exclusive (Mills 1956). Mills (1956) observed that men were running big corporations, the machinery of states and military establishments. The administrations of these big corporations were intertwined with the machinery of the state, which controlled the military (Mills 1956). These elite men running all three of these realms of power counselled each other and went from being career politicians to professional celebrities to Chief Executive Officers all with the power to distract the public (Mills 1956).

We agree that power is found in places where decisions are made and can be concentrated in one place over time. Walklate (2005) outlines how crime is found behind closed doors. We suggest this is a useful way to explore power as well. Looking behind closed doors supports the idea that power should be looked for in places that are the least accessible to observation (Lukes 1974). From our perspective, closed doors and power are bound together and inextricably linked. Closed doors are both literal and metaphorical. The literal closed doors are those which form a barrier to homes, gated communities, workplaces, clubs (working men's, freemasons, sports), institutions (i.e. prisons, care homes and local authorities), boardrooms and corporate suites. The metaphorical closed doors—places that are closed, but may not have a physical presence or are simply isolated—are those found in cyberspace, isolated communities, the 'wild'/environment, social strata (elite professions, royalty and aristocracy) and the corridors of state.

It is important to remember that knowledge of power relations, crimes and harms in places with both literally and metaphorically closed doors is limited. This is the case for crimes in places where decisions are made as well as the range of physical and virtual spaces discussed above. Because of the isolated, hidden and obscured and thus invisible nature of such places, throughout this book, we present what evidence there is in order to try to uncover the characteristics and scale of crimes and harms by the powerful. The so-called dark figure of crime in this field can only be estimated, but we argue, it is likely to be particularly high due to its invisible nature. Thus, as we said in Chap. 1, we do our best to answer: What crimes take place? Are there victims? Who can offend? Who can victimise? Who experiences victimisation? Who wields power? And importantly, how is that power used and for what purpose? Our case study approach throughout the book seeks to answer all of these questions across the range of crimes of the powerful that we detail.

How Is Power Used and Why?

Why when we talk about harm and crime, do we talk about power? We agree with Box, Pearce and others that power is crucial for perpetrating many harms and crimes. Power is also critical in determining legally and socially what are defined to be harms and crimes. Furthermore, power is an essential element to hide and conceal harms and crimes, and thus maintain power. Power then is used in the commission of harms and crimes, in the process to determine what is harmful and criminal, and in the concealment of harms and crimes in order to sustain power, wealth and status.

Box (1983) suggests that power is criminogenic. Where there is power, it will be used to commit harms and crimes. If power is relational, as detailed in the first section of this chapter, then power exists in every society. Since power is everywhere, harm and crime, according to the criminogenic argument, in some form or another also will be everywhere. Whereas democratic systems with checks and balances should be able to contain power, they will not completely solve the problems that come with it:

> There is no way that people determined to behave badly, and having mastered the shameless art of deception, can be prevented from occupying positions of power. There is probably no way in which positions of power can be designed so as to avoid contradictions that impose tremendous pressure on their incumbents to deviate from the path of decent behaviour. (Box 1983: 202)

Particularly since, as Gramsci (2014) proposed, hegemony—the ideological process by which the working class consent to their own domination by the ruling class—obfuscates power. This happens because there is a subtle diffusion of ideas supportive of the ruling classes in the institutions of civil society—religion, education, media—embedded in everyday practices (Gramsci 2014). Our point here is that whilst power is actively used to commit harms and crimes that benefit the powerful perpetrator, the powerful are also able to passively rely on the power structures in which they are enveloped to benefit and to maintain power, wealth and status.

Summary: How Are Power, Harm and Crime Connected?

Power, harm and crime are inextricably connected through the process of criminalisation, through the nature of offending and through crime control. The powerful define crime. Criminal law categories are ideological constructs (Sumner 1976) of the ruling class, the powerful. The criminal law and other regulations do not reflect what is truly harmful and only criminalise some victimisation (Box 1983). Problem populations that potentially or actually threaten the distribution of power, wealth and privilege are criminalised, demoralised and incapacitated (Box 1983). Spitzer (1975) argues it is the populations who challenge capitalist production to which this happens. For instance, only some types of avoidable killing are murder or manslaughter, like car accidents, but this is not the case in workplaces, where the responsibility is a corporation or a business (Box 1983). Like Pearce, Box (1983) notes there are some victories in legislation for the powerless. Thus, we see some restraints on the financial and banking sectors or an increase in environmental regulations. Overall though, criminalisation is controlled by and benefits the powerful.

Patterns of criminal offending then are directly linked to what is criminalised. Prisons are filled with working-class criminals for drug offences and property crimes, not with white-collar embezzlers or negligent Chief Executive Officers. Societal understanding of criminal behaviour is determined by their skewed knowledge of who is offending. Again, this is directly tied to the criminal law, but also the media have a significant part to play in amplifying the perception that crime is the purview of the working class rather than those with power, which we discuss more in Chap. 3 when looking at the features of invisibility. Furthermore, 'The process of law enforcement, in its broadest possible interpretation, operates in such a way as to *conceal* crimes of the powerful against the powerless, but to *reveal* and *exaggerate* crimes of powerless against "everyone"' (Box 1983: 5). The control of crime then is also integral in perpetuating the mistaken and manipulated notion that the powerless tend to be criminals, when in fact the powerful are likely to be responsible for much more harm and suffering.

Pause for Thought

- How would you define power?
- Who are the 'powerful' and who are the 'powerless'?
- How are harm and crime different? How are they the same?

References

Bachrach, P., & Baratz, M. (1970). *Power and Poverty: Theory and Practice*. New York: Oxford University Press.
BBC News. (2018). Windrush Generation: Who are They and Why are They Facing Problems? Retrieved November 7, 2018, from https://www.bbc.co.uk/news/uk-43782241.
Becker, H. (1963 [1973]). *Outsiders*. New York: Free Press.
Beetham, D. (1991). *The Legitimation of Power*. Basingstoke: Palgrave.
Blau, P. (1964). *Exchange and Power in Social Life*. New York: John Wiley and Sons.
Bolton, A. (2018). Grassley: No Corroboration of Kavanaugh Accusers' Allegations in FBI Report. *The Hill*. Retrieved November 9, 2018, from https://thehill.com/homenews/senate/409864-grassley-no-corroboration-of-kavanaugh-accusers-allegations-in-fbi-report.
Box, S. (1983). *Power, Crime, and Mystification*. London: Tavistock Publications.
Calhoun, C., Gerteis, J., Moody, J., Pfaff, S., & Virk, I. (2012). Introduction to Part IV. In C. Calhoun, J. Gerteis, J. Moody, S. Pfaff, & I. Virk (Eds.), *Contemporary Sociological Theory* (3rd ed., pp. 223–228). London: Wiley-Blackwell.
Chakravarty, A. (1996). On the Absence of "Power" in Marxist Theory. *Social Scientist, 24*(9/10), 77–80.
Dahl, R. (1957). The Concept of Power. *Behavioral Science, 2*, 201–215.
Dahrendorf, R. (1959). *Class and Class Conflict in Industrial Society*. Stanford: Stanford University Press.
Foucault, M. (1975) [1977]. *Discipline and Punish: The Birth of the Prison*. Trans. Sheridan, A. London: Penguin.
Gerth, H., & Mills, C. W. (1958). *From Max Weber*. New York: Oxford University Press.

Giddens, A. (1968). 'Power' in the Recent Writings of Talcott Parsons. Social Sciences Collection (pp. 258–272). London: SAGE.

Giddens, A. (1984). The Constitution of Society. Cambridge: Polity Press.

Giddens, A. (1987). The Nation-State and Violence, Volume Two of A Contemporary Critique of Historical Materialism. Basingstoke: Palgrave Macmillan.

Gordon, C. (1980). Preface. In C. Gordon (Ed.), Power/Knowledge: Selected Interviews and Other Writings, by Michel Foucault (pp. vii–x). New York: Pantheon Books.

Gramsci, A. (2014). On Hegemony. In Q. Hoare & G. Nowell-Smith (Eds. and translators), Selections from the Prison Notebooks of Antonio Gramsci (pp. 326–351). New York: International Publishers.

Lemert, E. C. (1951). Social Pathology: A Systematic Approach to the Theory of Sociopathic Behavior. New York: McGraw-Hill.

Liazos, A. (1972). The Poverty of the Sociology of Deviance: Nuts, Sluts, and Perverts. Social Problems, 20(1), 103–120.

Lukes, S. (2005). Power: A Radical View (2nd ed.). Basingstoke: Palgrave Macmillan.

Mills, C. W. (1956). The Power Elite. Oxford: Oxford University Press.

Nigam, A. (1996). Marxism and Power. Social Scientist, 24(4/6), 3–22.

Parsons, T. (1963). On the Concept of Political Power. Proceedings of the American Philosophical Society, 107(3), 232–262.

Pearce, F. (1976). Crimes of the Powerful: Marxism, Crime and Deviance. London: Pluto Press.

Petkar, S., & Rogers, J. (2018). Endless Knife Crime: London Stabbings of 2018—Latest Knife Crime Statistics and Attacks in Tuffnell Park, Clapham, Shepherds Bush and Tulse Hill. The Sun. Retrieved November 7, 2018, from https://www.thesun.co.uk/news/5251268/london-stabbings-knife-crime-statistics/.

Sewell, W. (1992). A Theory of Structure: Duality, Agency, and Transformation. American Journal of Sociology, 98(1), 1–29.

Shaw, D. (2018). Nine Charts on the Rise of Knife Crime in England and Wales. BBC News. Retrieved November 7, 2018, from https://www.bbc.co.uk/news/uk-42749089.

Spitzer, S. (1975). Towards a Marxian Theory of Crime. Social Problems, 22, 368–401.

Sumner, C. (1976). Marxism and Deviance Theory. In P. Wiles (Ed.), Crime and Delinquency in Britain (Vol. 2). London: Martin Robertson.

Walklate, S. (2005). Criminology: The Basics. Abingdon, UK: Routledge.

Weber, M. (1918). Politics as a Vocation. In H. H. Gerth & C. W. Mills (Eds.), From Max Weber: Essays in Sociology (p. 1991). London: Routledge.

The Invisibility of Crimes of the Powerful

3

Introduction

The enabling potential of power is further explored in this second substantive chapter. Here we outline the significance and importance of the ways in which some individuals and groups are enabled, whilst others are less able, to avoid detection, prosecution, punishment and accountability. This chapter explores how it is this happens. In 1999, Jupp et al. mapped the contours of what they termed invisible crime, victimisation and regulation and considered the commonalities associated with this range of acts, events and experiences. They suggested that there are seven interacting and overlapping features that help make or crimes more or less invisible. We begin the chapter by detailing these features—no knowledge, no statistics, no theory, no research, no control, no politics and no panic!—and setting them within the context of power. The chapter then explores how invisible crimes can be categorised into typologies with similar characteristics, which also overlap and intersect. These additional conceptualisations are explored by ourselves (with our co-editor Peter Francis) in a 2014 update of the original 1999 book. These spatial typologies are as follows: the body, home, street, environment, suite, state and virtual space (Davies et al. 2014). Together, these conceptualisations of the features of invisibility and spatial typologies provide a framework for the investigation of the range of crimes of the powerful in the individual chapters belonging to Parts I and II of this textbook.

© The Author(s) 2021
P. Davies, T. Wyatt, *Crime and Power*,
https://doi.org/10.1007/978-3-030-57314-0_3

The Seven Features of Invisibility

Jupp et al. (1999) innovatively proposed seven interrelated factors that make harms and crimes more or less visible to a range of audiences. These seven factors or 'features', as they called them, impact upon whether certain acts are considered criminal or not and whether the person committing the act is labelled as a criminal. Not all of the seven features need to be present or expressed for a harmful or criminal act to be invisible. Jupp and colleagues further their theory of invisible crimes by proposing there are 'degrees of invisibility'. The degree to which a harmful or criminal act is visible effects how that act is variously witnessed, detected and experienced. We will first detail each of the seven features before providing an example that will illustrate the degree of invisibility concept.

No Knowledge

The first feature of invisibility is that of 'no knowledge'. No knowledge includes no knowledge by individuals as well as no knowledge by the public that a harm has occurred or that a crime has been committed. This may happen for several reasons. For instance, there may be an awareness problem. In some cases of harms and crimes, the victims may not be aware that they have been a victim. This may be the case in identity thefts or exposure to pollution. People may have their personal information taken or be breathing toxic air and not know this has happened or is happening. Furthermore, other people may also not be aware that this has happened. Therefore, victims have to know that they are victims and others have to know about this victimisation for a harmful or criminal act to be visible. This may also be the case in victimisation of young people where the young person could be unaware that what someone has done to them, for instance, sexual assault (although this could be the case at any age), is wrong or criminal. Lack of awareness may also be because the perpetrator has hidden the knowledge about the harm or crime. We propose this is a core element when interrogating crimes of the powerful.

Another reason why there may be no knowledge is a normalisation problem. For numerous harmful and criminal acts, there is individual and public awareness that the act has taken place. Yet it may still seem normal, be accepted and not be challenged. The normalisation problem is evident in many instances of corruption. Paying a bribe or giving a gift to receive a public service is still routine in many parts of the world. Whereas this is technically criminal, the corruption continues and remains hidden in plain sight.

The problem of ideology is another reason why there may be no knowledge about a harmful or criminal act. In this case, some harmful and criminal acts are considered to be enterprising, so are tolerated or encouraged. Corporations who cut corners by dumping waste rather than treating it, or not making repairs to save money, are examples of ideologies that render harms invisible. Finally, a reason for a lack of knowledge about an invisible harm or crime may stem from collusion. There are cases of harm and crime where the victims may actually participate and/ or contribute to their victimisation. People who consent to be trafficked to search for more lucrative opportunities in other places may fall into this category. Whilst this is an incredibly complex topic, in some instances those being trafficked know they are doing something illegal, but act out of desperation. Some victims of trafficking upon being discovered may even deny they have been trafficked, so collude in their victimisation. The feature of 'no knowledge' then is a complex factor with varying degrees of expression. Knowledge ranges from none at all, to some, to full knowledge that the victim may actively assist in hiding.

No Statistics

The second feature of invisibility is 'no statistics'. As will be evident, no knowledge and no statistics are closely connected. There may be no individual, official or public knowledge if there are no data kept to support and verify the existence of harms and crimes. There are many harms and even crimes for which no official data are recorded. Corporate and environmental infractions and violations are just a few that are subject to the lack of statistics. Data are often not recorded for those harms and crimes that take place away from the public gaze. This is clearly applicable to corporate and environmental harms and crimes since they occur behind 'closed' doors or in isolated spaces. Furthermore, predominantly statistics are not collected for harms and crimes that are viewed as victimless. Again, corporate and environmental offences are often viewed in this light. Another reason for statistics not to be kept is that those who would be collecting the data are unsure or unable to capture the complexity of these harms or crimes. Many corporate and environmental harms require a significant amount of specialist knowledge that police forces' or regulatory agencies' staff may or may not have. This results in no information being recorded. No statistics then feeds into the lack of knowledge.

There may also be no statistics because of underreporting of crimes to the law enforcement or regulatory agency that is keeping the data. The dark figure of crime—the amount of crime that is not captured in official statistics—is thought to be substantial because for numerous crimes, victims do not come forward. Their reasons for not coming forward are varied, but in general, victims may be embarrassed, ashamed, afraid and/or worried that they will not be believed. Victims may also be afraid of or worried about the type of response—insensitive or dismissive—that they would receive from the police. Victims may also not know to whom to report an offence or think that reporting is too much hassle. In all of these instances, victims then do not tell the authorities what has happened. This is particularly evident in sexual offences, which will be discussed more in Chap. 7.

No Theory

Not all harms and crimes are the subject of theorising by criminologists or other experts. 'No theory' is the third feature of invisibility and, again, links to no knowledge and no statistics. Criminology as a discipline has been and continues, largely, to focus on street-level conventional crimes such as drug use and prostitution. Theorising about harms and crimes other than these tends not to take place. Theorising also may be lacking because of the complexity involved. There is clearly no single simple definition of crime. There is therefore no single simple theory to explain crime, its existence or its causes. For invisible crimes, which we would argue, are even more varied and diverse than street-level conventional crimes, theorising such a complex range of acts and omissions becomes a difficult task. The lack of theory related to invisible harms and crimes then may be in part due to their complicated multifaceted nature.

No Research

Also closely interlinked to no knowledge, no statistics and no theory is no research. These four features in particular have a mutually reinforcing interaction where scarce or no data can lead to limited knowledge and theorising. There may be no data because there is no research. As with the other features, there are several reasons why there may be no research. First, there are practical aspects to conducting research into crimes of the powerful and invisible crimes and harms. These practical aspects include, but are not limited to, the difficulty in gaining access to the closed spaces, which are the locations for crimes of the powerful. In addition, if access were to be gained, these locations may be far too dangerous to conduct research in. As mentioned in the other features detailed, crimes of the powerful are often very complicated. Research into these incidents then may be very time-consuming and most likely expensive. Access, danger, time and money then may prohibit this type of research.

Second, as mentioned in regard to no knowledge, the data being sought may be actively hidden by the offenders. Those being researched in studies into crimes of the powerful have a vested interest in hiding or withholding the data as it would expose their illegal and/or unethical actions. Research may well then be purposely and actively squashed in order to prevent generation of knowledge, statistics and theory. Likewise, the research may fall foul of political agendas. If politicians are in anyway linked to the actions to be researched, the study will not be funded. Funding may also not be given to projects that are politically sensitive or unpopular. Governments do not want to give money to research that would paint them in a bad light and most likely will not give money that paint their allies in a bad light either. Politicians also pander to the public by supporting projects that investigate individual-level mainstream crimes because these are the main source of fear for most people. We will return to this in more detail shortly. Therefore, no research may be the result of practical hurdles to conducting research about crimes of the powerful, but also no research may well stem from powerful actors, either because they are involved or because they hold the purse strings, not supporting studies about invisible crimes.

No Control

The fifth feature of invisibility is that there is no control. It may be that no control stems from the reality that there is no formal or systematic control for invisible crime even though possibly there is legislation in place. For instance, there are protocols for not selling illegal goods on the internet, but if in practice no actions are taken to stop the sale of illegal goods online, then there is essentially no control. The internet is a prime example of no control as locations with no physical space are particularly difficult to control. No control may also arise from the international nature of many invisible crimes and crimes of the powerful. Crimes that cross borders or are planned in one place and occur in another are challenging to regulate and control because of the lack of clarity over jurisdiction for the regulatory and/or law enforcement agencies involved. Without clear jurisdiction, there is little way for those agencies tasked with controlling crimes to act. No control may also be evident in crimes where there is the interaction of legitimate and illegitimate activities. The selling of illegal goods on the internet provides further support of this.

When illegal goods are mixed in with legal goods, it is sometimes impossible for law enforcement agencies to detect and then distinguish what is illegal from what is legal.

No Politics

Politics not only play a role in the research funding, or lack thereof, in relation to invisible crimes. They also are clearly instrumental in determining the law and order issues that are present in party platforms and agendas. In order to get (re)elected, party platforms tend to centre on public order and safe street initiatives as these are what voting constituencies tend to be the most concerned about. Individual victimisation and fear of such victimisation is an emotive topic that can sway voters to certain candidates who tout a tough stance on crime. This can come at the expense of invisible crimes, which remain ignored and neglected, yet, most likely, cause more damage and victimisation than the crimes that are central to party platforms. In addition, often there is an inseparable link between corporate lobbying and politicians. Politicians may shy away from holding the contributors to their campaigns accountable for invisible harms and crimes as this may directly affect the amount of money the politician receives. Powerful people and powerful corporations can manipulate politicians in this way to steer them away from actions that would bring to light hidden harms and crimes. There is often then no politics associated with invisible crimes and harms as focus on them is not going to help politicians stay or get into office.

No Panic!

Finally, invisible crimes and harms unlike mainstream conventional portrayals of crime do not cause panic. Panic in this context is Cohen's (2002) conceptualisation of moral panics. Moral panics are when the public, often driven by the media, are overly concerned with a particular type of harm or crime or group of criminals. This offence or offenders are the focus of intense fear and media coverage. The panic caused means that the act receives not only a significant amount of attention, it also can have resources diverted to it in order to prevent it. The Mods and Rockers are the classic example of the public and the media panicking over the actions and police being tasked with controlling the gathering of the two groups. An ongoing moral panic is the fear, which features in the media, that playing video games causes violence, unemployment and/or addictions, although there is little evidence linked to any of these moral panics (Grace 2019). In conjunction with the panic over the crimes, the offenders are labelled as folk devils—people who are deviant and cause trouble by engaging in anti-social and/or criminal behaviour. In terms of invisible crimes and harms, there is no panic. Tax evasion and pollution, for instance, do not create moral panics that prompt the public to speak out or get a tremendous amount of coverage by the media. In addition, offenders of invisible crimes, often business people or others with high status, are not made out to be folk devils and are not the focus of police attention and resources.

The Media

It is important to note that the media's role in crime, in general, is not isolated to crime's (in)visibility. The media has a complicated role to play in people's fear of crime as well. A complex interplay of the characteristics

- of the media message (random, sensational, location, content, whether justice was received, etc.);
- of the audience (belief in the reality of the message, apprehension of being a victim, etc.);
- and of the dependent measure (local vs. non-local, societal vs. individual violence, urban vs. rural, etc.)

all affect whether the media will impact upon a person's fear of crime (Heath and Gilbert 1996). As Heath and Gilbert (1996: 385) noted even before the rise of social media and the 24-hour news cycle, 'Media messages do not affect all people all of the time, but some of the messages do affect people some of the time'. Ditton et al. (2004) would seem to support this. In their study, they found people's fear of crime was not related to the randomness, sensationalism or localness, but appeared to predominantly be connected—and then only in a small way—to the interpretation of the media content as relevant to and by the consumer' (Ditton et al. 2004: 607). Thus, unpacking the relationship between media and fear of crime is difficult, as it requires understanding and uncovering people's interpretations of the content. Therefore, there is relevance, but it continues to be studied, so as to be better understood.

Summary

The seven features combine to form a complex interconnected web of interactions that can amplify invisibility. The presence or absence of one or more of the features in any given situation contributes to an overall degree of invisibility for that situation. So whereas there may well be knowledge about a crime or harm, like the Hillsborough Stadium football disaster, for instance, due to the strength of no research, no politics and no panic, the incident was not uncovered to be an invisible crime until much later. Not all features need to be present then for a crime to be classified as an invisible crime. The seven features function as a guide and template as to how we can explain (in)visibility and where we might investigate to uncover more injustices. Connected to this are our proposed typologies of spaces that frequently contain invisible crimes and harms.

Pause for Thought

- What are the seven features of invisibility?
- What are the different ways in which 'no knowledge' happens?
- What is meant by degrees of invisibility?

The Seven Spatial Typologies of Invisible Crimes

Invisible crimes and harms do not happen in all places and do not happen in the same way in the places where they do occur. We propose that there are seven typologies that help to explain why certain crimes and harms are invisible in certain areas. The seven typologies are the body, the home, the street, the suite, the environment, the state and the virtual (see Table 3.1). The examples in the table are by no means exhaustive; they serve to illustrate some harms and crimes that may fall under these typologies. In addition, the factors contributing to invisibility are not complete lists but begin to uncover the similarities and differences amongst and between these spaces. For each of the typologies there are characteristics that may be similar and yet there are also distinct aspects that make each of the spatial typologies unique in how invisibility is expressed. We will expand on the aspects in each of the typologies as well as provide examples that support our claims.

The Body

The body features in much victimisation that is both visible and invisible. Whereas much human victimisation often involves the victim's body, in some invisible crimes and harms the body is *specifically* targeted as a means of oppression, as a way of gaining and/or maintaining power and/or as a justification for some perceived

Table 3.1 The seven spatial typologies of invisible crimes

The typology and the harms	Some factors that may make these crimes and harms invisible

The body
Female genital mutilation
Rape/sexual assault
  – Men-on-men
  – Family member
Honour crimes
Theft of cells and DNA
Industrial farming
Lab experimentation
	Behind closed doors, shame, fear of not being believed, voiceless, power used to silence victims and quash information sharing

The home Domestic violence Child abuse Elder abuse Animal abuse	Behind closed doors, interpersonal hidden violence, normalised, accepted, fear of speaking out, invisible because of location
The street Hate crime Police discrimination and brutality Noise pollution Air pollution Waste water	Isolation, normalised, structural, institutional

The suite
Financial crimes
  – Ponzi schemes
  – Price fixing
Fraud
Social injustices
	Behind closed doors, isolation, criminogenic structures and cultures, privileged spaces, control information, need expertise and specialism

The environment Pollution Waste dumping Loss of biodiversity Deforestation Theft of nature Social injustices Ecocide	Isolation, voiceless, speciesist, economy central, commodification, need expertise and specialism

(*continued*)

Table 3.1 (continued)

The typology and the harms	Some factors that may make these crimes and harms invisible
The state	No physical space, control information, define crimes and concerns
Torture Police brutality War crimes Genocide Abductions/killings Fraudulent elections Social injustices Environmental injustices	
The virtual	No physical space, lack of regulation and control, need expertise and specialism
Trespass Black markets Deception and theft Sex offences Violence Terrorism	

greater good. Sexual assault is one such invisible crime where the body is the means of oppression and expressing power. It is a crime that is gendered in nature, where women are predominantly the victims (see Chap. 7), but also intersects with these women's other characteristics, such as race, age and sexuality. To take just one example, family honour is a powerful principle in many communities. Transgressions from honourable behaviour can result in physical, emotional and psychological harm to the person if the person is judged by their family to have transgressed these boundaries. The breach of honour can vary, but as Alexandra Hall (2014) found, it often stems from the adoption of what are perceived as Western attitudes and customs. This may mean wearing of Western-style clothing, which are deemed to be less modest or having close friendships or relationships with boys or men outside of the community. Breaches of honour can result in the person in breach (most likely a girl or woman) being physically, emotionally and psychologically harmed for violating the norms of the community. In extreme cases, girls have been killed in so-called honour crimes. Other invisible crimes where the body is targeted are female genital mutilation and theft of cells and DNA that then become patented by corporations.

It is not our intention to suggest or to sensationalise violence directed at bodies in certain communities over others. Sexual violence is, unfortunately, a feature of all societies and certainly not something 'other' to Western society. The use of honour killings as an example here is to highlight that such crimes are complex and are so because of the intersections of, in this case, culture and gender, but also because of traditions and relationships between family members and society, honour crimes can be particularly difficult to uncover.

Human bodies are not the only bodies that are subjected to violence to achieve oppression or as justification for some perceived greater good. Non-human animal bodies are also harmed and injured in invisible ways. Industrial farming of livestock and poultry takes place behind closed doors and often involves large-scale violations of animal welfare. Chickens, cows, pigs and sometimes sheep are confined to crowded unhygienic spaces and given high levels of antibiotics to fight off illnesses that are frequent in these conditions. These concentrated animal feeding operations (CAFOs) are justified from an economic perspective. The underlying principle that is also worthy under consideration as an invisible harm is the use of animal bodies to feed people. Related to this is the continued use of animals in medical laboratory experiments. There are the potential for benefits to human health from the experimentation on laboratory animals, but this is not guaranteed and science is developing alternative methods to test medicines and procedures rather than subjecting animals to painful procedures and death (Bekoff 2009). The use of animal bodies for food and experiments is a harm that needs further exploration.

Harms to both human and non-human animal bodies then continue because they are physically hidden from sight, either because they happen behind closed doors or because the victim hides the wounds to their body, but also because oppression and commodification of bodies is engrained in cultural practices. In all cases, the perpetrators of the violence hold power to keep their actions invisible to some degree. That may be because they purposefully withhold the information as in the case with animals who are unable to report their own suffering or because the perpetrator may achieve silence of the human victim through fear and intimidation. In addition, human victims may be ashamed to tell family, friends or the police that they have been victimised. There is no knowledge then for invisible crimes and harms targeted at the body because the victims do not or cannot speak out.

The Home

Other invisible crimes and harms that happen behind closed doors and may well involve violence perpetrated on people's and non-human animals' bodies are those that happen in the home. These differ from the typology of the body in that, though the body may be injured as part of the crime or harm, the body is not the main target or object of the injury. Thus, each typology may overlap and there may be multiple sites of harm (i.e. the body and the home) in the perpetration of a single crime. Violence against the body may also be part of a larger pattern of control or expression of power that may have diverse causes. For instance, physical abuse and assault are two of a range of actions undertaken to control victims of domestic violence or as means for the perpetrator to express their power. Similar methods are used within other invisible crimes and harms that happen within in the home, such as elder abuse, child abuse and animal abuse.

Here the location is not public, only private. It is not a space that is under scrutiny from anyone but close friends and family. As such, the space serves to keep crime and harm hidden unless victims or perhaps witnesses speak out regarding the suffering. As with the body, this may not happen because of fear and/or being intimidated by the perpetrator of the crime and harm. Shame also plays a part in victims' silence for crimes and harms happening in the home. In the specific chapters related to invisible crimes and harms taking place in the home, the diverse motivations that explain the abuse will become clear (Chaps. 7 and 8).

The Street

The third spatial typology is that of the street. Clearly, the street is a public space without the factor of a closed door influencing the types of invisible crimes and harms that take place. Even without being a private space though, the street is the location for numerous hidden injuries. Places on the street, and thus largely in the public sphere, can still be isolated in terms of physical space and lack of witnesses. This isolation is a factor in how hate crimes and police discrimination and brutality still occur. In the case of hate and police-related crimes and harms, their normalisation and at times institutional foundations also contribute to their hidden nature. For example, institutionalised racism in police departments both in the United Kingdom and in the United States seems to play a role in the significant disparity of ethnic minorities not only being stopped to be searched but also in ethnic minorities unnecessary and unjust deaths in confrontations with police. Whereas there is a certain amount of visibility related to police misconduct of this nature and to some extent hate crimes, arguably there is still an element of hiddenness as these injustices continue and are not the subject of significant control measures.

Crimes against the environment that are damaging to both the environment and to people are also taking place in the space of the street. Pollution of air is a pervasive invisible crime and harm in most streets as cars and other forms of public transport emit toxins of varying kinds and varying levels. Manufacturing can also be a source of air pollution in city streets. Noise pollution is also a problem in urban areas where again cars, but other city activities too, can make noise levels damaging to human hearing. The exact cause of such noise may be difficult to identify, thus adding to its hiddenness. Water can also be polluted in streetscapes especially in cities that lack the proper infrastructure to treat water and not having drainage systems that collect potentially contaminated run-off. In some instances, the run-off mixes with substances in the street becoming polluted and flowing into drains and eventually into streams, rivers and oceans.

Green/Environmental crimes that are hiding in plain sight in the street can do so because they are normalised. People have to travel so air pollution is a necessity. Our cities have always been built for water to simply pass through. Once water is in the drainage system it is out of sight and not the focus of efforts to make the water and the surrounding waterways clean. The deafening din of urban areas is taken for granted as part of city life. Invisible street crimes—hate and green as well as police discrimination and brutality—are hidden because they are normalised and structurally embedded in the way people interact and the way our cities' infrastructure are constructed.

The Suite

Invisible crimes and harms happening in 'suites' or company board and meeting rooms are also hidden because of a literal closed door. In particular, invisible financial crimes may be part of the everyday routines of corporations. Either the employees or the corporation as an entity may be instigating price fixing schemes or Ponzi schemes to rob people of their money. Due to the closed door and private sphere of businesses and corporations, it is difficult to make these injuries visible. Suites are privileged spaces to which only certain powerful people have access. Suites may not only facilitate various financial crimes, but may also provide the foundation of social injustices and employment or labour violations. For example, company policies and recruitment and promotion practices may be responsible for discriminatory actions against women, minorities and the disabled. As with institutionalised racism at police departments, such prejudicial actions may be part of embedded institutional approaches to business.

One of the main and most powerful factors of invisible crimes and harms taking place in suites is the power and influence of corporations and business people to control the flow of information. With closed doors, privacy and limited access, decisions—including criminal and harmful—are nearly completely hidden. Unless corporations choose to disclose information about their processes, or there is a whistle blower, injurious behaviour is likely to remain invisible. The other way these damaging practices may come to light is when there is a very visible accident. The BP oil spill provides an example. Company and individual employee's decisions to not make repairs and cut corners never would have become visible had an explosion and spill not occurred. The spill revealed though behaviour typical to the routine business of the companies involved and likely representative of the industry and other companies as well.

The Environment

By the environment, we are not referring to a person's surroundings, but to the non-built environment—those parts of the planet not made by people, although all spaces are now affected by human actions. The environment is the location of innumerable crimes and harms, which we would suggest, the vast majority of which are hidden. Probably more so than in any of the other spatial typologies, many spaces within the environment are isolated. Invisible crime and harms take place in areas that are largely inaccessible without expensive forms of transportation or without permission of companies and landowners. Some areas are nearly impossible to reach like the bottom of the ocean or high-mountain peaks. Yet technology has enabled these spaces too to be the site of harms and crimes. Crimes in the environment are in remote locations where people may rarely go and infrequently pass by. The victims of crimes in the environment are the environment itself and non-human inhabitants that live there. The environment and the non-human are voiceless so are unable to speak about the harms and injuries inflicted upon them. The environment—be it animals, plants, soil, rocks, minerals, water, air and so on—is commodified. The living and the non-living elements of the planet are natural resources to be used and sold by people, as the people need. Much of the commodification is invisible because it is normalised. People put price tags on timber, diamonds, land or whatever aspect of the environment they want to use without much regard for the process or questioning of the demand. The cost in terms of a healthy functioning ecosystem is not factored into the markets producing the commodities made from these natural resources. Even when damage to the environment is visible, it is rarely defined as criminal. The economy is the most important part of society, so the environment is allowed to be destroyed in order to maintain economic growth. Underlying this ideology is pervasive speciesism, which prioritises human concerns and wellbeing over everything else. Other life forms are usable and expendable for human desire and progress.

The types of harms and crimes that are taking place in the environment have both non-human and human victims. Pollution in all its forms—air, water, soil, noise, light—affects people, the environment and other species. Pollution also often travels, so if the source of pollution is cars in London, the air pollution created can be blown and move many miles to victimise and impact other people and areas. Other crimes in the environment are waste dumping and fly tipping. To save money on properly paying for the disposal of various kinds of waste (household, industrial, commercial), people and companies travel to remote locations and discard their waste in the environment. This can pollute that area and cause problems for the environment, other species and people.

Remote spaces though are becoming less common. The environment continues to be converted into spaces that support human life. This may be as a result of urbanisation, where more than half the world's population live in large cities rather than in rural areas as has historically been true, but also large-scale land conversion to support agriculture to feed people. This contributes to loss of biodiversity and species extinction and is a main reason for deforestation. Loss of other species can disrupt and destabilise ecosystems, which can affect the livelihood and wellbeing of people too. Deforestation is linked to global warming as well as soil erosion, both of which also negatively impact upon people and other species. Natural resources, like timber but also minerals, gems and metals, are extracted from the environment often by severely damaging the environment. This too affects human communities and environmental health. It is not uncommon for these natural resources to be illegally extracted and sold on black markets or laundered so that they can be sold in the legitimate market. The exposure to degraded, polluted and toxic environments is not experienced by all groups of people. Ethnic minorities, indigenous people and women are more likely to live in unhealthy environments. Therefore, there is an additional invisible harm taking place in regard to the spatial typology of the environment as this injustice is discriminatory in nature.

The environment is made up of complex systems that are still not completely understood. In order to document and evidence these harms and crimes, if they were to be uncovered, requires a certain level of expertise and specialism. Police departments and other regulatory agencies rarely have this sort of expertise or the technical skills to be able to identify crimes taking place in the environment. This is another reason why these harms and crimes remain hidden. Crimes in the environment also remain invisible because of jurisdictional issues. Many of the harms and crimes described above are transnational in nature. The added complexity of ascribing blame across borders means that harms and crimes can go undetected and unexplored. One of the main reasons for the invisibility of crimes in and to the environment is the powerful people and entities defining crimes do not recognise that the environment and other species are victims. A majority of the time this is the state, which is another space for hidden crimes and harms.

The State

The state as a space for invisible crimes and harms may well be the spatial typology that is most difficult to uncover and to challenge. Not only is there not necessarily a physical space where information can be gathered from or where protest can be lodged, but if there is an actual space, it is highly exclusive with very few people being given legitimate access. The people permitted access may well have an interest in keeping harms and crimes hidden. Furthermore, the state as an entity has control over nearly all, if not absolutely all, of the information that is generated and held by the various agencies, which make up the state. And of course possibly the most difficult hurdle in relation to crimes of the state is that the state has defined what a crime is in the first place. This means harms, which should be crimes, perpetrated by the state are purposefully ignored and actively kept hidden. Green and Ward (2004) propose seven categories of state crime and we would add to their list environmental injustices. State crime then, in addition to environmental injustices, can take the form of torture, police brutality, war crimes, genocide, abductions and killings, fraudulent elections and social Injustices.

As the state is a space, which we are discussing here, and an actor, which is the focus of the individual chapters, we will focus on the state's actions in much greater detail in Chap. 11. It is notable though as a location that the state shares similar factors, such as closed doors, power and influence with the suite discussed above. Also similarly, unless there is a whistle blower from within the ranks of a state agency, many of the atrocities happening within state spaces and sanctioned by state governments will remain hidden.

The Virtual

The newest space for crimes and harms to be hidden is within the virtual world of cyberspace. As with the state, there is no literal or actual physical space for the most part. Whilst the space may be new, the crimes that are committed in the virtual are not always themselves something new. Crimes committed in cyberspace are crimes that are computer assisted and crimes that are computer orientated. For crimes that are computer assisted, there is a real-world equivalent. For crimes that are computer orientated, the electronic infrastructure itself is the target of the crime or harm. Drawing on cybercrime scholars (Kleemans 2007; Jewkes and Yar 2010; Yar 2013), we propose there are six categories of virtual crimes: cyber trespassing, cyber black markets, cyber deceptions and thefts, cybersex offences, cyber violence and cyber terrorism.

Cyber trespassing may be what most people think of when they think of crimes in the virtual space. This includes incidents of hacking, where a person (hacker) uses a computer to gain access to the files on the computer of another person or an organisation. As with many cybercrimes, there is (was) a physical equivalent to hacking, but the sort of data being stolen or accessed by hackers is much less likely to exist in the physical realm any more. Other forms of cyber trespassing would be the various forms of malicious software or malware that computer criminals send, presumably largely at random, to people through email and online. Malware includes worms, Trojan horses, viruses and spyware that may lie in wait on the victim's computer system until a time where the malware can copy useful information to then access the victim's accounts or other private information.

Other crimes happening in the virtual world are cyber black markets, deceptions and thefts. Again, all of these forms of crimes also happen in the physical world. The internet has allowed though for these types of crimes to flourish and probably to proliferate. Online black markets include stolen goods, which have been stolen in the physical world, but are being moved and sold online, illegal drugs and pharmaceuticals, weapons, wildlife and pirated goods. Pirated goods is an interesting form of cybercrime since most mass media is now digital; the piracy too then becomes digital. Selling pirated goods online then becomes sites that give access to illegally downloaded or copied digital material. Here we see an overlap with cyber theft. Cyber deception may take the form of selling items online and claiming that they are made of one material, but in reality they are made of something else. Cyber deception may also be currency manipulation, where a government or central bank buys or sells foreign currency in the attempt to change or impact on the value of their own currency. In addition, deception online may be in the form of money laundering. In the virtual world, online companies and bank accounts are used to hide the illegal origins of money. Returning to cyber theft, presumably the most thought-of form of online theft is identity theft where, probably through the use of malware, cybercriminals are able to assume the identity and access the accounts of their victim.

Cybersex offences clearly have an equivalent in the physical world. In cyberspace and in virtual worlds like Second City, there are incidents of sexual harassment, sexual assault and rape (Kleemans 2007). Pornography, of children, women and animals, is also prevalent. A potentially new form of sex offence is revenge pornography. The offender, often a former sexual partner of the victim, posts online revealing or sexually explicit images of the victim without the victim's permission or knowledge. Potentially, this could have happened with printed photographs in the past, but clearly, with electronic communication, the number of people who could potentially see such pictures is exponentially more. Virtual worlds and electronic communication also enable grooming to happen. Grooming is where an offender misrepresents themselves online in order to deceive a potential victim. What has started in the virtual world then moves to an offline crime, when the offender meets the victim in the physical world.

Sex offences are not the only forms of violence that are perpetrated in cyberspace. Cyber bullying, harassment and stalking also take place. Again, the bullying, harassment and stalking that happen are in essence the same behaviour that occur in the physical world but are assisted by the use of a computer. Presumably with the anonymity and distance from victims, cyber bullying, harassment and stalking might be more prevalent than the real-world equivalents. It seems that many of the victims of cyber bullying, in particular, are young people. Unfortunately, this has led to several suicides, such as the case of 18-year-old Brandy Vela (Pasha-Robinson 2016). She shot herself after enduring years of cyber violence where the offenders created fake social media profiles of her saying she would have sex for free and including her mobile number.

Finally, there is cyber terrorism. This takes one of two forms. First, terrorist organisations have websites where they post fear-inducing material and sometimes themselves engaging in criminal acts. Streaming or having digital recordings of beheading prisoners is one example of this type of content. Second, cyber terrorists may attack the electronic and digital infrastructures of their targets. For instance, they may attempt to disrupt air traffic control or the network of a large bank. Not only could there potentially be the real-world disruption and chaos if such an attack were successful, just the fear and possibility that such an attack will be attempted can be seen as a terrorist act.

All of these cybercrimes are able to be hidden because of the lack of regulation and control that currently is in place in regard to the virtual world. The lack of regulation and control stems from the slow process of adding legislation that would provide the regulation and control that is needed, but also stems from the difficulty in actually trying to create regulation and control mechanisms that would be able to govern a vast space with no physical reality. In addition, the virtual is an ideal space for invisible crimes and harms to take place because the amount of expertise needed to uncover such activity is high. Few regulators have the specialism necessary to track the amount or type of cybercrimes that are happening let alone the skill set to gather evidence and hold cyber offenders accountable.

The seven typologies or sites of invisible crimes and harms can be both discrete and overlapping. As mentioned the site of the 'the body' may be related to 'the home' and similarly 'the virtual' may lead to harm against 'the body'. These typologies serve as a useful framework for conceptualising the common patterns and characteristics that emerge when researching crimes of the powerful and their invisible crimes and harms.

Pause for Thought

• What are the seven typologies of invisible crimes and harms?
• What are factors common throughout the typologies?

Summary

In this chapter, we have detailed two of the core theoretical frameworks that will be used as a basis for analysis throughout the coming chapters. The first is the seven features of invisibility, which we propose provide a way in which to investigate why it is that some crimes and harms remain invisible even though they cause injury and suffering. No knowledge, no statistics, no research, no theory, no control, no politics and no panic! combine in differing levels and intensities to create varying degrees of invisibility for a range of crimes and harms. The second theoretical framework is the spatial typologies—the body, the home, the street, the suite, the environment, the state and the virtual—have commonalities, which we argue makes it possible and at times likely for invisible crimes and harms to occur in these places. With our conceptual and theoretical frameworks outlined, we now turn to Part I 'Individual Power'.

References

Bekoff, M. (2009). Animal emotions, wild justice and why they matter: Grieving magpies, a pissy baboon and empathetic elephants. *Emotion Space and Society, 2*(2): 82–85.

Cohen, S. (2002). *Folk Devils and Moral Panics: The Creation of the Mods and the Rockers* (3rd ed.). London: Routledge.

Davies, P., Francis, P., & Wyatt, T. (2014). Taking Invisible Crimes and Social Harms Seriously. In P. Davies, P. Francis, & T. Wyatt (Eds.), *Invisible Crimes and Social Harms* (pp. 1–25). London: Palgrave Macmillan.

Ditton, J., Chadee, D., Farrall, S., Gilchrist, E., & Bannister, J. (2004). From Imitation to Intimidation: A Note on the Curious and Challenging Relationship between the Media. *Crime and the Fear of Crime. The British Journal of Criminology, 44*, 595–610.

Grace, K. (2019). Games Blamed for Moral Decline and Addiction Throughout History. *The Conversation*. Retrieved May 29, 2020, from https://theconversation.com/games-blamed-for-moral-decline-and-addiction-throughout-history-123900.

Green, P., & Ward, T. (2004). *State Crime: Governments, Violence and Corruption*. London: Pluto Press.

Hall, A. (2014). 'Honour' Crimes. In P. Davies, P. Francis, & T. Wyatt (Eds.), *Invisible Crimes and Social Harms* (pp. 81–101). London: Palgrave Macmillan.

Heath, L., & Gilbert, K. (1996). Mass Media and Fear of Crime. *The American Behavorial Scientist, 39*(4), 379–386.

Jewkes, Y., & Yar, M. (Eds.). (2010). *The Handbook of Internet Crime*. Cullompton: Willan Publishing.

Jupp, V., Davies, P., & Francis, P. (1999). The Features of Invisible Crimes. In P. Davies, P. Francis, & V. Jupp (Eds.), *Invisible Crimes: Their Victims and their Regulation*. Basingstoke: Macmillan Publishers.

Kleemans, E. (2007). Organized Crime, Transit Crime, and Racketeering. *Crime and Justice. A Review of Research, 35*, 163–215.

Pasha-Robinson, L. (2016). Teenager Killed Herself in Front of Parents after Relentless Cyberbullying. *The Independent*. Retrieved March 24, 2016, from http://www.independent.co.uk/news/brandy-vela-cyber-bullying-kill-shoot-herself-driven-suicide-texas-shotgun-a7451446.html.

Yar, M. (2013). *Cybercrime and Society* (2nd ed.). London: SAGE.

Part I

Individuals and Power Dynamics

In our effort to push and further your progress through the book, these shorter sections between the two parts of the book guide you to appreciate how the micro, meso, and macros levels of analysis are important. A snapshot analyses from any singular one of these levels is likely to produce an interesting case study, but only a partial reproduction of what is going on. We seek to make you confident to engage in deep case study analysis in order to get closer to capturing the lived reality of people's experiences of crime, harm and victimisation. This endeavour demands that we appreciate the complexity of the dynamics of power where the boundaries of levels of analysis and perspectives are blurred. Some criminological tools, concepts and theoretical constructs can help us get closer to achieving this type of rich criminological research. In part, we do this through the case study approach and in part we do this by reminding the reader of the complexity of the crime and power dynamics. We promised, that in the chapters that form the series comprising Part I of the book, we would provide proof that power exists and is expressed differently in different individuals. The characteristics of a person—their class, gender, race, religion and/or age (in addition to others)—and the complex interplay of these result in each of us potentially having power or being powerless and, equally important, result in the potential for us to be the focus of power from another individual or from a group. The personal characteristics of an individual can play a role in their offending and victimisation, and the visibility of both.

As we introduced in Chap. 2, power is a contested topic that does not have an agreed upon definition. The most straightforward way to conceptualise power maybe Giddens' (1984: 257) definition "the capacity to achieve outcomes" or Parsons' (1963) a capacity to achieve ends. The first three chapters served as an extended introduction to the remainder of this book. Whilst Chap. 1 introduced the reader to the text and outlines the structure and features, Chap. 2 focused on what power is and who the powerful are. Chapter 3 addressed how power is maintained and dwells on the idea of hidden crime and victimisation, invisible crimes and social harms. Collectively, these chapters have begun to explore what constitutes power. They introduced a range of well-known and oft used concepts related to power and domination and outlined how criminologists have tended to make links between power and crime, offending, criminalisation, crime control and the regulation and responses to crime, harm and offending. They began to consider where power is vested and concentrated, who has power and how it manifests. They clarified the differences between the 'micro' levels of power, the 'macro' levels of power and the 'meso/mezzo' levels of power covered in the book. To summarise, the term 'Crimes of the powerful' has been principally applied to the crimes of states, corporations, and syndicated crime and we characterise this as macro-level power. The power in each of these cases emanates out of huge control over core resources of markets. We are encouraging you to consider a broader conception of power and Part I of the book, in particular, helps you to do precisely this whilst preparing you for the further level of complexity whereby the micro, meso/mezzo and macro levels of power overlap in mutually constitutive ways.

Organised within two Parts, the remainder of the book addresses hugely consequential forms of crime, which have been traditionally relatively 'invisible' in relation to conventional forms of crime. Whilst we retain traditional content related to 'crimes of the powerful' in Part II in Chaps. 9–12, we preface this with Chaps. 4–8 that adopt a broader conception of power that encompasses that linked to class, race, religion, gender, and age. Although some of this power is institutionalised, deeply embedded and exercised systemically, for example via patriarchal systems, much of what is addressed in Part I also occurs in specific settings and contexts, for example, the workplace or the home. The disproportionate power of the male corporate manager, partner, or indeed father, is in this sense situational, and a form of micro power. At another level, although the broad patterns to crime and victimisation may suggest the weakness and vulnerability of some as compared to other populations, and that women and the elderly are collectively less powerful than men and the middle-aged, there are of course immensely powerful women (i.e. the late Margaret Thatcher) and elderly people (i.e. Rupert Murdoch, Donald Trump). Thus, there is value in exploring the meso levels of power and how these sometimes reside within or sit comfortably alongside micro and macro levels of power. Interpersonal relationships are where the confluence of different powers often manifest and this can result in physical violence, domestic abuse and coercive control. The combined personal characteristics of an individual—their class, race, religion, age and/or gender (though there are others as well)—can play a role in their victimisation and its visibility and their ability to victimise. Within the next few chapters comprising Part I, the case studies we examine therefore foreground discrete actors and actions whilst not forgetting the systemic nature and interconnectedness of the micro, meso and macro of much crime of the powerful. Thus, the first and next part of this book focusses on how individual characteristics or demographics of people—age, class, gender, ethnicity and race, religion, and so forth—are integral to the power a person may or may not have.

In Chap. 1 of this book, we explained how we would draw upon a number of perspectives, traditions and theoretical formulations throughout our examination of crime and power. In our efforts to help readers understand the significant factors at work, the first three chapters of the book, as noted above, have prepared you for the journey to appreciate how the micro, meso and macro levels of power overlap in mutually constitutive ways. We have also divided the book into two parts as described earlier in order to make this complex task of unpicking the dynamics of crime and power more manageable. However, we feel we should stretch your understanding further and this requires us to oscillate between various individual and group level power dynamics. Therefore, before reading the chapters that form Part I of this book, where there is a focus on individual characteristics, we want to expand on what we mean by our promise to examine what we have so far called the 'mutually constitutive ways' in which vectors of power intersect. It is timely therefore for us to introduce the theoretical construct *intersectionalities*. Intersectionalities is a theoretical framework for understanding class-race-gender-age-sexuality-etc. This theoretical underpinning has the potential to harness what brings about the points of confluence between crime, offending, harm and victimisation. These areas of criminological concern are bound together by dimensions of power and influence and, because it is important that we do not over simplify the personal individual features of our identity, it is also incumbent upon us to illustrate not only the complex interplay power plays in the mediation of these social problems but also the complex interplay of these characteristics that form our personal identity and the ways in which different qualities of power interact.

In order to help you develop your own critically informed, meaningful and original case studies, we provide an outline of the theoretical construct *intersectionalities*. Although you may not choose to adopt this theoretical framework wholesale, you may be inspired to firm up the theoretical underpinning of your own research. We now expand on the important sociological concept of intersectionality, the theoretical construct class-race-gender and the significance of these formulations in the context of criminology.

3.1   Intersectionalities

Let us start by thinking about social divisions in society. Social divisions provide a basis for shared identity and shared experience including experiences of oppression and subjugation. Iris Marion Young (1997) argued that, essential to redressing structural inequalities, and indeed what she explains as the five faces of oppression (Exploitation, Marginalization, Powerlessness, Cultural domination, Violence) (Young 2005), is that we appreciate social group distinctions. Social divisions are apparent in many societies and in the social sciences, familiar social categories include those identifiable according to class, race, gender, age, sexuality, disability, mental health and physical disability (Davies et al 2017). These social categories are not static, but rather dynamic and change over time, space and place. They are situated historically, culturally, economically, and politically. Messerschmidt (1993, 1994) brought home these ideas to criminology. Building on previous work, he examined the connections between violent crime and masculinity. In 1997, he pointed out:

> Gender, race and class are not absolutes and are not equally significant in every social setting where crime is realised. That is, depending on the social setting, accountability to certain categories is more salient than accountability to other categories. (Messerschmidt 1997: 113)

Messerschmidt introduces the idea of situation or context; indeed, he discusses crime as a 'situated accomplishment'. By this time, Kimberle Crenshaw (1989) had coined the term intersectionalities in her expose of the interplay between law, race and racial power in American society. Crenshaw and Young's thinking on the interplay between class and race and how these interlocking systems define women of colours' lives has prompted much theoretical development around the concept of intersectionality. There is now a variety of opinion about the salience of any single category or indeed if there is any one isolating factor from another in any given context, including the commission of crime. Nevertheless, it is important for us to consider how aspects of our personal characteristics intersect to create conditions of oppression, and, alternately, conditions of liberation that are specific to particular identities. Thus, whilst there is debate about *when* does *what* feature of our identity *if any* matter most and *what combination* of features is most toxic, there is little disagreement that power is an important part of these avenues of inquiry.

Other scholars have developed, refined and postulated variations of the theoretical construction of intersectionalities in the context of crime and offending.

Kathleen Daly (1993), for example, explains that the intersectionalities of class-race-age-gender or multiple inequalities variously combine "as intersecting, inter-locking and contingent" (Daly 1997: 33). Class, race, age, and gender are amongst the major social inequalities in our society. To be poor, to be black, to be young and to be female, simultaneously represents different distinct social categories with combined significance and relation to relative disadvantage, exclusion, marginali-sation and powerlessness (Davies et al 2017).

So for example, gender is therefore only one of a number of processes or social variables that are usually attributed to framing our experiences (Davies et al 2017) and which get to the heart of our social lives by tapping in to the lived everyday realities of people's experiences of social harm and criminal victimisation. Several contemporary theoretical, feminist inspired constructs, have been postulated (See Connell 1987, 1995, Messerschmidt 1993, 1994, 1997, 2004), which suggest that gender is sometimes highly salient in understanding both offending and victimisa-tion. 'Doing—gender', the theoretical formulation most extensively demonstrated by West et al (1987, 1995), was later extended to 'doing race' and 'class' (Daly 1993, 1997), so that a new understanding of 'difference' is that it is viewed as an ongoing interactional accomplishment. The focus on gender as something which is socially constructed sees gender as 'omnirelevant'. Moreover, it is something we are accountable for and any occasion offers the resources for doing it. Similarly, 'doing—difference' explains how gender, race and class operate simultaneously and like gender are a process.

In the first sentence of this section, we used the phrase 'shared identity'. A further useful concept emerging out of these theoretical formulations is the idea of 'multiple identities'. We have gone on to establish that some differentiations can become divisive categorisations and there are points of intersectionality. This cros-scutting feature means that individuals may share a common in-group membership on one dimension (i.e. gender), but belong to different categories on another di-mension (i.e. rage). Hence, we have multiple identities. We raise this in order to illustrate once again the overlaps between the chapters sandwiched within this part of the book: Individuals and Power Dynamics.

3.1.1   Part I: Chaps. 4–8

As we now explore in the forthcoming chapters, the level of power seems to be accumulative. The power that is inherent in being a mature, upper class, white man is historic and structural. As each of the chapters investigates, the power that comes with each of these characteristics does not necessarily stem from the actions of any one person, but are rooted in many years of economic, political, and social events and transformations. For instance, patriarchy—the male dominance of many societies—is not a new phenomenon, but is grounded in hundreds of years of men controlling societies as politicians and core decision makers. Thus, being a man in modern day society lends itself to being powerful without the individual man necessarily having taken action to grab power (Chap. 7). Similarly, the powerlessness often experienced by ethnic and racial minorities has a long complicated history linked to the subjugation of non-white people during the slave trade, European colonisation, and segregation (Chap. 5).

That power at the individual level is intractable from historic events and evolving social structures leads to new lived realities for vulnerable populations as the negative aspects of globalisation open up new or heightened opportunities for human trafficking, exploitation, and other forms of victimisation. If indeed power at the individual level is intractable from historic events and social structures, this leads to at least two important considerations for the next five chapters. First, and this becomes especially evident in Chap. 4 on Class, the intersections of key features of our identity can become toxic. Some have a head start in terms of ability to victimise and others have less capacity to resist oppression. One example used in Chap. 4 illustrates how high-social status and maleness can be used to manipulate and victimise.

Second, the historic and structural nature of much of a person's power means that this form of power when used to harm people and commit crime is particularly difficult to challenge. This has implications for the individual victims of a powerful offender, but also long-term implications for preventing the same sort of offences and oppressions from happening in the future by other people, who are similarly powerful. As we seen in Chap. 7 on gender, gender-based violence is not uncommon and the power of men to exploit women in society is a form of victimisation that has been the focus of attention for hundreds of years. To disrupt the power imbued by individual characteristics, radical transformations of society must be considered.

In the chapters on individual elements of power, we also explore how one's class, race, gender, religion, and age enables that person to render their actions visible or invisible. For instance, depending upon a person's individual characteristics, they may well have more power over knowledge. An individual's age, class, gender, ethnicity and race, and religion could mean they have access to more information, that more information is shared with them, or that they have control over what happens to information. In Chap. 8 on Age, we detail how young people, for instance, are unlikely to have the power that comes with having the control over knowledge. As we introduced in Chap. 3 on invisibility, the feature of 'no knowledge' links closely to the other seven features of invisibility, namely 'no theory', 'no research' and 'no control' (Jupp et al 1999; Davies et al 2014). So having the power over knowledge, which may originate from being of high-social status or being older, lends to power over (in)visibility in other ways too.

The feature of 'no panic!' demonstrates the intersectionality of not only individual characteristics, but also the intersectionality to group or collective power that we will discuss in Part II of the book. Older white men have historically dominated the media in the West. This is evident in who have been reporters and journalists over the last several decades, but also who has owned and controlled the media companies during that time. Since there are individually powerful men combined with powerful corporations in the media, it is no wonder that the news media—and now social media—are a powerful force within society with control over knowledge and information that has far-reaching consequences.

Now each of the chapters—Chap. 4 Class, Chap. 5 Race, Chap. 6 Religion, Chap. 7 Gender, and Chap. 8 Age—set within an historic and structural context will unpack the power of the individual characteristic, the intersection with other individual characteristics and the role of the seven features of invisibility in contributing to that individual characteristics' power.

Questions to Ponder
- What are micro, meso and macro levels of analysis?

How does one's class, race, religion, gender and age interact in relation to power?
What are your own intersectionalities?

References
- Connell, R. W. (1995). *Masculinities*. Oxford: Polity.

Connell, R. W. (1987). *Gender and Power*. Oxford: Polity.

Crenshaw, K. (1989). Demarginalizing the Intersection of Race and Sex: A Black Feminist Critique of Antidiscrimination Doctrine, Feminist Theory and Antiracist Politics. *The University of Chicago Legal Forum, 140*, 139–167.

Daly, K. (1993). Class-Race-Gender: Sloganeering in Search of Meaning. *Social Justice, 20*(1–2), 56–71.

Daly, K. (1997). Different Ways of Conceptualising Sex/gender in Feminist Theory and their Implications for Criminology. *Theoretical Criminology, 1*(1), 25–51.

Davies, P., Francis, P., & Greer, C. (Eds.). (2017). *Victims, Crime and Society* (2nd ed). London: Sage.

Davies, P., Francis, P., & Wyatt, T. (2014). Taking Invisible Crimes and Social Harms Seriously. In P. Davies, P. Francis, & T. Wyatt (Eds.), *Invisible Crimes and Social Harms* (pp. 1–25). London: Palgrave Macmillan.

Giddens, A. (1984). *The Constitution of Society*. Cambridge: Polity Press.

Jupp, V., Davies, P., & Francis, P. (1999). The Features of Invisible Crimes. In P. Davies, P. Francis, & V. Jupp (Eds.), *Invisible Crimes: Their Victims and Their Regulation* (pp. 3–28). Basingstoke: Macmillan Publishers.

Messerschmidt, J. W. (1993). *Masculinities and Crime*. Lanham, MD: Rowman & Littlefield.

Messerschmidt, J. W. (1994). Schooling, Masculinities and Youth Crime by White Boys. In T. Newburn & E. Stanko (Eds.), *Just Boys Doing Business?* London: Routledge.

Messerschmidt, J. W. (1997). *Crime as Structured Action*. Thousand Oaks, CA: Sage.

Messerschmidt, J. W. (2004). *Flesh & Blood: Adolescent Gender Diversity and Violence*. Lanham, MD: Rowman & Littlefield.

Parsons, T. (1963). On the Concept of Political Power. *Proceedings of the American Philosophical Society, 107*(3), 232–262.

Young, I. M. (1997). *Intersecting Voices: Dilemmas of Gender, Political Philosophy, and Policy*. Princeton, NJ: Princeton University Press.

Young, I. M. (2005). Five Faces of Oppression. In A. E. Cudd & R. O. Andreasen (Eds.), **Feminist Theory: A Philosophical Anthology** (pp. 91–104). Oxford, UK and Malden, MA: Blackwell Publishing.

Class, Status and Elites

4

Introduction

If one were to uncritically take official or national crime statistics as the only indication of who in society commits crime, that person would conclude that people of so-called low, under- or working-class status are the people perpetrating most crime. As Pearce (1976) argued, the picture is much more complex than that. In this chapter, we detail the reasons why it appears that people of lower socio-economic status are more likely to commit crimes. These reasons include the focus of crime studies and statistics on the lower socio-economic classes, the presumed links between crime and poverty, and, once again, the fact that who is defining crime are people of high social status. We, then, discuss the contributions of Edwin Sutherland, who proposed the concept of white-collar crime. White-collar crime challenges the typical focus on crimes committed by people of lower socio-economic status and introduces the notion that people of high social status are just as likely to commit crime, but these crimes may be different. White-collar crimes are not the only crimes committed by the elite. We provide a case study of the movie director, Harvey Weinstein, as an example of how people in the upper classes also commit crimes typically found in crime statistics. Yet, because of the power that comes with their celebrity high social status, Weinstein and people like him are able to shield themselves from accusations of crimes. We conclude with a discussion of the power of class and being one of the elite.

© The Author(s) 2021
P. Davies, T. Wyatt, *Crime and Power*,
https://doi.org/10.1007/978-3-030-57314-0_4

Crime and the 'Lower' Classes

Theft, drug abuse, sex work, interpersonal violence and so on—these are the topics that criminology has traditionally focused on researching and trying to prevent. These crimes are likely to be committed by people categorised in the 'lower' classes. We begin this section by unpacking what is meant by class and how it can be conceptualised.

What Is Class?

What 'class' is has been a topic of discussion by many if not all of the great thinkers in sociology, from which criminology tends to draw its foundation. Here we highlight some of the main elements of this discussion. For instance, Marx linked class to property, thus, in a socialist society where there would be no private property, there could be no classes (Giddens 1975). Marxism remains hugely influential in debates about power with myriad derivations on Marxist views about the role of law and theorising around crime, conflict and social control. In simple terms, Marxism is concerned about the capitalist mode of production, and within that system, the social division is between the oppressors and oppressed. The middle-upper-class bourgeoisie (the oppressor class) promote their own economic concerns, valuing property and the preservation of their own capital to preserve their affluent status quo. The proletariat in contrast are the lower strata, wage earners whose value is their labour value. Structural Marxism contends that the state functions to serve the long-term interests of the capitalist class. Instrumental Marxism views policy-makers in government and positions of power as sharing common class and business backgrounds, and that their decisions will reflect their own class and economic interests. The state, and the law, including the justice system, as an agent of that state, is an instrument or tool for those of the economically dominant class to use to further their own ends. In crime control terms, the state is a mechanism for regulating the tensions of class conflict between the proletariat and the bourgeoisie.

Whereas income and wealth clearly play a large part in defining and conceptualising class, other demographic characteristics—like race, religion and gender—likely play a role as well as we will explore throughout this chapter. Ossowski (1963 [1981]) summarises that class, which has been conceptualised throughout modern societies, broadly follows dichotomous categorisations: the ruled and the ruler, the poor and the rich and the exploited and the exploiter. What is referred to as the 'working class' are those who are exploited for their labour (Giddens 1975). Class may also be conceptualised as a gradation, again, usually framed in terms of income (Ossowski 1963 [1981]). Census data that provides income bands to choose from are an example of such a gradation. Ossowski (1963 [1981]) also proposed that class can be thought of as separate yet cooperative elements of society—the functional scheme. For instance, there are managers, skilled workers, unskilled workers and so forth. Such understanding of class is less antagonistic than dichotomous or gradated conceptualisations, which often focus on the conflicts that occur between the different classes (Giddens 1975).

Thus, we can say that definitions and conceptualisations of class are linked to the distribution of income, wealth and status (Barak et al. 2010). This is the case regardless of a dichotomous, gradated or categorised interpretation of class, since in each of these interpretations the categorisations are framed in terms of income, wealth or status (i.e. profession that defines class in Ossowski's function scheme). Income, wealth and status—class—are, of course as we allude to above, inextricably linked to race and gender, as very often ethnic minorities and women earn less income (Barak et al. 2010) or have supposedly lower status occupations. Whilst class is a crucial element to power, and therefore crime, Barak et al. (2010) suggest that class is less frequently discussed due to a combination of not wanting to or not being able to challenge the capitalist status quo where the wealthiest people are in power. The lack of class discussion may also be due to the difficulty in collecting information about class (i.e. lack of transparency of people's income and the taxes that they have paid). One case where data about the lower socio-economic classes is kept is in terms of crime and statistics.

Crime, Statistics and Poverty

As we have mentioned, not all harms are defined as crimes (which we return to in a moment). And, as important, even if an action is defined as a crime, this does not mean that it is a recorded offence. The shortcomings of police or 'official' crime statistics as generated by the police are well established. Such *counts* of crime are 'unqualified crime statistics' (see Tseloni and Duncan 2020 for more on police counts of crimes and crime statistics more generally). Police data is often fragmented, classifications may be duplicated or overlap, and there are, therefore, plenty of validity and reliability concerns, some of which we illustrate below. Police agencies may not (will not) record crimes that fall out of their remit and are likely not to record offences that are not typical street crimes. For instance, recordable offences that feed into the quarterly crime report produced by the Office of National Statistics for England and Wales consist of the crimes listed in Table 4.1.

Apart from fraud offences, sexual offences and possibly miscellaneous crimes against society, the crimes are visible, observable, public crimes. All of the crimes are also either acquisitive (related to theft and property) or interpersonal (violence between people). Again, apart from fraud, corporate crimes or businesses as perpetrators are largely absent from these crimes. Environmental, wildlife and non-human animal crimes are also missing. Essentially, crimes of the powerful—state, corporate, green, organised—are not recorded, or at least not recorded by local police agencies and constabularies. In particular, since businesses are treated completely differently in the criminal law than people (see Chap. 9 on corporations), these offences maybe recorded by other, less prominent, agencies, like an environment agency or not recorded as crimes at all. The picture of criminality that is then presented to governments and the public is one that is skewed in numerous ways. The crimes recorded and therefore those that receive media and law enforcement attention as well as funding for prevention are those perpetrated and experienced by people in the lower socio-economic classes. Furthermore, they tend to be crimes

Table 4.1 Crimes recorded by police constabularies in England and Wales

All other theft offences
Bicycle theft
Criminal damage and arson
Death or serious injury caused by illegal driving
Domestic burglary
Drug offences
Fraud offences
Homicide
Miscellaneous crimes against society
Non-domestic burglary
Possession of weapons offences
Public order offences
Robbery
Sexual offences
Shoplifting
Stalking and harassment
Theft from the person
Vehicle offences
Violence with injury
Violence without injury

occurring in urban settings, so experiences of residents of rural areas—regardless of their class—are largely missing from most countries' national statistics.

That these crimes are the focus of law enforcement creates further problems because it amplifies perceptions of the criminality of people in the lower socio-economic classes. This happens, in part, because conventional crimes, such as those in Table 1, are known to have a high incidence rate in areas of high poverty. Furthermore, statistical analysis of the residential areas of known offenders show recorded crimes are typically concentrated in areas of poverty (Newburn 2017). Thus, only crimes known to be correlated to poverty are the crimes that are the target of record keeping. This creates a feedback loop, where criminality is inextricably linked to poverty whilst ignoring crimes and harms that occur in other locales and involving other offenders.

There is even further bias to crime statistics. If high status and/or wealthy offenders are caught by the police committing one of the crimes from Table 1, their status and/or wealth may well give them political and financial protection from arrest (Sutherland 1949). If a person is not arrested, but only comes into contact with the police, this may be recorded internally by the police, but would not become a public statistic and certainly not part of crime statistics. So the power that comes with status and wealth can shield powerful individuals from becoming suspects, being arrested, being prosecuted, being convicted, being given harsh sentences and being sent to more secure facilities. Power lends advantages to those who have it throughout the criminal justice process.

To reiterate the bias of the statistics—in the words of Newburn (2017: 400):

> The general theories of criminal behaviour which take their data from poverty and the conditions related to it are inadequate and invalid, first, because the theories do not consistently fit the data of criminal behaviour; and second, because the cases on which these theories are based are a biased sample of criminal acts.

Newburn's first point addresses the problematic use of the research based upon the biased statistics. Drawing upon the work of Sutherland (1983), Newburn argues that theories explaining the causes of crime are generated from data that only looks at a portion of criminality—the portion that is visible and policed that occurs in lower socio-economic neighbourhoods. This focus on the lower classes also contributes to the reinforcement of the bias that offending is more prevalent in the lower socio-economic classes. Furthermore, a significant portion of criminality cannot be explained by poverty and its related challenges, as will become more evident when exploring white-collar crime (Sutherland 1949). That brings us back to the fact that it is the powerful who are defining what crime is in the first place.

Definitions of Crime

From both the introduction and Chap. 1 of this book, we have argued crime is a social construct that is mainly constructed by the powerful (Pearce 1976). Those individuals in positions of power are the people crafting the law. Who are these powerful people? By and large in the Western world, at least historically, policy-makers have been rich Christian white men and probably connected to positions of power such as the monarchy or the church, depending upon the country under examination. As this is a chapter discussing class in particular, those people's wealth and status are of the most interest (gender and race will be examined in Chaps. 7 and 5). The wealthy have greater access than other people to politicians who can make the laws favourable to the rich (Barak et al. 2010). This links to why it might be that businesses are treated differently within the criminal law than individual offenders. Policy-makers, possibly influenced by those in the upper classes, have shaped legislation such that is more lenient towards corporations and the wealthy.

High status and wealthy individuals can influence policy-makers in a variety of subtle—and sometimes not so subtle—ways. For example, wealthy individuals can donate large sums of money to election campaigns for politicians willing to create laws in ways that the wealthy support. Such financial support by the wealthy can also manifest through the lobbying process, where professional organisations try to influence policy-makers to draft laws in particular ways or keep laws as they are. The National Rifle Association (NRA) in the United States could well be an example of this. Wealthy donors support the NRA who then lobbies and financially supports politicians who will try to keep the status quo around gun laws. High status and/or wealthy individuals may also influence policy-makers by withholding or granting public endorsement of that particular policy-maker. Again, this is evident in the United States where famous celebrities support like-minded candidates (i.e. George Clooney endorsing Hillary Clinton for President).

The result of crime being defined in favour of the wealthy and people of high status is that street crimes—crimes happening in public spaces—are the actions and harms most likely to be defined as criminal and are the crimes targeted by government enforcement strategies. Furthermore, if white-collar activities are criminalised, then the powerful are able to minimise the damage it may cause them, despite the possibility that people may band together to challenge such efforts of the powerful (Pearce 1976). Overall, the criminal justice system is about controlling the poor and keeping them in check (Chambliss and Seidman 1982; Quinney 1977; Shelden 1999). That means that the crimes of the wealthy and of celebrities are often overlooked and hidden. As we will explore in detail after the case study, crimes of the wealthy are hidden in part because of the potent combinations of the seven features of invisibility we introduced in Chap. 3. Sutherland (1949, 1983) tried to change the overlooked, hidden nature of crimes of the powerful by introducing white-collar crime.

White-Collar Crime

'White-collar Crime is a crime committed by a person of respectability and high social status in the course of his occupation' (Sutherland 1949: 7).[1] The two core elements of this definition are the ability of the person to commit an offence because of their occupation and the status of the person committing the offence. First, Sutherland specified that the crime or offence being committed was not things like murder and/or adultery as these criminal or immoral behaviours are not likely to be linked to occupational procedures. Second, he suggested that confidence games and gambling offences committed by wealthy people in the so-called underworld (organised crime groups and gangs) are not white-collar crimes as these individuals are not respected and/or do not have a high social status. Thus, white-collar crime sits in this specific space of occupation and high status.

Sutherland (1949, 1983) introduced the idea of white-collar crime as he felt it was particularly problematic. In the first instance, white-collar crime is an important problem to tackle because in all likelihood it costs society and the victims of white-collar crimes several times more than the supposed 'crime problem'. The crime problem consists of crimes such as those in Table 1, and Sutherland suggested these types of crimes cost much less than white-collar crimes. Furthermore, white-collar crime is a problem, again more than street crime, because it violates trust in social institutions including the state, thus creating distrust, which can have far-reaching implications. There are recent examples from around the world of white-collar crimes linked to violations of public trust. Such violations can have a knock-on effect, reducing confidence and faith in other state institutions including those linked to the economy and justice systems. In particular, the distrust that comes from white-collar crimes can be tied to the lowering of social morale and the production of social disorganisation on a large scale. For example, the financial crisis in 2008 stemmed in part from wealthy, high-status bankers manipulating and hiding the fragility and instability of loans in the housing sector. Governments

---

[1] Sutherland does say 'his' occupation. Whilst this may be largely accurate in terms of who works in corporations and who holds positions of power, we realise a more accurate definition would include 'her' occupation too.

around the world had to financially bail out or prop up banks to keep the banks from collapsing. The white-collar crimes of the individuals involved in the financial sector had global consequences that are still being felt over ten years later in parts of the world that never recovered from this crisis. In contrast, conventional street crimes have little impact on social institutions or social organisation (Sutherland 1949). Similar to Pearce (1976), Sutherland highlighted similar concerns regarding who is able to define what crime is.

Why would crimes that are so harmful be ignored and overlooked? Sutherland gave three reasons as to why this might be the case: (1) the scattered effects of white-collar crime, (2) the trend away from a criminal justice system response to corporate crime and (3) the characteristics of the perpetrators.

The Scattered Effects of White-Collar Crime

Sutherland (1949) proposed that the public were relatively unorganised in their resentment of being victims of white-collar crimes. Such an unorganised response stems from the fact that white-collar crime is complex and the effects are diffused. Commission of a white-collar crime is not as straightforward or as visible as, for example, an assault on the street. A white-collar crime will happen behind closed doors and, in recent times, probably in a virtual space—some online manipulation or theft—that is difficult to trace and where it is difficult to see all of the consequences. In addition, consumer victims are scattered, unorganised and lacking in objective information. In the 2008 financial crisis mentioned earlier, the people who had been given predatory housing loans that they could not afford to repay were scattered around different parts of American states, different parts of the United States and around different parts of the world. They did not know that other people were in the same situation and there was no umbrella organisation that was unifying these people to take collective action. Furthermore, Sutherland suggested that no one consumer suffers a loss in a singular transaction that would prompt action. Again, this is evident in the 2008 financial crisis. People who were approved for housing loans that they would not be able to pay back did not suffer a single identifiable incident where they were misled. It was the approval process for the loans and the months or years of payments taken in aggregate that led to their victimisation.

Such complex victimisation and perpetration are not easily presented as news (Sutherland 1949). These complicated situations cannot be simplified and then expressed in terms of an appealing accessible moral sentiment. In addition, white-collar crime would not be covered by the media because these media outlets are controlled by the companies committing the offences (Sutherland 1949; Jupp et al. 1999; Davies et al. 2014). These complicated situations cannot be expressed in terms of a simple newsworthy soundbite. In addition, white-collar offences are regulated by new and specialised statutes, which means the police may not be trained to investigate such crimes and that the police may not have jurisdiction over white-collar crimes. Specialised statutes may be the remit of fraud agencies or financial regulators rather than local constabularies.

The Trend Away from a Criminal Justice System Response to Corporate Crime

As indicated, corporate offences in particular are nowadays regulated using non-criminal approaches. And, prior to the era of mass incarceration that began to take hold in the United States in the 1980s and later in the United Kingdom, there was an overall trend away from the use of penal methods. Sutherland (1949) noted that probation and casework methods of punishment were increasingly being relied upon. He argued that this was taking place for a variety of reasons. At the time—post-World War II, when trade unions were on the rise—there was an increase in the power of the lower socio-economic classes. Thus, there seemed to be a push towards less strict punishment of conventional crimes, which, as detailed above, has been observed to be more prevalent in the lower socio-economic classes for various flawed reasons. The increased power of the working class meant a challenge to their treatment by the criminal justice system. At the same time, Sutherland (1949) argued there was inclusion within penal laws of actions of the upper socio-economic classes. He suggested that this stemmed, at least in part, from the increased power of the working class, but also because of the increased social interaction among classes. Furthermore, there is a trend towards non-penal punishment because of the failure of other methods to reduce crime (Sutherland 1949). Finally, Sutherland (1949), as Foucault (1975 [1977]) would later argue as well, noted that there was a weakening of the ideology that pain could control people.

Sutherland's work on white-collar crime is thus seen as a segue into a regulatory approach and a position that locates the use of the criminal law alongside the other methods of controlling white-collar and corporate crime. The unique nature of corporations, it is argued, requires different forms of regulation than other kinds of law-breaking. The increasing prominence of civil damage actions and sanctions for these forms of deviance only serves to emphasise how these crimes can be dealt with differently to traditional crimes. Civil damage actions may be brought where the criminal law is not invoked or to supplement criminal cases. Either the state or the victims of the offenses, alone or in class actions, may bring these damage actions.

Although distinctions between criminal, civil and administrative sanctions remain, this variety of methods for dealing with such wrongdoing has become increasingly blurred with many scholars criticising compliance sanctioning, regulatory strategies and regulatory cooperation pointing towards the lack of or lax sanctions, inadequate and weak regulations, decreasing transparency of regulation and the failures and breaches of regulations (Croall 2017). Tombs (2016) illustrates, for example, how the rate of inspection and enforcement actions for environmental health, food safety and hygiene, and health and safety have all been falling as successive governments undermined independent and effective business regulation to the extent that he calls business harms 'social murder'. Evidence often derived from case study research is used in support of arguments calling for stricter enforcement, punitive methods of enforcement, greater use of the criminal law as a means of control and harsher penalties. Those concerned with the crimes of these powerful advocate the use of the criminal law not only to imprison offenders but also to provide the basis for financial remedies, such as forfeiture, profit-fines and restitution. To some extent this has occurred and there has been an increase in financial penalties for financial institutions facilitating money laundering and for other financial wrongdoing. The Financial Conduct Authority (FCA) is the financial conduct regulator in the United Kingdom. The FCA authority fines are published by calendar year. By 17 February 2020, the total amount of fines was £2,865,400. Anti-corruption watchdog activists claim that Britain's record in fighting economic crime over the past decade pales in comparison to the United States because of a combination of weak laws and a failure by regulators to impose heavy fines.

So white-collar crime and related corporate crimes are overlooked and ignored as part of an overall trend at the time that Sutherland was writing. What is interesting to note is that in the decades following, whereas the trend continues that white-collar crime and corporate crime are overlooked and ignored, conventional crimes—particularly drug use—are punished severely, with some offenders in the United States serving life sentences for drug-related offences. The implications of the trend away from a criminal justice system response to white-collar and corporate crime have not narrowed the gulf between the severity of sanctions imposed on perpetrators of white-collar and corporate crime as compared with perpetrators of the publically visible conventional crimes that are channelled through the criminal justice system. In regard to white-collar crime, an extremely wide range of regulatory bodies are involved and victims may not know which agency to approach. Many agencies, dealing, for example, with regulatory law, see themselves as being charged with maintaining standards, rather than prosecuting the guilty. The main reason why white-collar crime is hidden, however, has to do with who is the perpetrator.

Characteristics of the Perpetrators

White-collar crime, as defined above, is committed by respected high-status people. Such people tend to be feared and admired, and thus unlikely to be suspected of committing crimes and/or unlikely to be confronted about wrongdoing (Sutherland 1949). Furthermore, similar to the power wealthy people have in defining crime, policy-makers and law enforcement may be afraid to accuse or confront high-status people about criminal activity because it may threaten their own position or endanger political contributions (Sutherland 1949). In addition, it is possible that high-status individuals will be well-known to the public or to other powerful people. Being a celebrity is one way to gain high status and the protections—fear and admiration—that comes with being in the upper classes. Interestingly, Sutherland (1949) also proposed that white-collar crime is ignored because the offenders do not consider their actions as crimes and because they do not think of themselves as criminals. This demonstrates the power of labels in not only defining crime and criminals (Becker 1963 [1973]), but also in focusing (or not) government, law enforcement and public attention on particular harms and crimes. White-collar offenders are less often attributed the label of criminal, and the audience—the public and so forth—also do not label them as such. This combined with wealth and status leads to power that helps to keep the offending of the rich and upper classes hidden.

The Limitations of White-Collar Crime

The concept of white-collar crime is not without its flaws. Croall (2001) has pointed out that the definition of white-collar crime could be improved upon, as elements of it are quite vague. For example, the concepts of 'respectability' and 'high status' are not defined. Both of these concepts link to the element of occupation within the definition. Not all occupations are regarded the same, and, again, there is a vagueness around which occupations would actually facilitate white-collar offences. Thus, whilst the concept of white-collar crime introduced an important significant portion of criminality, further attention could be given to teasing out how and why people are deemed to be respectable and what elements play a part in high status. As we attempted to do in the section above defining class, we suggest there is an economic aspect to status, but celebrity, race, gender and even birth (royalty and aristocracy) play a role as well.

More Than Just White-Collar Crime

White-collar crime is a useful concept; it has been instrumental in challenging the myth and stereotypes that crime is a working-class problem or predominantly committed by people in the lower socio-economic classes. Yet, it does not go far enough in exposing the range of criminality of people in the higher socio-economic classes. White-collar crime predominantly focuses on economic and financial crimes. But the power that comes with an elite status enables many other crimes to be committed, hidden and denied.

> **Case Study 1: Harvey Weinstein**
> On 5 October of 2017, *The New York Times* published an expose covering decades of sexual harassment and assault claims from numerous women actors and women working in the film industry against the famous movie producer, Harvey Weinstein. Their investigation uncovered three decades worth of undisclosed allegations (Kantor and Twohey 2017). Of central importance in the newspaper article is the memo of Lauren O'Connor, an employee at The Weinstein Company. In addition to detailing Weinstein's abusive behaviour of trying to get massages or sexual favours and appearing naked in front of women, O'Connor says: 'I am a 28 year old woman trying to make a living and a career. Harvey Weinstein is a 64 year old, world famous man and this is his company. The balance of power is me: 0, Harvey Weinstein: 10' (Kantor and Twohey 2017).
> According to *The New York Times*, Weinstein's attorney 'explained to him that due to the power difference between a major studio head like him and most others in the industry, whatever his motives, some of his words and behaviors can be perceived as inappropriate, even intimidating'. The attorney describes Weinstein as 'an old dinosaur learning new ways' (Kantor and Twohey 2017). Yet, he scheduled meetings with women employees and actors in hotel rooms. Numerous accounts from these women say that they believed they were attending a business meeting but then found themselves alone in Weinstein's hotel room, where he made sexual advances. These sexual advances follow the same pattern: he asks the women if they will give

(continued)

Case Study 1: (continued)

him a massage or if they will watch him shower. He is often in a bathrobe or naked. Many women also say that they have been raped and forced to have oral sex (BBC News 2019).

On the day the article in *The New York Times* was published, Weinstein denied the allegations, but apologised for behaviour that caused anyone pain. He also threatened to sue *The New York Times* (BBC News 2019). Weinstein then takes a leave of absence to see a therapist (BBC News 2019). Three days after the article is published, Weinstein is fired by his company (The Weinstein Company, which he and his brother founded) (BBC News 2019). In the days and weeks after the story breaks, tens of women come forward to say that they, too, have been sexually harassed, assaulted and raped by Weinstein during their careers. He continues to deny any wrongdoing.

In the original coverage, *The New York Times* reported:

> Dozens of Mr. Weinstein's former and current employees, from assistants to top executives, said they knew of inappropriate conduct while they worked for him. Only a handful said they ever confronted him. Mr. Weinstein enforced a code of silence; employees of the Weinstein Company have contracts saying they will not criticize it or its leaders in a way that could harm its 'business reputation' or 'any employee's personal reputation'. (Kantor and Twohey 2017)

An unknown number of women over 30 years, who had lodged complaints or spoken about incidents of Weinstein sexually harassing or abusing them, accepted pay-outs. As part of the pay-out, they agreed to keep quiet about the incident and about the deal that had been struck (Kantor and Twohey 2017). It seems clear then that people, at least in Weinstein's inner circle, knew all along about his routine sexual misconduct (BBC News 2019). Weinstein was known to have a volatile temper and to be difficult to deal with, and so his behaviour towards women was lumped into this hostile part of his character (Kantor and Twohey 2017). Even though both of his companies (Miramax and The Weinstein Company) had people worried about his behaviour, nothing substantial was done to address it except to draft sexual harassment policies (Kantor and Twohey 2017) that do not appear to have been enforced.

The state of New York filed a class action lawsuit (a single civil case with numerous victims of the same offence) against The Weinstein Company for failure to protect its employees against harassment and abuse in February 2018 (BBC News 2019). In May of 2018, Weinstein turned himself into the

(continued)

Case Study 1:   (continued)

New York City police for criminal charges, including rape and other sexual assaults—that are separate to the class action lawsuit. He was released on a $1 million bail, a GPS tracker was fitted to his ankle, and his passport was taken (BBC News 2019). A New York grand jury indicted Weinstein for these criminal charges and so he stood trial in late 2019. Weinstein pleaded not guilty to all charges. Other charges were added to the criminal case from other accusers and some charges were removed for lack of evidence. In February 2020, news broke via several news media that Weinstein had been found guilty of a criminal sex act in the first degree and rape in the third degree (Aratani and Pilkington 2020). He was acquitted of three further charges, including the two most serious counts of predatory sexual assault, which carried a possible life sentence and an alternative count of rape in the first degree. In March 2020, he was sentenced to 23 years in prison.

The class action lawsuit in the United States—civil litigation—is the only option for the bulk of Weinstein's accusers. It was anticipated that it would likely be settled sometime in 2019 for $44 million, which will act as compensation to the victims (BBC News 2019). In late 2019, it was reported that a tentative agreement with Weinstein's accusers had been reached amounting to $25 million (*The New York Times* 2019). Eleven women in London alone have made claims against Weinstein (BBC News 2019), and more than 70 women from around the world have accused him of sexually harassing or assaulting them (Durkin and Pulver 2019).

Case Study Discussion: Hiding in Plain Sight

Kantor and Twohey (2017) pose the question probably on most people's mind when hearing about the extent of victimisation: 'How could allegations repeating the same pattern—young women, a powerful male producer, even some of the same hotels— have accumulated for almost three decades'? Media reports document what research studies have been showing for decades. Weinstein's power manifested in very particular ways to silence his victims and those who would support them. The ability to give or withhold acting roles and other employment on his movies was tremendous leverage over anyone aspiring to have a career in Hollywood. There are probably dozens if not hundreds of women who felt coerced into sexual acts with him to get a part. If people not targeted by his assaults objected to his behaviour, they were made to feel like outsiders (Kantor and Twohey 2017). Women coming forward now say that they did not do so at the time for fear of retaliation and because there were no witnesses. Many did not say anything because they felt embarrassed, but many did confide in their colleagues (Kantor and Twohey 2017). This happened to such a degree that women employees would try to attend meetings with him in pairs. Some women who did seek the advice of lawyers were told that they did not have a chance of winning (Kantor and Twohey 2017).

Furthermore, for people who were unaware of this insidious part of Weinstein's nature, he had a well-crafted public image that would make people doubt he would be a sexual predator. As Sutherland (1949) argued about white-collar criminals, people feared and admired Weinstein. Kantor and Twohey (2017) note he was regarded as a progressive left liberal, who supported women's rights and equality. He held political fundraisers for Hillary Clinton, when she ran for the US Senate in New York and when she ran for president of the United States. Weinstein had participated in at least one of the Women's Marches, and he funded the Gloria Steinem academic chair at Rutgers University, named after a famous and influential feminist activist and journalist. These competing images serve to discredit claims that Weinstein would sexually assault women. It is worth noting that criminal and civil actions were brought to bear on this case. Although the outcome of the criminal trial has been concluded, the civil suit lingers on. Weinstein's case is not the only example. Such serial sexual predation has been found in numerous other instances. Jeffrey Epstein, Roger Ailes, Jimmy Saville, Bill Cosby, Jerry Sandusky—the list goes on (see Chap. 7 on gender as well). The commonality between these cases is the power of the perpetrators. They are celebrities. They are men. They are wealthy. In terms of the seven features of invisibility that we introduced in Chap. 3, these powerful celebrities hold sway over many of the key features. In particular, powerful people control 'No knowledge'. The wider public knowledge of the victimisation is controlled not only by the perpetrator, who can threaten the victims to be silent, but also by the few people or organisations, who do know. As mentioned, Weinstein's colleagues kept silent about the victimisations because they feared retaliation and/or they did not want to risk losing their incomes. No public knowledge means 'no panic!'. The media do not know about the situation to expose it, but in some cases, the perpetrator controls the media (i.e. Roger Ailes former head of Fox News in the United States) or is connected to someone who does. There are also 'no politics' in these cases. As repeated throughout this chapter, politicians dare not risk their donations or their endorsements, by challenging or exposing the powerful when they commit crimes.

Pause for Thought

- Where does Weinstein's power come from?
- Why when people find out about crimes of the powerful do they not speak out?
- Which of the seven features of invisibility are relevant to the Weinstein case study?

Elitism and Crime

As Barak et al. (2010: 71) state, '"crime" refers to "crime on the streets" rather than "crime in the suites"'. Crime in the suites constitutes more than financial crimes; they include violence and abuse. Being one of the elite—from being wealthy, from being a celebrity or from holding a position of power—can be a shield from suspicion and investigation. Crimes committed by the elite or high-status individuals are a significant portion of the 'crime problem' though this is frequently actively hidden and/or unknown. Whereas street crime should continue to be the focus of reduction efforts, it should not be overlooked that crime is not exclusive to the working or lower socio-economic classes. Crime is committed, and to at times a startling degree (i.e. decades of sexual violence and theft of millions of pounds), by the upper elite classes.

Crimes of the powerful remain hidden and consequently unsanctioned for a plethora of reasons. A key feature of these crimes is a relationship of power between offender and victim. Ruggiero and Welch (2009) refer to the asymmetrical relationships in 'power crime', and Croall (2017) provides examples of the distinct and depersonalised relationships between victim and offender that facilitate yet mask such crimes. She explains that corporations, for example, have the power to exploit workers who need employment and a key element of state crime is the abuse of the power vested in the position of, for example, a soldier or police officer, who may use legitimate 'force', but abuse their power to engage in illegitimate violence such as torture or genocide. Powerful actors can also 'cover up' their crimes. Responsibility is often diffused and denied, offences are often tolerated within an organisational or corporate culture, or they may be concealed within the legitimacy of the organisation. In many cases, victims are unaware of any harm, such as being overcharged for substandard goods, and in others, such as pollution or tax evasion, the harm is so diffuse that there is no clear individual loss. Offenders' justifications may also involve victim blaming.

Stopping the invisibility of elite offenders is a daunting task. There are clear ways to ameliorate and reduce the crimes of the powerful: we can try to reduce the influence of wealth and money in politics; we can ensure that there is a free and independent press; we can challenge patriarchy and racism that disadvantage women and minorities from attaining positions that afford them higher social status; we can embed mechanisms for whistle blowers and victims to safely speak out. It is a difficult problem, but one that social scientists should not shy away from in order to reduce the suffering and victimisation that continues unchallenged.

Go Further

- What are other examples of a crime of the powerful stemming from class and/ or status?
- How can elite offenders be exposed or their power lessened?

References

Aratani, L., & Pilkington, E. (2020). Harvey Weinstein Sentenced to 23 Years in Prison on Rape Conviction. *The Guardian*. Retrieved May 23, 2020, from https://www.theguardian.com/world/2020/mar/11/harvey-weinstein-sentencing-rape-conviction.

Barak, G., Leighton, P., & Flavin, J. (2010). Class, Race, Gender and Crime: The Social Realities of Justice in America.

BBC News. (2019). Retrieved June 07, 2019, from https://www.bbc.co.uk/news/entertainment-arts-41594672.

Becker, H. (1963 [1973]). *Outsiders*. New York: Free Press.

Chambliss, W., & Seidman, R. B. (1982). *Law, Order and Power* (2nd ed.). Reading, MA: Addison-Wesley.

Croall, H. (2001). *Understanding White-collar Crime*. Buckingham, UK: Open University Press.

Croall, H. (2017). Victims of the Powerful. In P. Davies, P. Francis, & C. Greer (Eds.), *Victims, Crime & Society: An Introduction* (2nd ed., pp. 245–270). London: Sage.

Davies, P., Francis, P., & Wyatt, T. (2014). Taking Invisible Crimes and Social Harms Seriously. In P. Davies, P. Francis, & T. Wyatt (Eds.), *Invisible Crimes and Social Harms* (pp. 1–25). London: Palgrave Macmillan.

Durkin, E., & Pulver, A. (2019). Harvey Weinstein and Accusers 'Reach Tentative $44m Compensation Deal'. *The Guardian*. Retrieved June 07, 2019, from https://www.theguardian.com/us-news/2019/may/23/harvey-weinstein-accusers-reach-tentative-44m-deal.

Financial Conduct Authority (FCA). (2020). 2020 Fines. Retrieved May 23, 2020, from https://www.fca.org.uk/news/news-stories/2020-fines.

Foucault, M. (1975 [1977]). *Discipline and Punish: The Birth of the Prison*. Trans. Sheridan, A. London: Penguin.

Giddens, A. (1975). *The Class Structure of Advanced Societies*. London: Harper and Row Publishers.

Jupp, V., Davies, P., & Francis, P. (1999). The Features of Invisible Crimes. In P. Davies, P. Francis, & V. Jupp (Eds.), *Invisible Crimes: Their Victims and their Regulation*. Basingstoke: Macmillan Publishers.

Kantor, J., & Twohey, M. (2017). Harvey Weinstein Paid Off Sexual Harassment Accusers for Decades. *The New York Times*. Retrieved June 7, 2019, from https://www.nytimes.com/2017/10/05/us/harvey-weinstein-harassment-allegations.html.

Newburn, T. (2017). *Criminology* (3rd ed.). London: Routledge.

Ossowski, S. (1963 [2001]). *Class Structure in the Social Consciousness*. London: Routledge and Kegan Paul Publishers. Translated from the Polish by Sheila Patterson.

Pearce, F. (1976). *Crimes of the Powerful: Marxism, Crime and Deviance*. London: Pluto Press

Quinney, R. (1977). *Class, State, and Crime: On the Theory and Practice of Criminal Justice*. New York: David McKay.

Ruggiero, V., & Welch, M. (2009). Power Crime. *Crime Law and Social Change, 51*, 297–301.

Shelden, R. (1999). The Prison Industrial Complex and the New American Apartheid. *Critical Criminology, 10*(1), 3–5.

Sutherland, E. (1949). *White Collar Crime*. New York: The Dryden Press.

Sutherland, E. (1983). *White Collar Crime: The Uncut Version*. New Haven, CT: Yale University Press.

The New York Times. (2019). Retrieved June 21, 2019, from https://www.nytimes.com/2019/12/11/us/harvey-weinstein-settlement.html.

Tombs, S. (2016). *'Better Regulation': Better for Whom?* Centre for Crime and Justice Studies 14. London.

Tseloni, A., & Duncan, E. (2020). Tools of the Trade: Crime, Survey and Big Data. In P. Davies & M. Rowe (Eds.), *An Introduction to Criminology*. London: Sage.

Race and Ethnicity

5

Introduction

This chapter focuses on race and ethnicity. There are numerous ways in which power dynamics have combined to oppress peoples around the world such that they experience exploitation, marginalisation, powerlessness, cultural domination and violence (Young 2005). Inequalities, stigmatisation and the abuse of power have long been manifest in the experiences of people of colour and those from ethnic groups. Imperialism, Caucasian domination and the political economy of colonisation is an important contextual feature to much of this experience. Power struggles around race are documented throughout history, and post-civil rights activism, as we will explain and illustrate, continues in various parts of the world today. The foregrounded aspects of power in this chapter are illustrated and drawn out of a set of quite recent events that feature the loss of African American lives in the United States. There are of course many other events, injustices and signal crimes that might be selected as material ripe for a criminological case study to expose race, ethnicity and power issues from various countries around the world. A study of hate crime in England and Wales, for example, might focus on the bias-motivated violence against black youth following the racist murder of Stephen Lawrence in 1993 and the ensuing publication of the Macpherson Report in 1999 which found the Metropolitan police to be institutionally racist. Such a case study could draw on the compelling evidence from various parts of the criminal justice system to illustrate how black bodies are disproportionately represented in the criminal justice system and how black bodies are policed. Data on young people in custody, police

© The Author(s) 2021
P. Davies, T. Wyatt, *Crime and Power*,
https://doi.org/10.1007/978-3-030-57314-0_5

stop and search data and confidence levels in the police all suggest that criminology should remain attuned to the issues of race, ethnicity and power:

- During the period 2005/06 to 2018/19 the percentage of young people in custody who were Black more than doubled from 12.5% to 27.8%. Every year, a lower percentage of Black Caribbean people had confidence in their local police than White British people.
- The rates for the Asian, Black, and Mixed ethnic groups were higher than the national rate every year
- Between 2017/18 and 2018/19 there were 4 stop and searches for every 1000 White people, compared with 38 for every 1000 Black people.
  (Ministry of Justice 2020).

However, the case study that forms the basis of this chapter originates in the United States. It focuses on the Black Lives Matter movement. First, we locate this movement in historical context, and therefore the next section examines the political economy of colonisation. Our case study then commences. This social media inspired movement focuses on African Americans and how they are, and have been, routinely and systematically policed in racist ways. Black Lives Matter is a grassroots or locally led and inspired movement founded and grown by passionate activists fighting for justice. With that in mind, our approach to this chapter may be somewhat original in that we deliberately draw upon an (possibly) unusual mix of literature. We employ ethnographic and narrative type material from those involved in Black Lives Matter as well as some of the classic literature about race and crime. The combination of the two types of sources as well as the case study itself allows us to reflect on the history of the present in respect of race, ethnicity and power and leaves issues in the foreground that continue to be highly relevant in terms of criminological inquiry and research.

Below, after a brief but important historical contextualisation of colonisation, we provide a descriptive outline of the case study for this chapter. The remainder of the chapter dissects this in order to illustrate several dimensions to power. We do this with reference to slavery and the civil rights movement, contemporary racial profiling and an analysis of the role of the state and the synergies with the institutions of the police and other criminal justice system agencies. Whilst featuring an analysis of a contemporary movement, the chapter draws out the racialised history of the criminal justice system and the historical and culturally prejudiced ways in which African Americans have died in custody and had their bodies controlled and policed through the ages.

The Political Economy of Colonisation

We have already emphasised above that a historical perspective to this chapter is warranted. An appreciation of the imperialist, Caucasian colonisation by states such as Portugal, France and Britain, for example, in establishing and maintaining the slave trade, helps us understand the nature and contemporary legacies of such domination. The French colonial empire extended into North America, the Caribbean and India where French rule was established from the sixteenth century onwards. The Portuguese Empire was built by settlers in South America, Africa and Asia. That empire, commencing in the fifteenth century, survived for more than six centuries, until 1999 when Portugal returned Macau to China. British Hong Kong was a colony of the United Kingdom from 1841 effectively until 1997 when the one-country, two-system arrangement of governance commenced. The protests in Hong Kong in 2019–20 have roots in the colonial past of the country. The long duration and ongoing legacy of imperialist colonisation cannot be understated, and we will continue to stress the importance and seismic impact of such development trajectories throughout the chapter and in our critical reflections about the histori-cal roots of our racialised history in general and of the criminal justice system of today in particular. After we present the case study, we pick up on the historical trajectories in the section on slavery and civil rights. By introducing these contexts at the start of the chapter we hope to underscore not only the inequity established by imperialism, but how it is perpetuated through the evolution of globalisation today. We thus return to these ideas and the question of stolen lands in other parts of the globe during the colonisation of the 'New World'. Several concepts are worth defining at this point including colonisation and imperialism. The body of work on the political economy of colonisation is thus an important contextual fea-ture for us to pause and explore.

Colonisation and colonialism are inextricably bound up with the concept of power. Colonialism is where a country seeks to extend or retain its authority over other people or territories. *Economic* dominance tends to be the driver, and during the process of colonisation, the colonialist nation or the colonisers impose their economically determined policies and other social practices and cultural practices on the indigenous peoples of that land. The European settlement of North America dates back to the 1400s, and over the next 100 years or so, many permanent European settlements were established in the 'New World', which was already in-habited by many Native American societies. Settlers arrived from England establis-hing what became the Virginia colony. Others travelled on the Mayflower settling in New England and sprawling into New Hampshire and further afield with the establishment of colonies continuing into the second half of the seventeenth century. Thirteen British colonies were established during the seventeenth and early eighteenth centuries in what is now a part of the eastern United States. During this settlement, not only were indigenous peoples exploited economically, but also their cultural practices were eroded. The first half of the seventeenth century saw various legal systems that had developed over thousands of years being replaced under the influence of the new settlers. A new colonial system of law supplanted the traditional laws, and the modern American criminal justice system thus has its roots in the legal concepts carried by early English settlers to the New World.

Imperialism and colonialism are often used synonymously though some argue there are distinctions. Whereas colonialism is explained with reference to settlement practices which are driven by economic imperatives, as described above, imperialism is not only concerned with policy but also with the ideology of empire-building expansionism by military force or by wilfully gaining political and economic control of another country or area.

Bringing us back to the present, scholars are now elucidating how contemporary US mass incarceration is the current form of state-organised violence that compares to that which supported colonial violence (Stone-Mediatore 2019). According to Garland (2001: 4), 'imprisonment becomes *mass imprisonment* when it ceases to be the incarceration of individual offenders and becomes the systematic imprisonment of whole groups of the population'. Criminologically, there are big questions foregrounded by the demographic evidence of mass incarceration in the United States. The racial impact is blatantly evident. African Americans are incarcerated in state prisons at more than five times the rate of whites. Incarceration data reproduced in a factsheet by the Sentencing Project outlines what contributes to racial disparities at every level of the criminal justice system:

> Sentencing policies, implicit racial bias, and socioeconomic inequity contribute to racial disparities at every level of the criminal justice system. Today, people of color make up 37% of the U.S. population but 67% of the prison population. Overall, African Americans are more likely than white Americans to be arrested; once arrested, they are more likely to be convicted; and once convicted, they are more likely to face stiff sentences. Black men are six times as likely to be incarcerated as white men and Hispanic men are more than twice as likely to be incarcerated as non-Hispanic white men. (Sentencing Project 2019)

A welter of criminological questions flow from this evidence which directly connects to the racial and colonialistic history of imprisonment in the United States and the shift to the more recent trend towards imprisonment for private profit (Hallett 2004). Racial disparity evidence in matters of criminal justice are not confined to the United States. Black deaths in custody in Australia have been the subject of recent concern. A Royal Commission into Aboriginal Deaths in Custody was launched in 1987. Since it reported in 1991 research shows that 407 indigenous people have reportedly died in police or prison custody (*The Guardian* 2019).

As this extended contextualisation has shown, for us to fully appreciate the depth and breadth of the racial and ethnic divisions in society in the twenty-first century, our gaze must look to the past. However, to illustrate the extent to which race and ethnicity still matter in criminal justice contexts, we move our criminological gaze to the present. We do so by exploring racialised policing in the United States and our case study of the Black Lives Matter movement.

Case Study: Black Lives Matter

As noted above, Black Lives Matter is a grassroots movement founded and grown by passionate activists. The fight is to improve the material conditions of black people's lives. The movement is concerned with all aspects of injustice including systemic racism, economic inequality and mass incarceration. This case study taps in to the systemic racism inherent in American society, the justice system, and in particular it focuses on racialised policing. The case study examines the devaluing of black lives not only by the police but also by a society which accepts this form of racialised policing.

Trayvon Martin

On 26 February 2012, 17-year-old African American Trayvon Martin was walking to the home of his father's fiancé after having bought some sweets and a drink from a convenience store in Sanford, Florida (Botelho 2012). Martin was spotted by a volunteer of the local Neighbourhood Watch group, George Zimmerman. Zimmerman called 911 to report 'a real suspicious guy' (Botelho 2012). Zimmerman confirms to the dispatcher that he is following the person, and the dispatcher tells him that he does not need to do that. It is unknown why or how after the 911 call by Zimmerman that Zimmerman and Martin are in a confrontation. When the police arrive a few minutes later, Zimmerman's nose is (probably) broken and his clothing is wet (from being in the grass). Martin has been shot once in the chest and is lying face down on the grass. The police try to revive Martin, as do the paramedics, who arrive shortly after the police, but Martin dies (Botelho

2012). Zimmerman claimed that Martin attacked him and that he was defending himself. Zimmerman was not charged with second-degree murder until April 2012 after an online petition brought Martin's death to national attention (Botelho 2012). Second-degree murder in Florida is 'killing carried out with hatred, ill will or spite, but is not premeditated' (Carter and Yan 2013). In July 2013, after a month and half trial and 16 hours of jury deliberation, Zimmerman was found not guilty (Carter and Yan 2013).

In 2013, activist Alicia Garza, in response to Zimmerman's acquittal, wrote her now famous Facebook post 'A love letter to black people':

> The sad part is, there's a section of America who is cheering and celebrating right now. and that makes me sick to my stomach. We GOTTA get it together y'all, … stop saying we are not surprised. that's a damn shame in itself. I continue to be surprised at how little Black lives matter. And I will continue that. stop giving up on black life. … Black people. I love you. I love us. Our lives matter. (Lowery 2017)

Fellow activist Patrice Cullors plucked out the phrase 'black lives matter' and, together with another black activist, Opal Tometi, the #BlackLivesMatter movement was born (Lowery 2017). Lowery (2017) suggests though Black Lives Matter is thought of as a social media and activist movement, it may be better to think of it as an ideology. An ideology that challenges racial disparity and continuing injustices. Black Lives Matter became prominent following another shooting of an unarmed young black man.

Michael Brown

In Ferguson, Missouri (a suburb of Saint Louis, Missouri) in August 2014, a police officer came into contact with Michael Brown (18 years old) and another man in an apartment complex (*The Guardian* 2014). In the hours after the incident, it is unclear if Brown or the other man pushed the officer back into his patrol car where there was a struggle and one shot fired from the officer's gun. Somehow, the officer and the men end up back on the street, and the unarmed Brown is shot multiple times and dies (*The Guardian* 2014). In the days following Brown's killing, Ferguson is filled with vigils, protests and looting (*The Guardian* 2014; Swaine 2014). As details surface as to what really happened, the other man, Dorian Johnson (22 years old), states that the officer told him and Brown to 'get the fuck on to the sidewalk' since they were walking on the street (Swaine 2014). When they responded that they were almost to where they were going, Johnson says the officer opened his car door into Brown. The struggle then ensues and Brown is killed (Swaine

2014). The demonstrations and protests over the days afterwards sometimes turned to violent clashes between demonstrators and the police (Swaine 2014). In response to the event, the movement Black Lives Matter participated in and organised some of the demonstrations (Black Lives Mattes No Date). As Cobb (2016) notes,

> Darnell Moore, a writer and an activist based in Brooklyn, who knew Cullors, coordinated "freedom rides" to Missouri from New York, Chicago, Portland, Los Angeles, Philadelphia, and Boston. Within a few weeks of Brown's death, hundreds of people who had never participated in organized protests took to the streets, and that campaign eventually exposed Ferguson as a case study of structural racism in America and a metaphor for all that had gone wrong since the end of the civil-rights movement.

Darren Wilson, the officer who shot and killed Brown, was never charged (Mindock 2018). The failure to charge him was reviewed by the federal-level Department of Justice, but it was decided there was not enough evidence that the incident was not self-defence (Mindock 2018).

Freddie Gray

Although there are many incidents on which Black Lives Matter campaigned, one further incident is key to the movement's story. Freddie Gray was arrested in Baltimore, Maryland, on 12 April 2015 for making eye contact with a police officer and running away. His arrest was partially captured on a cell phone camera. The arrest saw him shackled and transported on the floor of a police van. On arrival at the custody suite, Gray was unresponsive. He died from a spinal cord injury a week later. His spine had been 80% severed at the neck and his voice box crushed. Following his death, the phrase 'I can't breathe' became associated with the Black Lives Matter movement, resonating with its wider political claims and grievances.

Initially, the officers involved in Gray's arrest were placed on paid leave. On the first weekend of May 2015, a spontaneous citywide celebration was sparked by the announcement that criminal charges would be brought against all six police officers involved in his death. Days earlier, there had been a rather different spontaneous demonstration of tense clashes between the people of West Baltimore and heavily armed riot police in response to the arrest video going viral and news of Gray's death. This series of events is now known as the 'Baltimore Uprising' (Kamat 2016). Kamat describes this as the logical outcome of designed residential segregation, police abuse, harassment and violence resulting in criminalisation, systemic racism and inequality. She concludes:

[U]ntil the broader culture of police impunity and the systematic criminalization of Black lives is addressed and changed, alongside a fundamental transformation of the economic priorities of the city to remedy the deep structural inequalities in Baltimore, the broad constellation of factors leading to the rebellion remain[s] unchanged. (Kamat 2016: 82)

In the United States, the Black Lives Matter movement grew throughout 2014, 2015 and 2016 following fatal shootings and arrests of African Americans by police around the country. As we write, black deaths in the United States continue to make worldwide news in 2020 as a white Minneapolis police officer is accused of killing George Floyd, a black man by kneeling on his neck while he was handcuffed. This has sparked days of demonstrations and protests in numerous US cities and around the world. The Black Lives Matter movement has international groups in Australia, Canada and Ghana, meaning there are more than 40 chapters worldwide. According to their website:

As organizers who work with everyday people, BLM [Black Lives Matter] members see and understand significant gaps in movement spaces and leadership. Black liberation movements in this country have created room, space, and leadership mostly for Black heterosexual, cisgender men—leaving women, queer and transgender people, and others either out of the movement or in the background to move the work forward with little or no recognition. As a network, we have always recognized the need to center the leadership of women and queer and trans people. To maximize our movement muscle, and to be intentional about not replicating harmful practices that excluded so many in past movements for liberation, we made a commitment to placing those at the margins closer to the center.

This extract illustrates an important aspect to of the ambitions of the movement and that is their commitment to all those at the margins. Thus whilst the movement continues to advocate and mobilise to fight the injustices and the ongoing violence targeted at black people as foregrounded in detail above, women, queer and transgender people face similarly abusive and violent experiences. The kaleidoscopic variety of ways in which race, ethnicity, gender, sexuality come together again signal the importance of recognising that our identity is not to a single homogenous group but comprises a complex matrix of characteristics. Intersectionalities theorising (as discussed in Part 1) is a helpful way of making sense of the experiences of those at the margins. As we outline next, there are so many violent incidents in the United States that Black Lives Matter and other organisations working towards an equal society have a challenging road ahead.

Pause for Thought

- What does the Black Lives Matter movement tell us about how power operates in contemporary American society?
- How does the website description of the Black Lives Matter movement intersect with gender, sexuality, religion and age?
- Why is race such an important dimension of exploitation in the United States?

Police Shootings in the United States

In order to analyse fully the biased and racist nature of police interaction with black people in the United States, it is necessary to have an overview of racial demographics of the country. According to estimates of the US Census Bureau (2018), white people make up 60.7% of the population of the whole country, black people 13.4% and Hispanic people 18.1%. The remaining population consists of American Indian and Native Alaskans (1.3%), Asian people (5.8%), Native Hawaiians and Other Pacific Islanders (0.2%) and people identifying as two or more races (2.7%). People of different races and ethnicities are not equally distributed across the country. In many Northeast and Midwestern states, over 77% of the population is white (Henry J Kaiser Family Foundation 2017). The South (Louisiana, Mississippi, Alabama, Georgia, North Carolina and South Carolina) and Delaware, Maryland, and Washington DC have the highest percentage of black residents, between 21 and 46%. California, Nevada, Arizona, New Mexico, Texas and Florida have the highest percentage of Hispanic people (26–49%) (Henry J Kaiser Family Foundation 2017). Urban areas also tend to have more ethnic minorities than smaller cities or rural areas.

With that in mind, Figs. 5.1 and 5.2 illustrate how many black, Hispanic and white people have been shot dead by police between 2015 and mid-2019. *The Washington Post*, a left-leaning newspaper based in Washington DC, has been collating every news report as well as police data related to fatal shooting incidents with police across the United States (see *The Washington Post* 2019 for each specific incident). As shown, nearly *a thousand* men in total are killed each year by police (Fig. 5.1). The number of women killed is drastically smaller (Fig. 5.2), around 40 each year. This amount is still more than all of the police killings in England and Wales for the last ten years (Inquest 2019). Admittedly, the US population is around 328 million (US Census Bureau 2018) and the population of England and Wales

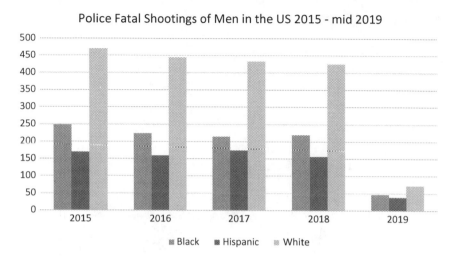

Fig. 5.1 Taken from *The Washington Post* 2019

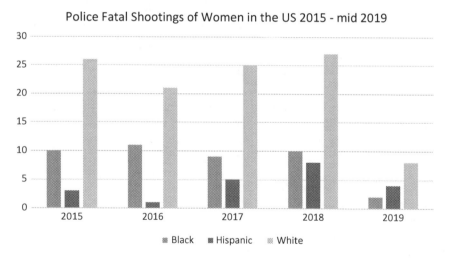

Fig. 5.2 Taken from *The Washington Post* 2019

less than 60 million, but even with that factored in, the US police seem far more violent.

And there appears to be a racial dimension to these killings (and clearly a gender disparity as we talk more about in Chap. 7). Black deaths account for 22–25% of the killings, for the years where there is a complete data set, even though black people are only 13.4% of the US population. White deaths total between 43 and 47%, yet they are over 60% of the population. Research by Arthur (2019) found that based upon police self-reporting of both amount of resistance encountered and level of force used in response to that resistance that police officers in Chicago responded with higher levels of force to black people even though the amount of resistance observed was less when compared to white people. The amount of resistance and level of force were on a four-point scale (the former was adapted from the Chicago police's six-point scale and the latter the same scale as the police):

> Passive resistance was measured as a 1, more active resistance like fleeing was a 2, physical assault was a 3, and deadly force like firing a weapon was a 4. … For officer use of force, verbal commands were measured as a 1, chasing or physical restraint was a 2, physical force like the use of a baton or stun gun was a 3, and firing a weapon was a 4. (Arthur 2019)

This coding took place for 60,000 incidents between 2004 and 2016. The patter that emerged is, as we mentioned, that officers tended to use more force against black people even though they resisted less than white people (Arthur 2019). More needs to be explored in relation to the aggressive response to black people in particular. Of course, we contend (and discuss more in Chap. 11 about states and power) that the police should not be killing people at all if possible and certainly not to the scale that is documented in Figs. 5.1 and 5.2 and Table 5.1. That, in the United States, there is a racial bias to these killings has a long complex history that we attempt to unpack in the next sections.

Table 5.1 Percentage of police fatal shootings of men in the United States by race 2015 to mid-2019

Year	Black	Hispanic	White	Total
2015	25	17	47	994
2016	23	17	46	962
2017	22	18	44	986
2018	22	16	43	992
2019 (through 1 June)	12	10	19	378

Slavery and Civil Rights

Black and brown bodies have been exploited in the United States for centuries flowing from the context of the political economy of colonisation we discussed earlier in the chapter. Native Americans had their land stolen and were killed as part of colonisation of the 'New World' throughout the 1600s until the 1950s when Hawaii and Alaska became US states. Largely, they have been marginalised and contained to reservations ever since. To capitalise on the land and opportunities for economic growth that came with this colonisation, black people were kidnapped from Africa, enslaved and forced to come to what would become the United States as well as other countries throughout the Americas. Slavery bitterly divided the United States with northern states being free and southern states allowing slavery until the US Civil War (1861–1865), which ended with slavery being outlawed, but left a legacy of racism and discrimination.

Even with slavery ending, black people in the United States were by no means integrated into society. The Reconstruction Era after the Civil War saw implementation of 'Jim Crow' laws in the former slave states and to a lesser degree in northern states too. Jim Crow is a derogatory, anti-black term. A body of state and local laws were designed to enforce racial segregation in all public facilities (schools, restaurants, restrooms, waiting rooms, entrances, lifts and cemeteries, etc.) and transport. Black people were forced to live in separate neighbourhoods and had separate hospitals, jails and care homes. Interracial marriage was strictly forbidden in most of the South. Restrictions were also put on voting by black Africans in the southern United States. These laws strictly governed how and where freed slaves, and later black people in general, could live, work and socialise. Former Confederate soldiers were the police and judges in these states, and so as far back as the 1870s, there is a clear discrimination by the criminal justice system against black people. The Jim Crow laws institutionalised racial segregation in the South as well as in the North (though again to a lesser degree) causing economic, educational and social disadvantage for African Americans and other people of colour.

Throughout the late nineteenth and early twentieth centuries, many brave black activists resisted Jim Crow laws in particular and a system in general that suppressed them, and the period is now recognised as the era of the civil rights movement. During these decades, anti-black violence was commonplace, including lynching by such groups as the Ku Klux Klan (History 2019). A race riot in 1908 in Springfield, Illinois, was the spark that brought together white and black activists to form the most widely recognised civil rights organisation—the National

Association for the Advancement of Colored People (NAACP 2019). Its mission is to ensure the political, educational, social and economic equality of rights of minority groups and to eliminate race-based discrimination (NAACP 2019). They first focused on eradicating lynching which had become an act of murder by hanging as a means of terrorising black people in order to enforce white supremacy. Even though the US Congress never passed anti-lynching legislation, the campaigns of the NAACP (2019) are thought to have contributed to the significant reduction of lynching. They were also instrumental in influencing the US government to provide protection and equal opportunities to black soldiers and labourers in the 1930s and 1940s.

One of the NAACP's (2019) greatest achievements is the landmark legal case, *Brown v Board of Education* (1954), where segregation of public schools was made illegal (though it did not accomplish the desegregation of schools in practice). The NAACP (2019) were also instrumental in helping the passage of numerous Civil Rights Acts in the late 1950s—late 1960s. Despite all of these legal developments, black people throughout the United States struggled, and still do, to be treated equally. The Civil Rights Era (roughly the 1950s and 1960s) was marred with violence and active resistance to equality as seen with the assassination of Martin Luther King Jr. and Malcolm X, who were both fighting for justice. Thus, our case study of Black Lives Matter sits on the backdrop of hundreds of years of black people's marginalisation within a system first designed, at least to some degree, on their exploitation. And that system has never reached a stage, where black people are viewed as equals.

Readers are encouraged to explore recent critiques of criminological inquiry itself which, drawing on critiques of social scientific knowledge more broadly (see, e.g., Connell, 2007), argue that as criminologists we have privileged theories, assumptions and methods based on empirical specificities of the Global North. Contemporary analysis of power relations in criminology suggests knowledge production be problematised. There are power relations embedded in the hierarchal production of criminological knowledge (Carrington et al. 2016). Narrative methodology is emerging as one avenue for exploring the experiences of minorities in different crime and justice contexts (see, e.g., Fleetwood et al. 2019).

The power of the system, and predominantly of white people (particularly police officers) in that system, is historic, enduring and institutionalised. The case study above illustrates how in many American cities, crime suppression efforts target African American communities and entraps, frisks, detains, beats, humiliates and destroys African American bodies (Coates 2015). Black men are at greatest risk of being killed, and the prosecution of their killers is highly unlikely, as evident in the Trayvon Martin and Michael Brown killings and many others. The targeting of black people, or non-white people in general, is a tactic of law enforcement in the United States, but other countries as well.

Contemporary Racial Profiling

Racial profiling occurs in different countries and contexts. As this chapter has emphasised, there is a long and significant history to this. The American Civil Liberties Union (ACLU 2019) defines racial profiling as follows:

> The discriminatory practice by law enforcement officials of targeting individuals for suspicion of crime based on the individual's race, ethnicity, religion or national origin. Criminal profiling, generally, as practiced by police, is the reliance on a group of characteristics they believe to be associated with crime.

It is, however, important to unpick the institutional nature of the problem. Racial profiling speaks to ideas about race, ethnicity and religion that are embedded in societies and our major social institutions and structures, including those of policing. Examples of racial profiling are stop and frisk strategies based upon race to look for contraband or basing traffic stops for minor violations upon race assuming more significant violations will also be found (ACLU 2019). Such profiling is not limited to the United States; the United Kingdom, particularly in urban areas, also employs stop and search tactics underpinned by race. Since the September 11th attacks of 2001, racial profiling is also a key strategy of airport security around the globe focusing on Muslims (ACLU 2019). As is evident from the last example, law enforcement refers to the broad range of actors, who are both employees of the state and of private companies contracted as security services.

Such policing, including that which involves stopping and frisking or searching people of colour and from particular racial and ethnic groups, increases the likelihood or being cited and arrested in the United States and produces an accumulation of distorted data. Aggressive police presence, surveillance, harassment and excessive interventions rely on discretionary policing based on 'reasonable suspicion' as defined by police in action, suggesting bias-driven, racialised policing is at work in the African American communities of Florida, Missouri, Ohio, New York, Maryland, South Carolina, Louisiana, Minnesota, California and many other states (US DoJCRD 2015). Racially coded data is produced, distorted and continuously reproduced directly affecting black bodies in an aggressive police surveillance overreach. 'Black data marks human "threats" with permanent digital suspicion and targets communities of color. Black data leads to aggressive use of police force, including deadly force, and new forms of invasive surveillance' (Guthrie Ferguson 2017: 4). Such racism drives the systematic response to crime.

The Impact of Zero-Tolerance Policing

Race has become a central point of debate in the aftermath of the Ferguson and Baltimore uprisings, where the interactions and patterns of racism and brutality are forging a cultural shift in policing. Here we begin to further unpack the case study by connecting with modern ethnographic contributions that attend to the unintended consequences of 'tough on crime' policing. Drawing in particular on the work of Goffman (2009, 2015), but also on critics of racially coded data, we consider the effect that a near unified endorsement of zero-tolerance policing (alongside the increase in 'mass imprisonment' in the United States) is having on poor minority, inner-city neighbourhoods. Zero-tolerance policing, or broken windows policing (Wilson and Kelling 1982), is characterised as an arrest-based approach to crime control (Lum 2009). This approach has been used widely in the United States and the United Kingdom under the rationale that by reducing crime and disorder, people's safety and security will be increased (see Bratton 1998 among many others). Lum (2009: 794) suggests 'This tactic encourages officers to *reduce* their discretion to arrest, resulting in the use of arrest for all types of crimes—especially "quality of life" and disorder misdemeanours—in order to reduce violence more generally'. Furthermore, she states, zero-tolerance policing 'may result in abuses of authority, illegal use of force, and a transformation of policing culture into one that could be inflexible or overly repressive' (Lum 2009: 794). As we consider the effects of this approach to policing, we shall be encouraging reflection on the broader sociological questions about control and adaptations to control as well as punishment and surveillance in the modern era.

Control and Adaptations to Control

An ethnographic account by Goffman (2015) documents life in the inner-city ghetto neighbourhood '6th Street', Philadelphia, Pennsylvania. Her book gives a rich account of the ways in which the highly punitive approach to crime control and policing has created a generation of fugitives. Her work (2009, 2015) illustrates the state's omnipresence in today's American ghetto. Penal policies see citizens watched, hovered over and beamed upon by search lights from police helicopters, under hyper-surveillance by cameras on street lamps and police, brutally controlled, chased, searched, questioned, entrapped, repressed and arrested by law enforcers, such that effectively they are deprived of citizenship and condemned within a fugitive community. The intense 'checkpoint or flashpoint system' of supervision through probation and parole results in violations and the issue of warrants for arrest or for missing court or for unpaid court fees and other minor infractions such as breaking a curfew or for failure to turn themselves in for a crime (Goffman 2009). Probation and parole terms it seems are unworkable. They impede the kind of life it nominally encourages: one with a steady job and committed relationships. The current criminal justice system in the United States, she contends, connects with black inner city youth in a way that transforms residents into 'arrestable' or 'dirty' populations, 'poor black neighbourhoods into communities of suspects and fugitives' (Goffman 2015: 8).

In response to state control, Goffman (2009, 2015) contends that a climate of suspicion has been fostered in such neighbourhoods, and a culture of fear, created by an increase in policing and supervision and erratic policing tactics, sees residents in poor black neighbourhoods develop skills to avoid civic and public institutions—schools and hospitals—as well as their own and family member's homes. They cultivate secrecy and unpredictability and do so because of their precarious legal standing. The threat of imprisonment transforms social relations. Men learn that holding a legitimate job or accompanying their pregnant girlfriends to the hospital to give birth are pathways to imprisonment because employers become 'last known' addresses in police databases and hospitals require records to be kept. 'The fact that some young men may be taken into custody if they encounter the authorities is a background expectation of everyday interaction in this community' (Goffman 2009: 344). When wanted men and their families are burgled or experience other forms of victimisation, they hesitate to use the resources of the law—the police or the courts—to protect themselves for fear they will be arrested and sent to jail. Jarringly evident, she suggests, in this kind of existence is the *powerlessness* of the black community to avoid confrontation with the police and that far too often these interactions are deadly or lead to imprisonment.

But Black Lives Matters also speaks of a different form of power and one that is positive, as we mentioned was possible in Chap. 2. The movement has become a salient political force, drawing enormous attention from all sides of the political spectrum at the local and national levels (Williamson et al. 2018). 'From August 2014 to August 2015, at least 780 BLM protests occurred in 44 states and 223 localities; 14% of all U.S. cities with more than 30,000 inhabitants saw at least one BLM protest in this time period' (Williamson et al. 2018: 401). Williamson et al. (2018) found that Black Lives Matter protests are more common in locations where police have previously killed more black people per capita. They suggest this supports other research, which indicates that in areas with high incarceration rates people are likely disengaged politically. Yet, those areas with indirect contact with incarceration are more likely to be mobilised into social action. In some instances then, the adaptation to control may be one of positive resistance as we also saw in the discussion of the civil rights movements.

Connections to the Past

The movement Black Lives Matters has brought to the surface decades, even centuries, of frustration and tension about racially discriminatory law enforcement practices and a racially prejudicial criminal justice system. As Goffman (2009: 354) concludes, 'Young men on the run in Philadelphia can tell us something about how power operates in contemporary society'. These young men live amidst modern discriminatory policing practices, and yet, these systematic, unconstitutional, legalised forms of oppression and racism have been endured by African Americans over a much longer period of time (Guthrie Ferguson 2017).

In a book-length letter to his adolescent son Samori, Coates (2015) writes about being young and black in Baltimore and recalls how the law did not protect young people when he was growing up. In his son's generation, he writes 'the law has become an excuse for stopping and frisking you, which is to say, for furthering the assault on your body' (Coates 2015: 17). The destruction of the black body is a key theme that runs through Coates' communication. The permanence of racism and what it means to be a black man and have a black body in a hegemonically white world is driven home with reflections on police brutality and state violence. Following references to Michael Brown, Eric Garner, Renisha McBride, John Crawford and Tamir Rice, Coates (2015: 9) refers to the police as 'destroyers' who, 'will rarely be held accountable...... destruction is merely the superlative form of a dominion whose prerogatives include friskings, detainings, beatings, and humiliations'. He emphasises the unrestrained nature of policing and continues 'All of this is common to black people. And all of this is old for black people. No one is held responsible' (Coates 2015: 9). The dominant theme is the power of the state to murder and take black life with impunity, without being held to account and without consequences.

Punishment and Surveillance in the Modern Era

A majority of encounters with the police for black people do not end in the horrific ways described in the case study. That is not to say, however, that there are no other negative outcomes. In addition to high numbers of fatal encounters, black people in the United States are also disproportionately represented in the criminal justice system. This is linked to racial profiling that we outlined earlier, which likely means black people come into contact with law enforcement more frequently. According to Gramlich (2019), there are 475,900 black federal and state inmates; there are 436,500 white inmates and 336,500 Hispanic inmates. These numbers do not include inmates in county jails, who are serving sentences of less than one year. The number of black inmates has been decreasing in the last decade, but clearly black people are still over-represented (13.4% of the overall population, but 33% of the prison population).

There are two particularly important points to raise in relation to power and punishment in the United States. The first is that the United States has the largest prison population in the Western world. The mass incarceration—nearly two million people at any one time—has significant impacts on communities and individuals. It is a very specific display of power. As we discussed in Chap. 1, incarceration is both visible and invisible. The community is certainly aware of people imprisoned and knows where these prisons are, but at the same time the punishment is hidden, since prisons are closed spaces. The state has the power to take away people's liberty and freedom and the power to largely keep these spaces away from public scrutiny.

Second, the power the state has to take away people's liberty and freedom is discriminatorily applied and targeted more often on black and brown bodies. The surveillance of the state seems to be racially cast (Guthrie Ferguson 2017). A growing body of work suggests that the criminal justice system has become an instrument that reproduces disadvantage (see Waquant 2009). So African Americans, who are still struggling with the legacy of slavery and segregation, not only have an oppressive history to overcome, but many of them must also contend with a criminal justice system that further deprives them of equality. The state's power reinforces their marginalisation.

Though a Foucauldian analysis might be developed, according to Goffman (2009) the ways that poor black men are watched and supervised in the American ghetto sees a form of power being exercised such that its residents do not live as tightly controlled and disciplined subjects. Power is exercised over wanted men in Philadelphia in a rather different way. This form of power is occasional, incomplete and for the purpose of identifying candidates for extreme sanction. This analysis compares ghetto residents' experience to that of other semi-legal or illegal people including undocumented immigrants, who are at risk of being deported, Jews in fear of being sent to concentration camps, deserters from the army and escaped slaves. Such precarity and vulnerability renders individual people invisible and powerless in the face of state denial (Cohen 2001, see also Chap. 11 on the 'state').

Summary

Power is integral to race relations. Although we have focused on race relations in the United States, and particularly with the police and the criminal justice system, we suggest this is likely the case around the world. Race and power in contemporary society cannot be uncoupled from a complex global history of oppression and exploitation of particular people in particular geographies. There has been progress in achieving equality and justice for marginalised people, but state power still often reproduces and reinforces powerlessness. Whereas the power is often exerted by a collective or a group such as the state, that power affects both individuals of a certain race and groups of people of a certain race. This impact on individuals is why we have included a discussion of race and power in Part I about individual power, even though clearly there is significant overlap to Chap. 11 in Part II about group power of the state.

Race is also included in Part I, because the power of the state in regard to race is exerted by individuals. In our case study, the officers who are killing black men are typically white officers. The white officers have the power to target whomever they like when patrolling, stopping and searching. Individuals respond with excessive use of force more often to black people than to others. The officers then benefit from the historic power of their race and institution by not being held accountable for killing citizens or being acquitted of any wrong doing.

Whilst this power has devastating consequences—nearly 1000 killings by police in the United States each year, nearly 2 million people in prisons, the effects on families, friends and communities of these losses—the response and adaptation to the oppression and injustice is an inspiring display of power in its own right. Black Lives Matter and other activist social movements are disrupting existing power structures and (hopefully) contributing to lasting improvements to communities around the world. In the case of Black Lives Matter, they not only want to end anti-blackness but also work to end the marginalisation for others as well such as gay, lesbian and transgender people. Thus, we see that positive power also intersects across individual characteristics like gender-race-sexuality-religion-age. In some instances, powerlessness can be overcome particularly when people act as a collective. This is crucial to overturn complex power structures that have deep historic roots from which those still in power continue to benefit.

Go Further

- How do we account for the undeniable improvement in race relations on some fronts and the apparent intractability of racism on other fronts?
- Is defunding the police a solution to help stop racism?

References

American Civil Liberties Union (ACLU). (2019). Racial Profiling Definition. Retrieved June 05, 2019, from https://www.aclu.org/other/racial-profiling-definition.
Arthur, R. (2019). New Data Shows Police Use More Force Against Black Citizens Even Though Whites Resist More. *Slate*. Retrieved June 05, 2019, from https://slate.com/news-and-politics/2019/05/chicago-police-department-consent-decree-black-lives-matter-resistance.html?fbclid=IwAR10udpDTlScsnRr7E7ybsMhHIohlt7CnHRv-TEK-744zd1OI20lr6wmgPWc.
Botelho, G. (2012). What Happened the Night Trayvon Martin Died? *CNN*. Retrieved June 04, 2019, from https://edition.cnn.com/2012/05/18/justice/flor ida-teen-shooting-details/index.html.
Bratton, W. (1998). *The Turnaround: How America's Top Cop Reversed the Crime Epidemic*. New York, NY: Random House.
Carrington, K., Hogg, R., & Sozzo, M. (2016). Southern Criminology. *The British Journal of Criminology, 56*(1), 1–20.
Carter, C., & Yan, H. (2013). Why this Verdict? Five Things that Led to Zimmerman's Acquittal. *CNN*. Retrieved June 04, 2019, from https://edition.cnn.com/2013/07/14/us/zimmerman-why-this-verdict/.
Coates, T. (2015). *Between the World and Me*. New York: Text Publishing Company.
Cobb, J. (2016) The Matter of Black Lives. *The New Yorker*. Retrieved June 04, 2019, from https://www.newyorker.com/magazine/2016/03/14/where-is-black-lives-matter-headed.
Cohen, S. (2001). *States of Denial: Knowing About Atrocities and Suffering*. Cambridge: Polity Press.
Connell, R. (2007). *Southern Theory: The Global Dynamics of Knowledge in the Social Science*. Sydney: Allen & Unwin.
Fleetwood, J., Presser, L., Berg, S., & Ugelvik, T. (2019). *Emerald Handbook of Narrative Criminology*. Bingley: Emerald.
Garland, D. (2001). Introduction: The Meaning of Mass Imprisonment. In D. Garland (Ed.), *Mass Imprisonment: Social Causes and Consequences* (pp. 1–10). London: Sage.
Goffman, A. (2009). On the Run: Wanted Men in a Philadelphia Ghetto. *American Sociological Review, 74*(3), 339–357.

Goffman, A. (2015). *On the Run: Fugitive Life in an American City*. Chicago: University of Chicago Press.

Gramlich, J. (2019). The Gap between the Number of Blacks and Whites in Prison is Shrinking. Pew Research Center. Retrieved June 06, 2019, from https://www.pewresearch.org/fact-tank/2019/04/30/shrinking-gap-between-number-of-blacks-and-whites-in-prison/.

Guthrie Ferguson, A. (2017). *The Rise of Big Data Policing : Surveillance, Race, and the Future of Law Enforcement*. New York: New York University Press.

Hallett, M. (2004). Commerce with Criminals: The New Colonialism. *Criminal Justice Review of Policy Research, 21*(1), 49–62.

Henry J Kaiser Family Foundation. (2017). Population Distribution by Race/Ethnicity. Retrieved June 05, 2019, from https://www.kff.org/other/state-indicator/distribution-by-raceethnicity/?currentTimeframe=0&sortModel=%7B%22colId%22:%22Location%22,%22sort%22:%22asc%22%7D.

History. (2019). Jim Crow Laws. Retrieved June 05, 2019, from https://www.history.com/topics/early-20th-century-us/jim-crow-laws..

Inquest. (2019) Fatal Police Shootings. Retrieved June 05, 2019, from https://www.inquest.org.uk/fatal-police-shootings.

Kamat, A. (2016). The Baltimore Uprising. In J. T. Camp & C. Heatherton (Eds.), *Policing the Planet* (pp. 73–82). London: Verso.

Lowery, W. (2017) The Long Read: Clack Lives Matter: Birth of a Movement. *The Guardian*. Retrieved June 04, 2019, from https://www.theguardian.com/us-news/2017/jan/17/black-lives-matter-birth-of-a-movement.

Lum, C. (2009). Community Policing or Zero Tolerance? Preferences of Police Officers from 22 Countries in Transition. *The British Journal of Criminology, 49*, 788–809.

Mindock, C. (2018) Ferguson Shooting: Four Years after the Michael Brown's Death, How have Things Changed? *The Independent*. Retrieved June 05, 2019, from https://www.independent.co.uk/news/world/americas/michael-brown-ferguson-shooting-missouri-death-shot-darren-wilson-trump-obama-police-a8481456.html.

Ministry of Justice. (2020). Retrieved May 27, 2020, from https://www.ethnicity-facts-figures.service.gov.uk/crime-justice-and-the-law/courts-sentencing-and-tribunals/young-people-in-custody/latest.

Stone-Mediatore, S. (2019). How America Disguises its Violence: Colonialism, Mass Incarceration, and the Need for Resistant Imagination. *Critical Review of International Social and Political Philosophy, 22*(5), 542–561.

Swaine, J. (2014). Michael Brown Shooting: 'They Killed Another Young Black Man in America. *The Guardian*. Retrieved June 04, 2019, from https://www.theguardian.com/world/2014/aug/12/ferguson-missouri-shooting-michael-brown-civil-rights-police-brutality.

The Guardian. (2014). Vigil for St Louis Teenager Killed by Police Descends into Violence. Retrieved June 04, 2019, from https://www.theguardian.com/world/2014/aug/11/vigil-st-louis-teenager-killed-police%2D%2Dviolence.

The Guardian. (2019). Retrieved May 22, 2020, from https://www.theguardian.com/australia-news/2019/aug/23/indigenous-deaths-in-custody-worsen-over-year-of-tracking-by-deaths-inside-project.

The National Association for the Advancement of Colored People (NAACP). (2019). Nation's Premier Civil Rights Organization. Retrieved June 05, 2019, from https://www. naacp.org/nations-premier-civil-rights-organization/.

The Sentencing Project. (2019). Criminal Justice Facts. Retrieved May 22, 2020, from https://www.sentencingproject.org/criminal-justice-.

The Washington Post. (2019). People Shot Dead by Police in the United States. Retrieved June 04, 2019, from https://www.washingtonpost.com/graphics/national/police-shoo-tings/.

United States Census Bureau. (2018). Population Estimate 2018. Retrieved June 05, 2019, from https://www.census.gov/quickfacts/fact/table/US/PST045218.

United States Department of Justice Civil Rights Division. (2015). Investigation of the Ferguson Police Department, Department of Justice/Civil Rights Division.

Waquant, L. (2009). *Prisons of Poverty.* Minneapolis: University of Minnesota Press.

Williamson, V., Trump, K., & Einstein, K. L. (2018). Black Lives Matter: Evidence that Police Caused Deaths Predict Protest Activity. *Perspective on Politics, 16*(2), 400–416.

Wilson, J. Q., & Kelling, G. (1982). Broken Windows The Police and Neighborhood Safety. *The Atlantic On-line, 211,* 29–38.

Young, I. M. (2005). Five faces of oppression. In A. E. Cudd & R. O. Andreasen (eds.), *Feminist theory: a philosophical anthology* (pp. 91–104). Oxford, UK Malden, Massachusetts: Blackwell Publishing.

Religion

6

Introduction

This chapter focuses on religion at both the individual and total institution levels. Power is foregrounded in the shape of the historically oppressive nature of religion and religious institutions. There are numerous ways in which the abuse of power has come to light in Christian and other faiths and cultures. Power struggles around religious identities are documented throughout history and continue in various parts of the world today with different states of confusion and turmoil manifesting. The foregrounded aspects of power in this chapter are illustrated and drawn out of case examples that are non-conventional in terms of what criminologists might usually think about as illustrative of crime and victimisation in society. The case studies are those of Ireland's Magdalen Laundries and the Bon Secours Mother and Baby Home in Tuam, Ireland. These cases, and the issues they raise, are contextualised both historically and contemporarily. There are, as with the cases selected in other chapters in this book, a number of potential examples that could be selected which implicate the role of the Church (or equivalent) and the state in hiding abuses of power. A catalogue of Church, clergy and culture-related case studies spring to mind and are thrown up when doing internet searches on various combinations of these terms in conjunction with those of power and abuse, injustice, crime and victimisation. Indeed, there are cases that could be selected from several countries where religious and secular institutions have been complicit in perpetrating serious criminal and non-criminal abuses including sexual abuse of boys, girls and young people that have been rendered invisible through silencing and cover-ups. Ireland

© The Author(s) 2021
P. Davies, T. Wyatt, *Crime and Power*,
https://doi.org/10.1007/978-3-030-57314-0_6

is not the only criminogenic country in this regard. From Archbishops and other high-ranking senior Catholic clerics and figures in Argentina, Australia, Austria, North, Central and South America, Vienna and several other European countries, sexual abuse involving the clergy is not a new phenomenon. A major scandal in twentieth-century Britain was that of the Reverend Harold Davidson from Norfolk, who went on trial in 1932 on a charge of immoral conduct with women over a ten-year period between 1921 and 1931. He was found guilty on all counts—molesting, importuning, making improper suggestions and immoral conduct. He was defrocked in 1932 from the Church of England for bringing grave scandal on the Church (Brown 2006). Several more recent exposés of shameful historical practices have been exposed and subsequently have been written about by scholars, including criminologists. See, for example, the work of Liz Stanley (2016) on state violence against children in New Zealand and discussion of indigenous victimisation in Australia, Canada, New Zealand and the United States (see Cunneen and Rowe 2015). We justify the particular case study examples of Ireland's Magdalene Laundries and the Bon Secours Mother and Baby Home in Tuam as the issues they raise have both historical and contemporary interest and relevance and they reach across far-flung geographical spaces. They also enable us to illustrate how gendered power operates in the Church and how hierarchies of power operate within these mostly all-female total institutions.

Below we provide a descriptive outline of the case studies for this chapter. The remainder of the chapter dissects these cases in order to illustrate several dimensions to power, most notably the role of the state and the synergies with the new morality established in Ireland via the Catholic Church and Magdalenism. We broaden the scope to consider these institutions as places of confinement and punitive control drawing on classic authors' contributions by those writing about the sociology of imprisonment, total institutions, penality and punishment (Sykes 1958; Goffman 1968; Foucault 1975/1991; Ignatieff 1978). Contemporary feminist-influenced scholarship is also drawn on (Howe 1994; Fischer 2016; Luddy 1992, 1997; Wecker 2015; Jordan 2012).

Case Study: Ireland's Magdalen Laundries and the Bon Secours Mother and Baby Home in Tuam
Magdalen Laundries—Historical Background and Contemporary Developments and Discourse
Ireland's Magdalen laundries—sometimes referred to as Magdalen asylums—have become a topic that has become familiar not only to the Irish public over the last 15 years or so, but also further abroad. Dissemination of

(continued)

(continued)

these institutions' histories has been achieved in film, drama and in literature as well as other medium, including scholarly reviews and critique. *The Magdalene Sisters* film (2002) directed by Peter Mullen is but one portrayal of Ireland's Magdalen asylums in popular culture. Together these various contributions display an antinomy of views about the institution of these Laundries (Simpson et al. 2014).

Magdalen Laundries operated in Ireland between 1922 and 1996, though the first opened in around 1765–1767 in Dublin. At this time, the institution provided refuge for women (Wecker 2015). By 1835, there were about a dozen such institutions in Dublin, and, established by women philanthropists, skills were taught such as laundry work, lace making and needlework (Fischer 2016). From their eighteenth-century beginnings, it is widely agreed that these shelters for girls and women in Ireland and other parts of the world transformed into institutions of confinement and punitive control and the term 'Magdalen Laundries' was coined. They were run most often by nuns under Roman Catholic orders until the late twentieth century. The last Magdalen laundry ceased operating as a commercial business on 25 October 1996. The name Magdalen—sometimes spelled Magdalene—Laundries is a biblical one which refers to Mary Magdalene, and, by adopting Mary Magdalene as the patron saint, compassionate sentiments are evoked (Simpson et al. 2014) towards prostitute women, who were viewed as having fallen from grace similar to the biblical character. Young women and girls were put into these institutions and confined for a variety of reasons. Unmarried mothers with 'illegitimate' babies and children out of wedlock were the largest group, deemed 'fallen women', 'difficult' and 'out of order' because they were sexually active, promiscuous, prostitutes, seduced women, sexually abused and victims of incest and rape. Others were homeless, vagrants, ex-convicts, alcoholics or simply poor. All were seen as a threat to the moral fibre of Irish society and were 'outcast' women (Luddy 1992). Estimates suggest as many as 10,000 women spent their days praying, repenting and working in silence in the Magdalen Laundries. On entry women's hair was cut and thereafter all contact with the outside world was limited. Life within these institutions saw further restrictions put on women and girls who were not able to leave easily and were forced to work for no pay, typically in laundry-based work. They were stripped of their identity, denied their given names and assigned new ones, typically names of biblical origin such as names of saints. Their children were usually sent for adoption and many women spent their entire lives in such confinement as penitents.

(continued)

(continued)

Bon Secours Mother and Baby Home in Tuam

Having read an article in the *Tuam Herald*, Catherine Corless, who had been researching a similar type of institution to the Magdalen Laundries— the Mother and Baby Home located in Tuam—began corresponding with a former resident. Corless, an independent historian, engaged in years of investigative research of the Bon Secours Sisters run home which led to her unearthing and exposing the tragedy and the extent of what happened there. In 2014, she published an article documenting the discovery of the remains of hundreds of babies at the site in Tuam. The buried remains were unmarked and unregistered. She reported the deaths of 798 babies at the home and that the main causes of death were congenital debilities, infectious diseases and malnutrition.

In 2014, the *Belfast Telegraph* was just one of many newspapers that reported on the mass baby grave in Tuam:

'Mass baby grave in Tuam, Galway: Sisters of Bon Secours nuns "have no burial records"'

The Sisters of Bon Secours nuns in charge of Mother and Baby Home in Tuam, Co Galway, where the burial of hundreds of babies in a septic tank mass grave has been uncovered have said they no longer hold the burial records.

The nuns, which operated the home, said they were shocked and deeply saddened by reports of the burial of 798 infants from 1925 to 1961.

The statement from the Bon Secours nuns failed to confirm, deny or give any detail about the existence of the mass grave.

There are similarities between the two types of institutions described above. Those who may have fallen pregnant outside of wedlock, but who were nevertheless considered redeemable, were hidden away in mother and baby homes, while women and girls who had experienced more than one pregnancy were consigned to Magdalen Laundries, their children often fostered or adopted by Catholic families in the United States (Fischer 2016). Women were thus subjected to all manners of judgements including judgement according to their level of sinfulness.

Several scholars address the Magdalen Laundries from a variety of disciplines, including politics (Simpson et al. 2014), women's studies (Fischer 2016, Wecker 2015) and history (Luddy 1992, 1997; McCormick 2005). These writers have their own agendas for choosing to draw on Magdalenism and the Magdalen Laundries, and there are often very different and contrasting views at stake, especially with regard to the positive or negative intentions of the Magdalen asylums and whether or not the sisters who ran them had sinister intentions (McCormick 2005). There is a sharp contrast also in public and mediated opinion, where some represent the Laundries as 'spiritual, educational and healthy havens in a welfare less world' and others see them 'as devices for drudgery akin to gulags, camps, or slavery' (Simpson et al. 2014). However, what most of these discussions have in common is that they variously address the role of the state and state power. Scholars have considered the role of the state as moral controller, aggressor, usurper, robber, subjugator, silencer, human rights violator and its institutions as disciplinary. Most assessments agree that the institutions, to a greater or lesser extent, were sites where the abuse of power was exercised.

The Magdalen Laundries have been subjected to both academic critique and public criticism, and, at the time of writing, a statutory Commission of Investigation (established in 2015) into Mother and Baby Homes is still underway to investigate and report to the Minister for Children and Youth Affairs in Ireland. The remit requires the investigation to establish, amongst other things, the circumstances and arrangements for the entry of single women into these institutions, the living conditions and care arrangements experienced by residents during their period of accommodation in them, and mortality and post-mortem practices and procedures in respect of children or mothers who died while resident in these institutions. The investigation covers the period from 1922 to 1998. The Terms of Reference require it to examine the reporting of deaths and burial arrangements in relation to 14 named institutions. In the spring of 2019, the Commission issued a Fourth Interim report and requested further extensions for submitting the final report (Mother and Baby Homes Commission of Investigation 2019). This appears to be due to the fact that more time is needed to conduct surveys of children's burial grounds in at least one location (Sean Ross Abbey).

Magdelenism and the Role of the State

In a book-length study, Smith (2008) dwells on the collective guilt that Irish society bear with regard to the Magdalen Laundries and in particular on the continued failure to confront and acknowledge the abuses that took place in them. His assessment is especially critical of the responsibility and collusion of the Catholic Church and the Irish state in the twentieth century. Here, we unpick these claims of collusion and draw out the role of the state as moral controller as well as the gendered nature of this morality.

The Catholic Church and the New Morality

The major religious trend of the last quarter of the twentieth century was that the Christian faithful dwindled in mainland Britain. This decline was more modest in the north of Ireland, but on the whole there was a marked rejection of faith-based morality. According to Brown (2006), the period between 1974 and 2000 shaped British secularisation, and the prevalence of scandal and hypocrisy had already affected many denominations, including the Catholic Church, as priests were accused of abusing boys and this was a factor in this shift towards secularisation. Secularisation did not feature in the Republic of Ireland where scandal and hypocrisy were dealt with rather differently. To understand this, it is important to have an appreciation of historical developments. The history of Ireland's transition from British rule in the early 1920s to partitioned sovereignty saw a new—different from British—nation-state emerge:

> Underpinning the construction of Ireland's newly emergent nation-state was a national imaginary that needed to clearly differentiate Irish identity from British identity, a task undertaken through recourse to the themes of purity, chastity, and virtue. The corollary of each of these, impurity, licentiousness, and vice, were attributed to the morally corrupt former coloniser, allowing the distinctness and superiority of Irish identity to be secured with particular reference to moral purity, bolstered by Catholic social teaching. (Fischer 2016: 822)

Smith (2008) suggests that in a bid to produce and enforce a new national identity premised on moral and sexual purity, the Catholic Church and Irish state colluded to impose strict Catholic social mores and values. This was in part enacted through women's bodies. Women's potential impurity and lack of virtue were significant threats to the creation of the new Irish nation. All women were potential transgressors and those who did transgress were seen as bringing shame on their families, communities and potentially the nation itself. Women of 'bad character', prostitutes and the 'wrens' of the Curragh (Luddy 1992, 1997) were typically inmates of the Magdalen Laundries. Luddy has written extensively on women, prostitution and philanthropy in nineteenth-century Ireland (see, e.g., Luddy 1992, 1997). Although there are differences of opinion about her assessment of the

Magdalen Laundries into the twentieth century (see, e.g., Wecker 2015), Luddy offers some useful insights into the broader historical context of post-famine Irish society, and she emphasises how a key element of philanthropy in Ireland was the denominational nature of its development.

The most extensive network of Magdalen asylums were provided by Catholic nuns. Within the Catholic hierarchy, the behaviour of nuns was governed by men. 'Ultimate authority on convent life, and hence in the Magdalen asylums, rested with priests and bishops' (Luddy 1992: 345). Nevertheless, it was as nuns that women achieved the highest status in Irish society. Outside of the Church, in the laity, women conformed to the ideals of the Irish constitution in the domestic sphere as wife and mother (Wecker 2015). Nuns were considered most likely to reform the Magdalens. The vows of chastity and commitment to purity, austerity and holiness by the Catholic nuns made them an ideal role model for the penitents, particularly prostitute women who were ostracised in the new morality and emerging moral order arising from the purity movement, which was active from the 1880s. This movement promoted an ideology of sexual abstinence, and the Church, the family and community all imposed and reinforced ideas of modesty, respectability, sexual virtue and chastity, amongst young girls. Focusing on prostitution, Luddy (1997) contends that the establishment of the Magdalen asylums provided a place and site for the containment of these 'fallen women'. The asylums allowed these women to be contained and hidden away from view, in what Smith (2008) has called the Nation of Ireland's 'architecture of containment', and separated so that they would not contaminate and spread disease or immorality amongst the public, keeping respectable women and girls away from public shame and the 'unrespectable'.

The new moral order was at the heart of Ireland's identity as a nation and moral purity literally governed all Irish Catholic women's lives. Magdalenism, the Catholic Church, the Magdalen Laundries and institutions, such as the Bon Secours Mother and Baby Home in Tuam, all played a key role in pitting moral purity and sexual virtue against shame. Commenting on an online newspaper article about the Magdalen Laundries, one member of the public suggested:

> These religious orders were not doing any of this to help Irish society or help the state in its early years, they were doing it because it was an opportunity to consolidate their power and influence. (Simpson et al. 2014: 262)

Indeed, the majority of the critical comments reviewed by these researchers concerned the Church's historical power within Irish society and its abuse and corruption.

Pause for Thought

- How do the case studies show that power is distributed across a wide range of individuals, institutions and groups?
- How does religion exert power over individuals and over society?

The All-Powerful Total Institution: Containment, Punishment and Discipline

As we have already seen, academic scholarship on the Magdalen Laundries often makes reference to these institutions as places of confinement and punitive control. There is a rich tradition on the sociology of imprisonment, and students of criminology are steered towards the classic contributions by Sykes (1958) and Goffman (1968). In *The Society of Captives*, Sykes (1958) undertook his fieldwork in a maximum security prison in the United States, and his work explores the prison as an institution of domination and totalitarian control, where inmate culture was determined by the inherent deprivations of prison life. In *Asylums*, Goffman (1968) extended the focus on the prison as a total institution suggesting it was just one among a range of 'total institutions'. For Goffman, such institutions are 'a place of residence and work where a large number of like-situated individuals, cut off from the wider society for an appreciable period of time, together lead an enclosed, formally administered round of life' (1968: 11). This definition applies equally to asylums, mental hospitals, monasteries and other places of mass incarceration or containment, including convents, and Magdalen Laundries. On entry into the Laundries, the practices listed by Goffman took place, including the removal of personal possessions, assigning of uniforms and new identities, cutting of hair. The regulation of inmates' routine activities also took place by imposing a strict regime often involving a combination of hard physical work and reformative ideals.

In addition to the classic and contemporary scholarship already cited above by Sykes and Goffman, all of which have inspired a rich tradition of sociological and criminological writing, students of criminology and criminal justice are also directed towards those who have been concerned about penality and the techniques of punishment and the control of the body. As mentioned in Chap. 2 about power, Foucault's (1975/1991) *Discipline and Punish* argues that power is not simply held by the powerful, but it flows throughout the social body, through the surveillance, rules and assumptions about social behaviour. In the Magdalen Laundries, a particularly controlling form of instrumental power is exercised over women in prison-like institutions, where exhausting work and intense surveillance combine to effect physical, psycho-social and symbolic discipline over and through bodies. Ignatieff's (1978) *A Just Measure of Pain* is another classic contribution. In this instance, the study is concerned with the isolation of prisoners and the desire to improve minds through scripture and hard work, again echoing the new moral purity code evident in Irish institutions and the hard physical laundry-based work that was conducted in them. These works, too, have inspired a range of scholarship, which you might variously draw upon to dissect the religious and cultural institutions of the Magdalen Laundries and Bon Secours Mother and Baby home.

Let us briefly focus on two ways in which the Magdalen Laundries operated as powerful and totally controlling institutions. First, we explore the power to contain the penitents/inmates and second we consider the power to discipline and punish.

Containment

The Magdalen Laundries were places of confinement and containment. Women were locked away, often for very long periods of time, with restrictions on their movement and there was little opportunity to leave. Once confined, the women were contained, hidden away from public view, abandoned and rendered invisible. In addition to not being able to enter the outside world, the women in these institutions were not allowed contact, visits or letters, from their family and friends. Thus, containment is twofold, stemming from physical removal from the community and from any social contact. Their experiences of containment can be likened to the experiences of those in reformatories and penitentiary institutions. Further restrictions were imposed on inmates via often brutal and punitive disciplinary regimes.

Discipline and Punish

Feminists, including Howe (1994) inspired by Foucault, suggest women are regulated and disciplined throughout society and, by and within, its institutions. The existence of the laundries at all though indicates that that there is a societal level of control over women's behaviour and bodies even before women who step out of the new moral order are placed within these institutions. Once in the Laundries, women were governed via the moral purity in the new Irish state where sexual purity was 'enacted and problematized through women's bodies' (Fischer 2016: 822).

Sexual impurity was dealt with by taking control of bodies. This was effected by removing women's bodies to the Magdalen Laundries and by restricting and shaming them within their walls through a disciplinary regime that was highly gendered in nature. Thus, women 'also learnt to govern themselves through protestations of faith, religious discipline and bodily exhaustion' (Simpson et al. 2014: 258). Sin was to be washed away through penitence and laundry work, scrubbing and ironing clothes brought in from other institutions (Simpson et al. 2014). The type of work was hard and arduous physical work (on the body). It also had mind and soul (spiritual) dimensions to it:

> The alleged sins committed by women and girls confined in Magdalen Laundries were read as stains upon their very character and bodies, stains that could be removed (though never quite) through repentance and the backbreaking work of washing away stains from dirty laundry. (Fischer 2016: 835)

Magdalenism, the Catholic Church and the new morality, total containment, punitive regimes and disciplinary codes all ensured a state-controlled discourse and a state-controlled narrative legacy of the Magdalen Laundries and the Bob Secours Mothers and Baby Home in Tuam. The assessment offered by one feminist scholar very recently suggests that in Ireland a system of institutionalisation that was especially punitive, pervasive and persistent (Fischer 2016: 829) was ushered in. Another concludes 'By silencing and locking away women who deviated from the accepted moral code, this action allowed for a narrative of fiction to develop' (Wecker 2015: 275).

Silence and Denial

Those received into and accommodated within the Magdalen Laundries were forcibly silenced within the laundry walls. Feminist-inspired scholarship has long argued that silence is a hallmark of oppression drawing attention to the various ways in which women are silenced and within the context of patriarchy there is a long history of the silencing of women's voices. In her powerfully emotive book on experiencing rape, *After Silence*, Raine (1998) discusses silence as part of the power-shame complex. 'Rape has long been considered a crime so unspeakable, so shameful to its victims, that they are rendered mute.........They must also carry the burden of silence and shame' (Raine 1998: 6). Jordan (2012: 254), a passionate advocate for victims of sexual assault and rape, has written about the historical silencing of women's voices and 'why such loud and resounding silence continues to surround the crime of rape'. The enforced silence in the regime at the Magdalen Laundries is one such example of oppression of women through their bodies. Silence and silencing serves to block these women out and shut them off such that the outside world can turn a blind eye, blank them out, refuse to see and know about atrocities and suffering behind the walls. The web of oppression takes on several guises including economic exploitation as we shall illustrate with reference to the labour performed. Silence and silencing are both tools used by the powerful to render their harms and crimes invisible, as we see in these examples.

To extend our analysis on silence and denial let us focus on the Bon Secours Mother and Baby Home in Tuam. An email from the Public Relations representative for the Bon Secours sisters sent to a would-be documentary maker of the Tuam Home was replete with denials:

> When the ;O My God—mass grave in West of Ireland' broke in an English owned paper (the Mail) it surprised the hell out of everybody, not least the sisters of Bon Secours in Ireland, none of whom had ever worked in Tuam and most of whom had never heard of it.
> If you come here, you'll find no mass grave, no evidence that children were ever so buried, and a local police force casting their eyes to heaven and saying 'Yeah, a few bones were found—but this was an area where Famine victims were buried'. (The Journal, 13 October 2014)

Drawing again on criminological scholarship, Sykes and Matza (1957) and Cohen (2001) both discuss denial in some depth. Sykes' and Matza's work was developed in response to what they saw as a sociological determinism in criminological theory. Three of Sykes and Matza's (1957) 'techniques of neutralization' contain the word 'denial'. Denial of responsibility is achieved by obedience to authority. A superior authority makes the (moral) decisions and the offender simply carries out their duties, so the blame does not lie with them but with those in authority. In this case, it is the Catholic Church—the bishops and so forth—who are responsible for creation of the Laundries. Therefore, the nuns who enact the punishment for moral transgressions are not responsible for the harm and suffering that they are inflicting upon the women 'penitents'. Denial of injury is claimed to neutralise the guilt the offender may feel over the suffering their actions have caused. Narratives that deny causing suffering may well include that hard physical work, like laundry-based work, is not an injury, but a reform technique or that containment is not harmful, but for the penitent's own good. Finally, Sykes and Matza (1957) propose that there is denial of the victim. 'Fallen women' cannot be victims or are deserving of what they get because of their own actions.

In his book-length exemplification of *States of Denial*, Cohen (2001) is concerned with explaining the apparent public indifference to media images of distant suffering through forms of denial. He identifies three categories of denial: literal denial, interpretive denial and implicatory denial. Literal denial is 'factual' or 'blatant' denial. There is a refusal to acknowledge the facts, nothing happened. The letter from the Bon Secours sisters is an example of this, denying that the incident ever happened at all. Interpretive denial is different in that the raw facts are not being denied but, rather, they are given a different meaning. There are elements of this as well in the letter from the Bon Secours sisters. If there are bones, then maybe they were from people who died in the famine not babies from contained mothers. What is denied or minimised in the category of implicatory denial are the psychological, political or moral implications that conventionally follow. The implications of containment and hard physical labour are not suffering but reformation. Similar to Sykes' and Matza's (1957) denial of injury and denial of the victim, what happened was justified. These techniques of neutralisation are used by offenders and states as a way of denying guilt in relation to violations of human rights.

As detailed above, Sykes' and Matza's and Cohen's categories of denial resonate in the context of the Magdalen Laundries. In particular, Cohen's theorising links silence with denial in ways, which are starkly evident in these examples. Codes of silence in the state and the Church range from strict, formal and enforced to barely collusive denials. Denying the truth of women's words serves as a muting device; the collusion between the state and the Church sees both these institutions as muting agents. The Church and the state engaged in collective denials and, through cultural slippage, information about the Magdelen Laundries, and in particular about the babies at Tuam, just disappeared. 'Slow cultural forgetting works best when powerful forces have an interest in keeping people quiet' (Cohen 2001: 133).

Power and Activism

Much of this chapter has focused on the abuse of power at state and institutional levels, all of which speaks to the significance of macro levels of power and of its structural and systemic overtures. It has also illustrated how power permeates from those macro levels to the mezzo levels within institutions (the Laundries and the Home) and micro levels of power at individual levels (the nuns). This closing section of the chapter builds on the idea of alternative narratives and truths. In doing so, the chapter ends on a more positive note about power and activism.

Whilst the assessment above focuses on the powerfully oppressive and negative overtures of silence and denial, Wecker (2015) revisits the rhetoric of silence and argues it is a form of power signifying positive resistance and survivorship. As noted earlier, in the context of not reporting rape, and in the silence of those suffering atrocities, the sufferers' silence is traditionally presumed to be a weakness. Wecker (2015) argues this fails to reflect the rhetorics of feminine silence, where it can provide clues to power struggles previously obscured. Wecker argues that continued silence can be interpreted not as a continued enforced silence but as a 'silence of will'. The latter silence—a self-contained silence—is a powerful choice, a deliberate action. In the same way that rape victims might silence themselves during and after their ordeal, for other survivors and victims, their silence performs a critical function. Wecker argues it is not simple passivity in such situations, rather it is purposeful, expressive power, and this perspective on women's silence might be used to reclaim Magdalenism. Such an approach affords the survivors an opening 'to reverse the stigma previously associated with Magdalen penitents and declare their truth' (Wecker 2015: 277).

Speaking truth to power has become a popular way to describe taking a stand and mobilising society around change. The 1955 book *Speak Truth to Power: A Quaker Search for an Alternative to Violence* published by the American Friends Service Committee is commonly cited with respect to this adage. Activist movements are wedded to the idea of advocacy and there is a well-established tradition of its history of use in feminist research/activist work and in political and cultural contexts other than religious contexts. For example, Scraton (2013), reflecting on two decades of research, writes about the politics of denial, liberating truth, and challenging power, securing acknowledgement and pursuing justice in his article about Hillsborough (Sheffield, UK), the legacy of the FA Cup semi-final and the death of 96 men, women and children in a crush in April 1989. Contrasting the official discourse with alternative accounts from bereaved families and survivors, he exposes the 'view from below'. 'Hillsborough illustrates the capacity of state organisations to engage in discourses of deceit, denial and neutralisation that protect and exonerate those in positions of power, those who stand highest in established hierarchies of credibility' (Scraton 2013: 24).

Scraton became wedded to exposing the truth of Hillsborough for over 30 years. In respect of the case studies at the heart of this chapter, a movement called Justice for Magdalenes (JFM) was established in 2003. JFM started a political campaign in 2009 with two objectives. The objectives were to bring about an official apology from the Irish state and to establish a compensation scheme for all Magdalen survivors. In 2013, these objectives were realised, and since then the organisation has transformed into a research-oriented and educational group. The stance of the JFM was that the Irish state

- was aware of the nature and function of the Magdalene laundries;
- was aware that there was no statutory basis for the courts' use of the laundries;
- enacted legislation to enable the use of one laundry as a remand home;
- was aware that children and adolescent girls were confined in the laundries as late as 1970;
- maintained a 'special provision' whereby women giving birth to a second child outside marriage at a Mother-and-Baby could be transferred directly to a Magdalene laundry;
- paid capitation grants to Magdalene laundries for the confinement of 'problem girls';
- never inspected, licenced or certified these home as 'Approved' institutions; and
- has yet to produce records for the women it referred to the laundries.

In 2013, the official apology was forthcoming and a press release made it clear: 'The responsibility to ensure that justice is delivered to survivors of the Laundries now rests with all members of Irish society, including Church, State, families and local communities' (JFM 2013).

Activism, activist movements and the mobilising of collective action is a way of exposing alternative rhetorics of silence. The above illustrates the strength of collective power to resist and challenge at state and institutional levels, with some speaking truth to power through the persistence of individuals.

Summary

With a focus on case examples that are religious and/or culture oriented, this chapter has exposed how individual characteristics like religion, but gender, race and age as we will see in the next chapters, can be a source of power and potentially powerlessness. People, in this case women, enmeshed in religious societies can be controlled by religious institutions and because of their religious beliefs. The Church (or other religious organisation) holds power within communities because of their long history, their centrality to many communities and their influence over many people's behaviours. Religious figures are individually powerful because they can, to some degree, control what happens to those in their congregation. This is very clear in the Magdalen Laundries and Tuam home for Mothers and Babies, where Catholic women who had strayed from the doctrine are forced into and punished in religious institutions often indefinitely.

Religion as an individual characteristic may also be tied to powerlessness. Again, this is evident in the examples presented here because in the Catholic faith, women are not in equal positions of power to men. Women have a specific expected moral behaviour that is placed upon them by the church and by individuals within the faith; the bishops and priests speak about the morality, and the nuns at these facilities were key to bringing the 'fallen women' back into the fold. As believers, or at least followers of the Catholic faith, the women likely subscribed to these moral expectations themselves and viewed the Church leaders and figures as powerful. They may well have felt powerlessness under the weight of the Church and the individual and societal level power it wields.

As indicated, power linked to religion is beyond the individual. The Church as an institution is a powerful institution. This may be particularly true in the Irish context, where religion is a prominent element of national identity. As seen time and again with church-related 'scandals' like the epidemic occurrences of paedophilia, religious institutions are powerful enough to hide their crimes, protect the offenders, silence the victims and render these horrific incidents invisible. This is not different for the Magdalen Laundries and Tuam Mother and Baby Home. In addition this chapter variously addressed the role of the state and state power. It has explored the abuse of power, and it has examined in some detail the role of the state as moral controller, aggressor, usurper, robber, subjugator, silencer and human rights violator and has shown how state institutions might be considered disciplinary in nature. In these cases, the state likely colluded with the Church. Religion, religious institutions and cultural practices and oppressions have links of course to other forms of oppression, including economic exploitation and repression. The latter forms of exploitation are carried into the next chapter where we examine gender and power. Religion, religious institutions and cultural practices are thus important areas for us to scrutinise in our exploration of how power can be wielded, by whom and through what mechanisms, practices and structures.

Go Further

- What do you understand by the term 'architecture of containment'? What are some examples?
- Is silence an instrument of repression?
- In what ways can the Church and state collude to neutralise historical harm and abuse?

References

Brown, C. G. (2006). *Religion and Society in Twentieth-Century Britain*. London: Pearson Longman.

Cohen, S. (2001). *States of Denial: Knowing about Atrocities and Suffering*. Cambridge: Polity Press.

Cunneen, C., & Rowe, S. (2015). Decolonising Indigenous Victimisation. In D. Wilson & S. Ross (Eds.), *Crime, Victims and Policy: International Contexts, Local Experiences* (pp. 10–32). London: Palgrave.

Fischer, C. (2016). Gender, Nation, and the Politics of Shame: Magdalen Laundries and the Institutionalization of Feminine Transgression in Modern Ireland. *Signs: Journal of Women in Culture and Society, 41*(4), 821–843.

Foucault, M. (1975/1991). *Discipline and Punish: The Birth of the Prison*. Harmondsworth: Penguin Books. (originally published in French in 1975.)

Goffman, E. (1968). *Asylums: Essays on the Social Situation of Mental Patients and Other Inmates*. Harmondsworth: Penguin Books.

Howe, A. (1994). *Punish and Critique: Towards a Feminist Analysis of Penality*. London: Routledge.

Ignatieff, M. (1978). *A Just Measure of Pain: The Penitentiary in the Industrial Revolution, 1750–1850*. London: Macmillan.

JFM. (2013). Press Release Press Release: 17th May. Justice for Magdalenes to End Its Political Campaign.

Jordan, J. (2012). Silencing Rape, Silencing Women. In *Handbook on Sexual Violence*. ISBN: 9780415670715.

Luddy, M. (1992). An Outcast Community: The 'Wrens' of the Curragh. *Women's History Review, 1*(3), 341–355.

Luddy, M. (1997). 'Abandoned Women and Bad Characters': Prostitution in Nineteenth-century Ireland. *Women's History Review, 6*(4), 486–503.

McCormick, L. (2005). Sinister Sisters? The Portrayal of Ireland's Magdalene Asylums in Popular Culture. *Cultural and Social History, 2*, 373–379.

Mother and Baby Homes Commission of Investigation. (2019). Retrieved March 21, 2019, from http://www.mbhcoi.ie/mbh.nsf/page/Latest%20News-en.

Raine, N. V. (1998). *After Silence: Rape and My Journey Back*. New York: Three Rivers Press.

Scraton, P. (2013). The Legacy of Hillsborough: Liberating Truth, Challenging Power. *Race & Class, 55*(2), 1–27.

Simpson, A. V., Clegg, S. R., Lopes, M. P., Cuhna, M. P., Rego, A., & Pitsis, T. (2014). Doing Compassion or Doing Discipline? Power Relations and the Magdalen Laundries. *Journal of Political Power, 7*(2), 253–274.

Smith, J. M. (2008). *Ireland's Magdalen Laundries and the Nation's Architecture of Containment*. Manchester: Manchester University Press.

Stanley, E. (2016). *The Road to Hell: State Violence Against Children in Postwar New Zealand*. Auckland: Auckland University Press.

Sykes, G. (1958). *The Society of Captives: A Study of a Maximum-security Prison*. Princeton, NJ: Princeton University Press.

Sykes, G., & Matza, D. (1957). Techniques of Neutralization: A Theory of Delinquency. *American Sociological Review, 22*(6), 664–670.
Wecker, E. C. (2015). Reclaiming Magdalenism or Washing Away Sin: Magdalen Laundries and the Rhetorics of Feminine Silence. *Women's Studies, 44*, 264–279.

Gender

7

Introduction

This chapter foregrounds gender-related dynamics of power as related to crime and victimisation and broader forms of economic repression that especially impact upon women. It starts from a position that accepts the patriarchal nature of Western society. The chapter explores the gendered nature of power in the context of crime and victimisation, and connected to this, one of the case study examples focuses on domestic abuse using the Sauvage case in France. Saudi Arabia's Women's Driving Ban features as the second case study. These examples variously and respectively illustrate the gendered nature of serious and harmful victimisations and the far-reaching effects of the Saudi Arabian guardianship system, which has long curtailed women's independence. The lifting of the driving ban in Saudi Arabia is part of a wider set of socio-economic liberal reforms, which will enable more women to enter the workforce. Both examples illustrate the complex interplay between gender and other social factors, which impact on our life chances. The reader is encouraged to think carefully about the interplay of these features of our individual identity, drawing on intersectionalities theorising (see Part I) in order to help assess the extent to which gender is especially significant.

In order to clarify our focus on gender, first we explain the differences between sex and gender-based dichotomies, binary and non-binary categorisations. We do so in order to lay the foundations for a sophisticated analysis of gender and power. The next two sections continue to provide contextual framing for the analysis of the case studies giving a theoretical framework for the discussions that follow. These

© The Author(s) 2021
P. Davies, T. Wyatt, *Crime and Power*,
https://doi.org/10.1007/978-3-030-57314-0_7

sections focus on gender, power and domestic abuse and emphasise how gender is part of the complex of social structural power. As noted above, the whole chapter commences from a position that accepts the patriarchal nature of Western society, and we take time to outline the concept of patriarchal power before we move to explore how individual power is mediated by gender, all within the context of a patriarchal power structure. In this part of the chapter, we therefore consider gender and individual power. We adopt the use of a case study of violence and abuse and other illustrative material to emphasise the different manifestations that such power can take ranging from physical to a controlling and coercive complex of psychological, emotional and financial weaponry. An extended discussion of the first case study leads into the second which focuses on Saudi Arabia's ban on women's driving. This is used as a segue for considering gender, culture, ideology, legal, familial, economic and political power.

The Sex/Gender Dichotomy and Binarism

In patriarchal societies (see below), cultural and social cues, imperatives and expectations tend to be overlaid upon sex-based distinctions. Here we explain some of the similarities and distinctions between sex-based and gender-based analyses unpicking what these terms and concepts mean before employing the use of some further gender-based concepts later in the chapter.

Walklate's (2004: 94) description of sex/gender differences remains a useful starting point: 'sex differences, i.e. differences that can be observed between the biological categories, male and female' are not necessarily a product of gender. 'Gender differences are those that result from the socially ascribed roles of being male or being female, i.e. masculinity and femininity'. Sex and gender therefore introduce oppositional associations: male/female, masculine/feminine. The concepts 'gender dichotomy' and 'binary category' refer to the additional socially constructed distinctions that are ascribed to male and female roles. For example, for women some of the socially ascribed cues associated with femininity include close affinities with all things family, home-based, nurturing, selfless and caring-oriented. Emotions, sensitivity and irrationality, passivity and subservience and weakness have become typical cultural expectations associated with womanliness and femininity. In contrast, for men some of the socially ascribed cues associated with masculinity include an over-riding concern with the business of work and economic productivity in order to provide and support dependents but also as a marker of independence, strength, purposefulness and rationality. A host of additional gender-matched characteristics and scripts could be added to these, all of which produce and reinforce gender dichotomies (Davies 2011).

Cisgender (people who agree with their gender assigned at birth) identity is privileged so that it is often seen as the way gender ontologically 'is' or should be. Cisgender normativity legitimises binary expressions of gender—male/female, masculine/feminine—whilst marking difference and 'othering' towards gender non-conformity (Johnson, 2013). Gender binary categories are exclusive, whereas non-binary is a spectrum of gender identities that are not exclusively masculine or feminine, but may be in between, fluctuating or with no gender identity. LGBTQ research in the context of hate crime is beginning to address these more nuanced dynamics of gender and power (Pickles 2018).

Having considered the distinctions between sex and gender, we can now begin to appreciate the differences between a simple sex-based approach and a more re-fined gender-based analysis. To illustrate the distinctions and associations between both types of analysis, we draw on Braithwaite's (1989) famous checklist of 13 facts about crime. The first two on the list are the most enduring features about crime:

1. Crime is committed disproportionately by males.
2. Crime is perpetrated disproportionately by 15–25-year-olds.

The first of these undisputed 'facts'—that males are disproportionately the of-fenders—surely implies that any theory of crime should address this. However, Braithwaite (1989: 50), lamenting the failure of the dominant criminological theo-ries to do this, observes: 'It is amazing that such basic, potent and uncontroversial correlates of crime and age and sex remain totally untouched by most of the domi-nant theories'.

Over 20 years later, commentators continue to reinforce this first most basic fact about men and crime and further emphasise the serious, violent and recidivist na-ture to men's offending: 'Men commit crime at higher rates than women, are invol-ved in more serious and violent offending, and are more prone to recidivism' (Heidensohn and Silvestri, 2012: 336).

A sex-based analysis of crime would measure and examine the female share of offending as compared with the male share. Although such a comparison produces some very interesting crime and victimisation patterns that reveal 'gendered cri-mes', for an explanation of why and how these patterns are reproduced, a *gender-based* analysis is necessary. A gender-based perspective adds another dimension to our understanding of how power can be exercised. In complementing a sex-based approach, the analysis becomes gender-wise. Thus, sex-based analyses are important in knowing male and female patterns to crime and victimisation, but what matters for understanding these patterns and broader forms of repression, powerlessness and vulnerability is a gender-sensitive approach.

Gender, Power and Feminisms

This chapter draws heavily on feminist influenced thinking to explore gender and power. However, in academia, sound thought is based on good theorising. The 'good theory' test demands that to be used for maximum effectiveness, theories must make sense (logical consistency), explain as much crime as possible (scope) and be as concise as possible (parsimony). Most importantly, the theory must be true or correct (validity) (Akers 2012). Ultimately, the good theory test demands that a theory must have some real-world applications and policy implications. A variety of feminisms exist (see Davies 2007 for a summary and Cain 1990) and thus there are diverse views on the dynamics of gender and power, yet the common factor is that each perspective challenges the conventional, the traditional and the status quo agendas. A liberal feminist approach challenges sexism and promotes equality. Equality-based arguments are based on the belief that parity—non-discrimination—is seen to result from men and women being treated the same. The affinity with a human rights concern that all should be treated equally, fairly and with dignity is clear. Radical feminism challenges men's sexual power over women and argues for the foregrounding of women's knowledge. Socialist feminism dwells on the interplay between patriarchy and capitalism insisting the intersectionalities of class-race-sex-gender-age be accounted for in the search for social justice. A post-modern feminism accommodates different standpoints and gives voice to diversity. Rather than a unified 'sisterhood', there is a range of feminist voices each asking the 'woman question'. They all strive for women to have a voice rather than be silent or silenced. This chapter draws on several of these different feminist positions as well as masculinities theories to examine equality and gender symmetry/asymmetry before the law, feminist jurisprudence, radical critiques about male power and the human rights dimension to the problem of seeking justice.

The Gender Order and Social Structural Power

In order to grasp the idea of the gender order and how specific types of masculinities are privileged and perpetuate deep-seated beliefs that are prejudicially sexist and bias in gender-specific ways, it is important that we outline some additional key concepts. We begin with two: *patriarchy* and *hegemonic masculinity*. We go on to illustrate how these concepts help explain how the gender order is perpetuated such that the violent and recidivist nature of men's offending can be better understood.

Patriarchy

The term patriarchy derives from the Greek word patria meaning father and arché meaning rule. A patriarchal social system is one in which the father or a male elder has absolute authority over the family group. As noted at the beginning of this chapter, we commence from a position that accepts the patriarchal nature of the social order—that is, the law or rule of the father—that establishes male domination in an institutional and cultural sense in Western societies. The use of the concept of patriarchy in the social sciences has been widespread, and it remains an enduring if thoroughly critiqued and contested one. At the heart of the concept of patriarchy is the male-dominated society with gender hierarchies and systems of male domination and female subordination typifying power arrangements. It is this broad social context and the social structural conditions whereby gendered social arrangements prevail that makes the concept of patriarchy so key to understanding how patterns of crime and victimisation and wider experiences of social and economic repression are connected to patriarchal power.

Activist scholarship proposes that violence against women be understood in historical context. Challenging patriarchal state responses (such as the 'rule of thumb'; see Box 7.1) and the legality of rape within marriage (see below) continues to be part of feminist activists' strategy for change. Such rulings illustrate how patriarchal power has dominated the legal and broader institutional approaches to not only the governance of interpersonal violence but also the institution of the family more broadly. Patriarchal power is thus exercised in repressive and oppressive ways that extend beyond the individual to social and state institutions (see also Chap. 6 in this volume).

Box 7.1   The Rule of Thumb
The 1857 'rule of thumb' stricture purportedly emanates from an English judge's ruling allowing a man to beat his wife with a stick so long as it was no thicker than his *thumb*. The 1860 Law of Coverture lends weight to this ruling whereby at the point of marriage, a husband became legally responsible for the actions of both his wife and children. This meant he was entitled to use physical or verbal abuse to control their behaviour.

Space precludes us from providing a comprehensive timeline relating to the shifts in legislative provisions relating to English matrimony, family violence and abuse, but it is worth pointing out that it was not until 1991 that marital rape in England was criminalised. Before this date, it was a husband's legal right to rape his wife as marriage implied consent for sexual intercourse. Thus, after more than two centuries in which men could not be convicted of raping their wives, the English courts finally held that husbands were liable to conviction. The anachronistic common law was overturned and for the first time a woman had legal protection from marital rape. However, despite the courts overturning the spousal rape exemption such that in law husbands no longer have legal immunity for raping their wives, in practice there are extremely few examples of prosecutions and even fewer successful ones. Spousal rape thus remains a hidden and denied crime.

Patriarchy has proven to be a powerful if controversial theoretical concept. It continues to be drawn upon to convey the extent to which power operates at several levels. Patriarchy explains not only the brutal crime of rape but also how our society is conditioned. Social psychologists have recently been highly critical of this ideologically based view of intimate partner violence (Dixon et al. 2012), whilst Hunnicutt (2009: 553) has suggested resurrecting 'patriarchy' as a theoretical tool:

> The concept of patriarchy holds promise for theorizing violence against women because it keeps the theoretical focus on dominance, gender, and power. It also anchors the problem of violence against women in social conditions, rather than individual attributes.

However, she goes on to caution there are multiple sites of power and labyrinthine power dynamics in patriarchal systems such that violence against women 'cannot be understood as a simple formula of "oppressor and oppressed." Patriarchal systems must be envisioned as "terrains of power" in which both men and women wield varying types and amounts of power' (Hunnicutt 2009: 555). Within this patriarchal view, even the most oppressed can alter relations of power.

The Man Question

Connell's (1987) work on a tripartite structure of gender relations and the gender order has been particularly influential in the context of gender and power. For Connell, hegemonic masculinity helps explain a hierarchical ordering of male social power. Hegemonic masculinity is

> the configuration of gender practice which embodies the currently accepted answer to the problem of the legitimacy of patriarchy which guarantees (or is taken to guarantee) the dominant position of men and the subordination of women. (Connell 1987: 77)

As noted above (and elsewhere in this volume, see, e.g., Chap. 8), there has been a focus on the male sex in dominant theories of crime. However, it has been maleness rather than masculinity that has been paid attention to. The different ways in which youthful male criminality might be informed by their understandings of themselves *as men*, and that these understandings might be problematic has only been paid greater attention in the last 20–30 years or so. The 'man question' (Naffine 2008) had been little researched, examined or theorised despite the claim that this is the most troubling and pressing question for criminology and criminal justice. Part of the man problem is the socially constructed distinctions that are traditionally associated with and create expectations around men and being male. Antonio Gramsci's (1978) work on cultural hegemony has been brought in to wider use such that the concept of hegemonic masculinity is used to understand how men be men, who men are, what they do, how they perform and live up to being a man. Jefferson (2001: 138) defines hegemonic masculinity as 'the set of ideas, values, representations and practices associated with "being male" which is commonly accepted as the dominant position in gender relations in a society at a particular historical moment'. Connell (1987) identifies the hegemonic position of males as follows: multiple performed masculinities are hierarchically ordered with dominant masculinities giving men who perform them esteemed cultural status and power. Hegemonic masculinity is constructed in relation to subordinated or marginalised masculinities, which are oppressed and exploited masculinities, and hegemony is both an achievement and an expression of social power. Thus, hegemonic masculinity is a particular and often damaging and criminal way of achieving, or 'doing', manhood.

According to Connell (1987), the ways in which men express their masculinity in contemporary society is connected to the powerful position held by the presumption of normative heterosexuality. This social system of power preserves heterosexuality as 'the norm'. This form of manhood constrains all men's social existence, othering gender non-conformists. Hegemonic masculinity is a culturally idealised and ascendant form of masculinity, which promotes particular expressions of masculinity (Connell 1987) providing for men to 'do gender' (West and Zimmerman 1987). Under Messerschmidt's (1993) formulation and extension of this idea, crime is a form of structured/situated action/accomplishment. As introduced in the introduction to this part of the book, the 'situated accomplishment' essentially refers to the context in which the crime is committed. If crime is used as a resource for 'doing-gender' (West and Zimmerman 1987), crime by men is a means of accomplishing masculinity (Messerschmidt 1997, 1995). In respect of young men, crime offers 'lads' and men a 'daring opposition masculinity' (Messerschmidt 1994: 97). Men and boys achieve masculinity through the doing of violent crimes and property crime. Masculine power is exercised through the medium of football hooliganism, rioting, arson, fire-raising/setting, violence, aggression, racism, hate crime, car theft, joyriding, road rage, gang crime, burglary, robbery, rape and corporate crime. In the edited book *Just Boys Doing Business?*, Newburn and Stanko (1994) pull together a range of contributions that variously explore boys doing the business of crime, thus foregrounding the overwhelmingly male nature of criminality, inequality, poverty, marginalisation and deprivation and, through a masculinities-influenced lens, men *as men*. Campbell (2008), for example, discusses how the youthful men in Cardiff of the 1950s and 1960s

> would have stayed on the right side of respectability because they earned enough to live and stay legal. One generation later the men's relationship with the world had changed: instead of being defined by work, it came to be increasingly defined by crime. With alternative sources of employment abolished, scavenging, stealing or redistributing stolen goods were hardly surprising sources of income.

More recently, Holligan and Deuchar (2014) have similarly argued that for young men who have become marginalised through the collapse of heavy industry and the lack of meaningful opportunities for employment, violence may provide a means of 'doing masculinity' when other resources are unavailable. In relation to a similar age group, the psycho-social roots of violence in the context of young offenders have been called upon to explain what it means to be a man in the context of incarcerated violent Scottish teenage offenders (Robinson and Ryder 2013). Though the man question may no longer be neglected, much 'malestream' criminology continues to operate on a presumption of maleness.

Gender and Individual Power

The hierarchical ordering of certain expressions of masculinity examined above has paved the way for a deeper understanding of masculinities and their respective powers in the social order. Well into the twenty-first century, even feminist-inspired literature on violence against women has continued to portray men as an 'unproblematic given' (Hunnicutt 2009: 559). Within the context of a patriarchal society, theories of violence against women must also directly address male power at an individual level and within hidden spaces.

As discussed in Chap. 3, understanding of the crimes of the powerful can be linked to a cluster of features of invisibility. The hidden nature of much serious violence is committed against women in the unsafe privacy of their own home. The domestic sphere renders these experiences hidden from view and invisible, omitted from the more traditional and orthodox counts of violent victimisation. The more closed and private the location, the more likely it is that the experience of what goes on there remains hidden from formal social control mechanisms and agents. The home and family context is thus exposed as especially problematic with regard to 'knowing' about what really happens. Making visible what happens in places where witnesses are non-existent or witnesses are highly vulnerable and indeed victims themselves—women, children and companion animals—makes the violence that happens there highly underreported, under-recorded and misunderstood as Case Study 1 will illustrate.

Case Study 1: The Sauvage Case, France
Early in 2016, news headlines across France reported that the French President, Francois Hollande, had pardoned and ordered the release of a woman who had served three years of a ten-year prison sentence that had been made in 2014 for the murder of her husband. The decision of the courts was upheld on appeal in late 2015 when the state rejected her plea of self-defence. Magistrates in a French court, however, refused to release her.

The day after her son hanged himself, in September 2012, Jacqueline Sauvage shot Norbert Marot three times in the back with a rifle. Marot was described in the reports as a violent alcoholic who had abused and raped Sauvage and her four children for many years during their 47-year marriage.

As *The Guardian* newspaper (2016) reported, 'Sauvage's case has cast a spotlight on the tricky and controversial legal argument known as 'battered woman syndrome'. It raised legal questions about the plea of self-defence in the context of men's violence against women and children in the home. According to French law, for an act to be considered self-defence it must be seen as proportional and in direct response to an act of aggression. Killing in response to repeated acts of violence suffered over decades, as in Sauvage's case, did not meet this test.

The Sauvage case raises a number of important questions surrounding equalities in law, the adequacy of the French criminal law in this area but also important issues concerning gender and power. In respect of French criminal law, the gendered law of self-defence and the adequacy of legal responses to battered women who kill have been called into question. The links between victimisation and offending are now better recognised, and this is in part seen in the new coercive control legislation in many jurisdictions around the world. Feminist-influenced jurisprudence is making progress. However, law in practice needs to reflect this. In light of the ongoing persistence of gendered stereotypes, critics suggest the need for law reform (Fitz-Gibbon and Vannier 2017). Under French criminal law, a defendant is not criminally liable for his or her actions if committed in self-defence; thus an act of lethal violence is excused from legal sanction, where the defendant reasonably believed there was no alternative save to injure or take the assailant's life. However, the courts tend to view reasonable response in relation to a specific physically violent event. Domestic abuse is not a single one-off event in most women's abusive relationships. It is an ongoing and often accumulative experience of abuse. In the Sauvage case, the courts failed to appreciate the prolonged ongoing nature of such abuse. Where there is a time gap between the original unlawful assault and the defendant's response, the courts, as in this case, interpret the response as disproportionate.

The Sauvage case '...highlights the impact of practitioner misunderstandings of family violence and gendered narratives of victim blame evident in French criminal law' (Fitz-Gibbon and Vannier 2017: 334). The case has broader relevance to criminal law reform in other countries too. As the proposals for further new legislation in the form of a Domestic Abuse Bill in England and Wales progress through the consultation phase in 2019–2020 via the Public Bill Committee, there is strong pressure to strengthen the legal protection for survivors of domestic abuse. One of the key areas for reform is provisions for those who are driven to commit offences in self-defence.

Pause for Thought

- How does this case study support the view that the French courts interpretation of self-defence in cases of women's extreme violence is outdated and inadequate?
- How does this case illustrate that the spectre of patriarchal power is still apparent in the legal interpretation of French law?

Coercive Power

Definitions of domestic abuse (DA) have long been contested. The most recent UK definition implemented from March 2013 is a cross-government definition of domestic violence and abuse.[1] It is defined as

> any incident or pattern of incidents of controlling, coercive, threatening behaviour, violence or abuse between those aged 16 or over who are, or have been, intimate partners or family members regardless of gender or sexuality.

This definition heralds a more comprehensive definition of such abuse and includes the various forms that such violence encompasses. Most significantly the definition now captures the coercive control element to such violence, and it extends the coverage to include young people aged 16 and 17. Intimate partner violence as well as violence involving children and parents is included. The abuse can encompass, but is not limited to

- psychological,
- physical,
- sexual,
- financial and
- emotional.

Controlling behaviour relates to a range of acts designed to make a person subordinate and/or dependent by isolating them from sources of support, exploiting their resources and capacities for personal gain, depriving them of the means needed for independence, resistance and escape and regulating their everyday behaviour. Coercive behaviour concerns an act or a pattern of acts of assault, threats, humiliation and intimidation or other abuse that is used to harm, punish or frighten a victim. Public awareness campaigns, interventions and legal reforms have done much to challenge gendered partner violence (see extract from one such campaign in Box 7.2). However, research with young people reveals significant acceptance and tolerance of interpersonal violence if perpetrated by men within the parameters of an intimate heterosexual relationship (McCarry 2010).

---

[1] See: https://www.gov.uk/guidance/domestic-violence-and-abuse#domestic-violence-and-abuse-new-definition.

Box 7.2   Sam (Boy 2) and Alice—Teenage Relationships
- *Boy 1*: 'Mate, where you been? You need to tell the boss where to stick it—you should be having fun!'
- *Boy 2*: [to Girl] 'What did I tell you?'
- *Girl*: 'What do you mean?'
- *Boy 2*: 'I mean you dressing like this.'
- *Girl*: 'Stop...'
- *Boy 2*: 'Do you really want people to think you're a little slut?'
- Girl: 'Please, please stop. I was just trying to...'
- *Boy 2*: [Interrupting Girl] 'Just don't dare make a scene.'
- *Girl*: 'Please, stop. I was just trying to look nice.'
- *Boy 2*: 'Do you really think that any other guy is gonna look at you the way I do?'
- *Girl*: 'Please... Come on.'
- *Boy 2*: 'Do you think you look good, do you? You think you look good dressed like that?'
- *Girl*: 'Stop...'
- *Boy 2*: 'Well you don't. You look disgusting.'
- *Boy 1*: [Voiceover] 'Recognise abuse when you see it? (Get the facts at mtv.co.uk/thisisabuse. Date: Fri Feb 15 10:14:44 GMT 2013)

This conversation is part of a teenage relationship abuse campaign about what abuse is. The 'This is Abuse' campaign is targeted at 13–18-year-old boys and girls. It encourages teenagers to rethink their views on violence, abuse, controlling behaviour and what consent means within their relationships. Consider the conversation above and reflect on the following:

- Is this abuse?
- Does coercive control help us to understand why self-defence should be upheld in Case Study 1?
- To what extent do you agree that violence against women is a product of patriarchal social arrangements and ideologies?

Before continuing reading, think about what other systems of domination reinforce patriarchal views of intimate partner violence.

Discussion

Case Study 1 and the plight of the Sauvage family illustrate that cases of sexual abuse and family violence are hampered from becoming visible and brought to successful conviction by very powerful 'silencing agents' (Jordan 2012). These include the victim's own personal difficulty in naming and defining what has happened. The police can also be effective silencers. Victims do not come forward for fear the police will not believe them, and if their cases go to court, victims' fear of the courts and concerns about facing challenging cross-examinations, together with controversial interpretations of the law, mean that the courts can also be effective silencers of rape. Other silencing agents include formal and informal supports even friends and peers as shown in the conversation above. Researchers, academics, the media, the police, Crown Prosecution Service and courts are implicated in rendering the crime of rape under prosecuted and victims being denied justice. Prosecution and conviction rates are impacted via the disbelieving of complaints and by courts giving men's explanations greater credence than those of women complainants (Brown and Walklate 2012: 3). The legal controversy evident in the Sauvage case illustrates the difficulty in accepting women's extreme violence might be legally defensible.

The same case illustrates that rape myths—commonly held beliefs about rape that are ill-informed and misconceived—remain prevalent. Rape within the Sauvage household illustrates the myths that rape within marriage is not real rape, is preventable, and that women are less traumatised by rape by a non-stranger. A gendered analysis renders some of the sex-based differences in levels and impacts of crime and victimisation, fear and worry understandable. Most rapes and sexual assaults are perpetrated by people known to the victim: partners, ex-partners, relatives or friends—most usually—men of a particular manhood.

Gender, Culture and Economic Power

Our next case study broadens the vista of gender and power to non-Western contexts. It takes us to Saudi Arabia and its ban on women's driving. As you read the case study, think about the broader significance of the existence and lifting of the ban and the far-reaching effects of the Saudi Arabian guardianship system.

Case Study 2: Saudi Arabia: Women's Driving Ban

Since June 2018, women in Saudi Arabia have been able to possess a driving licence and enjoy new freedoms flowing from a landmark decision by the ruling monarchy to lift restrictions on females travelling alone. On 26 September 2017, King Salman issued a statement recognising the right of Saudi women to drive in keeping with Sharia law. Although the law never explicitly banned women from driving, Saudi women were unable to make major decisions without the permission of a male 'wali'—an official guardian, typically a father, brother, uncle or husband. In effect, this prevented women from driving alone legally. The indirect ban caused huge restrictions on the mobility of families and stifled women's freedoms. If they wanted to travel, work or access healthcare, they had to be accompanied by a male guardian or have their written permission.

The lifting of the driving ban is part of Crown Prince Mohammed bin Salman's bid to modernise some aspects of Saudi society through the Vision 2030 programme to diversify the economy away from oil and open up Saudi society. Saudi Arabia was the only country left in the world where women could not drive. The lifting of the driving ban represents a new freedom for women who have long lived under repressive laws. Prior to the lifting of the ban, dozens of women were arrested for defying the ban in Riyadh in 1990 and several women's rights activists were detained in prison for their activism, which included online campaigning for change.

Saudi Arabia is often cited as an example of a country where culture is heavily infused by religion. The Islamic legal tradition sees Sharia law shaping the legal and political confines of what constitutes crime, justice and punishment. The driving ban persisted for decades via a combination of religious diktats and social pressure. Saudi law implements a strict form of Sunni Islam known as Wahhabism with strict guardianship laws and gender segregation rules being part of the cultural experience. The dominant cultural traditions, with a strong religious base, require Saudi Arabian women to adhere to strict dress codes, and association with unrelated men remains heavily restricted by the Islamic legal code.

There has been a growth in the social science literature about the position of women in Muslim societies. As a body of research, this literature is diverse and in turn reflects the diversity of the social, economic and political experiences of the half a billion Muslim women who inhabit some 45 Muslim-majority countries

(Offenhauer 2005). One of the major themes in this literature sees women's disadvantaged status as a hindrance to development. The disadvantaged status is evident in various spheres of Muslim women's lives: ideology, law, family, economy and politics (Offenhauer 2005). Feminist analysis of the history of women in Saudi Arabia debunks the two stereotypical images of Saudi women. At one extreme, they are excluded victims of their own patriarchal religion and society. At the other, they are wealthy, glamorous, cosmopolitan, educated survivors of discrimination imposed on them by that same society (Al-Rasheed 2013). Feminist analysis has gone on to show the harmful orientalist and racialising effects of presenting Middle Eastern and Islamic societies as backward around gender in comparison to the West (Grigsby 2015). Harmful orientalism refers to colonial relations between Europe and its Muslim colonies. The Middle East and Asia are constructed as barbaric, in contrast to the civility of European modernity. Such colonial narratives serve the ideological purpose of legitimising neo-imperialist practices and maintaining positional superiority of the West in relation to Islam and Muslim societies (Schmidt 2014). Orientalist representations of Muslim women as backward and oppressed are simplistic and can service to increase wider anti-Muslim rhetoric and prejudice, even Islamaphobia.

Pause for Thought

- What is the significance of guardianship laws in Saudi Arabian society?
- How is the lifting of the driving ban linked to wider cultural reforms and economic change?

Summary

This chapter has foregrounded gender-related dynamics of power as related to crime and victimisation and broader forms of social and economic repression. It started from a position that accepts the patriarchal nature of Western society. Commencing with an explanation of the differences between sex and gender-based analyses, the chapter then explored social structural and patriarchal power as well as different and complex terrains of individual power. Gender matters in the criminalisation and justice-seeking process. Gender matters in terms of understanding women's rights campaigns for equality. The Sauvage case in France and the Saudi Arabian ban on women's driving have been used to explore the historical, traditional, social, cultural, institutional and individual factors that render some extremely vulnerable to domestic and sexual abuse, and thus in need of justice, and wider forms of repression, like not being allowed to drive, which is a rather different type of harm and unjust experience, but one that also limits equality.

Overall, this chapter has illustrated how gender is relevant when studying harms and crimes and an integral part of power. Using a gendered lens, through feminist or masculinities theories, exposes power differentials between men and men, and men and women, as well as between people of non-binary genders. Gender entwines and intersects with legal, cultural and religious (see also Chap. 6 in this volume) histories, traditions and practices to produce ideological and lived realities that constitute oppression that curtails some women's independence, and some non-binary people's and non-hegemonically masculine men's independence too, through various control mechanisms. Gendered power is evident in much physical and sexual abuse, but is also a factor in social and economic repression, all of which combine to maintain control for the powerful

Go Further

- To what degree is gender on a par with class with respect to understanding the offending patterns of young men?
- Can hegemonic and subordinate masculinities explain women's behaviour?

References

Akers, R. L. (2012). *Criminological Theories* (2nd ed.). Abingdon: Routledge.

Al-Rasheed, M. (2013). *A Most Masculine State: Gender, Politics and Religion in Saudi Arabia*. Cambridge: Cambridge University Press.

Braithwaite, J. (1989). *Crime, Shame and Reintegration*. Cambridge: Cambridge University Press.

Brown, J. M., & Walklate, S. L. (Eds.). (2012). *Handbook on Sexual Violence*. Abingdon: Routledge.

Cain, M. (1990). Realist Philosophy and Standpoint Epistemologies or Feminist Criminology as a Successor Science? In L. Gelsthorpe & A. Morris (Eds.), *Feminist Perspectives in Criminology*. Milton Keynes: Open University Press.

Campbell, B. (2008). Boys will be Boys. In K. Evans & J. Jamieson (Eds.), *Gender and Crime: A Reader*. Maidenhead: Open University Press.

Connell, R. W. (1987). *Gender and Power*. Oxford: Polity.

Davies, P. (2007). Women, Victims and Crime. In P. Davies, P. Francis, & C. Greer (Eds.), *Victims, Crime and Society* (pp. 165–201). London: Sage.

Davies, P. (2011). *Gender, Crime and Victimisation*. London: Sage.

Dixon, L., Archer, J., & Graham-Kevan, N. (2012). Perpetrator Programmes for Partner Violence: Are They Based on Ideology or Evidence? *Legal and Criminological Psychology, 17*, 196–215. The British Psychological Society.

Fitz-Gibbon, K., & Vannier, M. (2017). Domestic Violence and the Gendered Law of Self-Defence in France: The Case of Jacqueline Sauvage. *Feminist Legal Studies, 25*(2), 313–335.

Gramsci, A. (1978). Selections from the political writings 1921–1926. Hoare, Q. (Ed.). London, England: Lawrence and Wishart.

Grigsby, H. (2015). Women2Drive Movement Contemporary Saudi Consciousness on Women's Position in Society. Short Paper.

Heidensohn, F., & Silvestri, M. (2012). Gender and Crime. In M. Maguire, R. Morgan, & R. Reiner (Eds.), *The Oxford Handbook of Criminology* (5th ed.). Oxford: Oxford University Press.

Holligan, C., & Deuchar, R. (2014). What Does It Mean to be a Man? Psychosocial Undercurrents in the Voices of Incarcerated (Violent) Scottish Teenage Offenders. *Criminology & Criminal Justice, 15*(3), 361–377.

Hunnicutt, G. (2009). Varieties of Patriarchy and Violence Against Women Resurrecting "Patriarchy" as a Theoretical Tool. *Violence Against Women, 15*(5), 553–573.

Jefferson, T. (2001). Hegemonic Masculinity. In E. McLaughlin & J. Muncie (Eds.), *The Sage Dictionary of Criminology*. London: Sage.

Johnson, J. R. (2013). Cisgender Privilege, Intersectionality, and the Criminalization of CeCe McDonald: Why Intercultural Communication Needs Transgender Studies. *Journal of International and Intercultural Communication, 6*(2), 135–144.

Jordan, J. (2012). Silencing Rape, Silencing Women. In J. M. Brown & S. L. Walklate (Eds.), *Handbook on Sexual Violence*. Abingdon: Routledge.

McCarry, M. (2010). Becoming a 'Proper Man': Young People's Attitudes about Interpersonal Violence and Perceptions of Gender. *Gender and Education, 22*(1), 17–30. https://doi.org/10.1080/09540250902749083.

Messerschmidt, J. W. (1993). *Masculinities and Crime*. Lanham, MD: Rowman & Littlefield.

Messerschmidt, J. W. (1994). Schooling, Masculinities and Youth Crime by White Boys. In T. Newburn & E. Stanko (Eds.), *Just Boys Doing Business?* London: Routledge.

Messerschmidt, J. W. (1997). *Crime as Structured Action*. Thousand Oaks, CA: Sage.

Naffine, N. (2008). The 'Man Question' of Crime, Criminology and Criminal Law. *Criminal Justice Matters, 53*(1), 10–11.

Newburn, T., & Stanko, E. (Eds.). (1994). *Just Boys Doing Business?* London: Routledge.

Offenhauer, P. (2005). *Women in Islamic Societies: A Selected review of Social Scientific Literature*. Washington, DC: Library of Congress.

Pickles, J. (2018). *Bridging Communities: Exploring Experiences of 'Hate' within Community, Voluntary, and Criminal Justice Sectors*. Unpublished theses. Northumbria University, Department of Social Sciences.

Robinson, R. A., & Ryder, J. A. (2013). Psychosocial Perspectives of Girls and Violence: Implications for Policy and Practice. *Critical Criminology, 21*, 431–445.

Schmidt, S. (2014). The Framed Arab/Muslim: Mediated Orientalism. In *(Re-)Framing the Arab/Muslim: Mediating Orientalism in Contemporary Arab American Life Writing* (pp. 137–190). Bielefeld: Transcript Verlag. Retrieved June 5, 2020, from www.jstor.org/stable/j.ctv1xxs1s.6

The Guardian. (2016). Retrieved September 8, 2016, from https://www.theguardian.com/world/2016/feb/01/french-president-pardons-jacqueline-sauvage-over-killing-of-violent-husband.

Walklate, S. (2004). *Gender, Crime and Criminal Justice*. Cullompton: Willan.

West, C., & Zimmerman, D. H. (1987). Going Gender. *Gender and Society, 1*(2), 125–151.

Age

8

Introduction

The power to establish or attribute an identity as an offender or a victim is a key thread running throughout this chapter on age. The chapter focuses on the opposite ends of the age spectrum. The review of young and older people's relationships with crime and victimisation explores the myriad ways in which the power to impose, resist and achieve victim or villain status varies significantly according to how young or how old we are and throughout our life course. It is important to note that the norms associated with both young and older people are continually evolving. Thus, over time the criminalisation of actions or response to victimisations seen as 'typical' for either group has and will change across contexts with different outcomes for various populations.

The chapter will address the conundrums associated with young people and children as victims and offenders, patterns and risks to offending and victimisation, and theoretical explanations that have been postulated to account for the enduring age/crime curve to offending. Popular representations and cultural constructions of children, young and older people as perpetrators and victims of crime will be examined. The chapter furthers a critical approach to the study of crime and power. It does so by introducing how a critical reading helps reveal the dynamics and working of power relations. The chapter will address age-related vulnerabilities to crime and victimisation; indeed conceptualisations of vulnerability are explored to show how vulnerability is used as a proxy for illustrating differences in power relations. As the chapter progresses, we will be debunking some of the enduring

© The Author(s) 2021
P. Davies, T. Wyatt, *Crime and Power*,
https://doi.org/10.1007/978-3-030-57314-0_8

stereotypes surrounding age and crime and challenging the dichotomies between offenders and victims drawing on the concepts of the 'ideal victim' and 'othering'.

The chapter commences with a critical discussion of age as a socially constructed and evolving concept. With the caveats about the socially constructed nature of age categorisations in mind, the chapter then begins to unpick young and older peoples' relationships with crime and victimisation. As we do so, ideology and the links between power, powerlessness and vulnerability are explored. The sometimes complex age and risk dimensions to vulnerability are considered against the backdrop of the ideal victim problem and in the context of popular imagery, stereotypes and myths.

Constructing Age as a Social Category

In beginning to explore what makes age, and specifically young age and older age, categories significant when studying crime and power, it is important to first problematise age as a social construction. Both of these social groupings—those in older age and the younger generation—comprise diverse populations. The older age bracket may span more than 40 years. At the opposite end of the age spectrum, those in the younger or youthful age population span a period of almost 30 years with age categories being variously constructed around babyhood and preschoolers, children, teenagers and young adults. There is a need, therefore, to critically identify age as a socially constructed and evolving concept that impacts on how those defined as 'elderly' offenders or victims, or 'young' offenders or victims are conceptualised as such and are responded to. As 'categories', older and younger people together may span an age band of almost 70 years, and as such, they represent a cross-section of the population divided by gender, class, race, nationality, sexuality, ability, income, health status and so on. Neither population are representative of a homogenous group at the extreme ends of the age spectrum. 'Old age', 'the elderly', 'the young' and 'childhood' are fluid concepts, and the case studies explored below illustrate how this is evident historically and contemporarily.

Defining 'Old' and 'Young'

The World Health Organization's (2019) way of defining old age is used in many developed countries to understand this period of life as beginning at the chronological age of 60. This, however, does not map on to larger societal recognition of when someone becomes 'old' and of course as mentioned this is not the same in every country. For instance, the age to receive a state pension in the United Kingdom is fairly continually being moved later in life from 66 in 2020, with plans to move it to 67 in the coming years. Historically, there have been different ages for women and men. Pre-2018 in the United Kingdom, women could retire at 63 and men at 65 though the new rules set one age for everyone. Whereas in the United States, the retirement age is the same—66 and rising—the 40-million member strong American Association for Retired Persons (AARP) is open to anyone over the age of 50, a significant difference from the government set retirement age. The fact that pension ages are changing to be later in life is possibly linked to two factors. First, people are living longer, so not only will people still have a substantial number of years in retirement even should that day come later in life, but people also need to work longer to pay for decades of retirement life. The latter is linked closely to the second factor in that governments need their citizens to work longer to pay into pension schemes for large cohorts of older people, who will all be drawing on pension funds at the same time. The redefining of old age is not only an economic concern but also reflects evolving societal shifts in conceptualising who we think of as 'old'.

In early life, there are a number of milestones that demarcate when we are no longer 'young' or at least that indicate society recognises a person has reached a supposed level of responsibility. Some of these points in life are the age when people are able to: start school, leave school, drive a car, drink alcohol, buy tobacco, work, travel abroad alone, vote and get married. These events, too, occur at different ages around the world. In the United States, for instance, the eligibility to drive is usually at age 16, when the age to be able to drink alcohol is 21. In contrast, in the United Kingdom, both of these are allowed at age 18. Defining young and old is inextricable from a society's social construction of these times in life. Age—both young and old—as a factor, is integral to the study of crime.

Criminal Responsibility

Criminal statistics have long been collated so that the age of the offender is captured and observations are frequently made about the age when offending 'peaks'. Young people are variously defined in public policy and legislative discourse. The term 'youth justice' is generally understood to refer to the set of arrangements pertaining to children below 18 years of age in conflict with the law, which recognises youth as up to the age of 21 (Bateman 2017). At various points in time, legislative provisions have allowed for different sentencing disposals according to the age of the offender. For example, the 1948 Criminal Justice Act, though best remembered for abolishing corporal punishment, introduced detention centres and attendance centres for offenders between 12 and 21 and extended the use of borstal (a specific type of youth detention centre in the United Kingdom and the Commonwealth) for this age group (Mair 2017). In the early 1980s in the United Kingdom, when the British Crime Survey (BCS) was introduced, it, too, collected data, which would be comparable with the categories used by the police to collect information about crime and offending. Although young people have until recently been excluded from participating in the BCS (now the Crime Survey of England and Wales (CSEW)), surveys have specifically been conducted with young people (Anderson et al. 1994), and the CSEW now routinely includes a survey of 10–15 years old.

The age of criminal responsibility is bound up with the legal principle of *doli incapax*. This principle refers to incapacity in regard to committing an offence. The concept of the age of criminal responsibility is spelled out in the United Nations Convention on the Rights of the Child (UNICEF 1990—see Box 8.1). In the United Kingdom, the age of criminal responsibility is the lowest in Europe with European Union member states setting the age of criminal responsibility between 14 and 16 and in other parts of the world the age is set at 18 (see Box 8.1).

Box 8.1   United Nations Convention on the Rights of the Child
United Nations Convention on the Rights of the Child
   Adopted and opened for signature, ratification and accession by General Assembly resolution 44/25 of 20 November 1989 entry into force 2 September 1990, in accordance with article 49
   A child means every human being below the age of eighteen years unless under the law applicable to the child, maturity is attained earlier.
   Article 40
   1. States Parties recognize the right of every child alleged as, accused of, or recognized as having infringed the penal law to be treated in a manner consistent with the promotion of the child's sense of dignity and worth, which reinforces the child's respect for the human rights and fundamental freedoms of others and which takes into account the child's age and the desirability of promoting the child's reintegration and the child's assuming a constructive role in society.
   2. To this end, and having regard to the relevant provisions of international instruments, States Parties shall, in particular, ensure that:

(*continued*)

Box 8.1 (continued)

(a) No child shall be alleged as, be accused of, or recognized as having infringed the penal law by reason of acts or omissions that were not prohibited by national or international law at the time they were committed;

(b) Every child alleged as or accused of having infringed the penal law has at least the following guarantees:

   (i) To be presumed innocent until proven guilty according to law;

   (ii) To be informed promptly and directly of the charges against him or her, and, if appropriate, through his or her parents or legal guardians, and to have legal or other appropriate assistance in the preparation and presentation of his or her defence;

   (iii) To have the matter determined without delay by a competent, independent and impartial authority or judicial body in a fair hearing according to law, in the presence of legal or other appropriate assistance and, unless it is considered not to be in the best interest of the child, in particular, taking into account his or her age or situation, his or her parents or legal guardians;

   (iv) Not to be compelled to give testimony or to confess guilt; to examine or have examined adverse witnesses and to obtain the participation and examination of witnesses on his or her behalf under conditions of equality;

   (v) If considered to have infringed the penal law, to have this decision and any measures imposed in consequence thereof reviewed by a higher competent, independent and impartial authority or judicial body according to law;

   (vi) To have the free assistance of an interpreter if the child cannot understand or speak the language used;

   (vii) To have his or her privacy fully respected at all stages of the proceedings.

3. States Parties shall seek to promote the establishment of laws, procedures, authorities and institutions specifically applicable to children alleged as, accused of, or recognized as having infringed the penal law, and, in particular:

(continued)

> **Box 8.1   (continued)**
>
> (a) The establishment of a minimum age below which children shall
>   be presumed not to have the capacity to infringe the penal law;
> (b) Whenever appropriate and desirable, measures for dealing with
>   such children without resorting to judicial proceedings, providing
>   that human rights and legal safeguards are fully respected. 4. A
>   variety of dispositions, such as care, guidance and supervision or-
>   ders; counselling; probation; foster care; education and vocational
>   training programmes and other alternatives to institutional care
>   shall be available to ensure that children are dealt with in a man-
>   ner appropriate to their well-being and proportionate both to their
>   circumstances and the offence.

Age, Crime and Victimisation in Context

A rise in crime generally is observed from the mid-1950s onwards, most dramatically amongst 17- to 20-year-old males (young adults). Little change in offending is recorded for elderly people. In the 1960s, the welfare/punishment debate about how to deal with juvenile offenders gathered momentum. The age of criminal responsibility was raised to ten in the United Kingdom's Children and Young Persons Act 1963. In 1969, another Children and Young Persons Act was passed. Measures were designed to phase out detention centres and borstals and introduce a new approach for juveniles, including intermediate treatment and a preference for care rather than criminal proceedings. However, as Mair (2017) observes, most of this welfare-oriented approach was never implemented, and the intention to raise the age of criminal responsibility to 14 was never implemented (Table 8.1). Short sharp shock detention centres were set up for young offenders during the Thatcher era (1979–1990), and the 1982 Criminal Justice Act introduced youth custody, encouraged the use of senior attendance centres for young adults and supervision orders for juveniles and day centres and specified activity requirements to the probation order, in an effort to make the order more demanding and thus encourage its use as an alternative to a custodial sentence, all of which saw the use of custody for young offenders tail off (Mair 2017).

Whilst many American states do not have a minimum age for prosecutions, across the United States the age varies between 7 and 12 years. For example, in Oklahoma and North Carolina, it is seven years, in Wisconsin ten years.

The above begins to illustrate the politicised nature of the youth justice discourse. In the United Kingdom, further evidence of this is seen in the impact of key episodes

Table 8.1 Age of criminal responsibility around the world

Country	Age of criminal responsibility
England, Wales and Northern Ireland	10
Scotland	8
India, South Africa	7
Australia	10–14
Republic of Ireland, the Netherlands	12
Turkey	11
France, Poland	13
Germany, Italy, China, Japan, Chile	14
Russia	14–16
Denmark, Norway	15
Luxembourg, Belgium, Brazil	18
Spain, Argentina	16

on the development of policy. The murder of two-year-old James Bulger in Liverpool in 1993 by two boys, themselves barely over the age of criminal responsibility, paved the way for a more punitive approach to criminal justice (see Case Study 1). The Criminal Justice and Public Order Act 1994 was clearly a punitive measure introducing secure training centres for 12–14-year-olds, and doubling the maximum sentence in a young offenders' institution for 15–17-year-olds. Similarly, the Crime (Sentences) Act 1997 introduced mandatory 'three strikes' sentences modelled on those in California. As Bateman (2017) observes, this was patently not an evidence-based response to shifts in the volume or nature of young people's behaviour but had, nonetheless, profound implications for the treatment of some of society's most deprived children (see Box 8.2). Other developments in youth justice, for example, the 1998 Crime and Disorder Act which introduced a range of measures, many focused on young people, can also be explained by swings in political mood rather than patterns of youth crime or demonstrable effectiveness.

Box 8.2 'Youth Justice'
Youth justice constitutes the state's response to youth crime and to children in trouble.

In one sense, such an articulation is uncontroversial, and at a simplistic level, the youth justice landscape is readily delineated. An overview of the distinct organs of youth justice provision in England and Wales can be sketched out, the range of criminal sanctions available to children can be described, and the extent to which the treatment of children diverges from, or replicates, that for adult offenders can be compared.

(continued)

Box 8.2   (continued)

However, such identification of youth justice with process implies a non-ideological reaction to children's challenging behaviour and, thereby, obscures an array of questionable assumptions about the nature of youth crime and the deeply political determination of responses to it. One way of illuminating such assumptions is to ask why a distinct system of justice for children is necessary.

Answers to that question typically draw on a binary distinction between welfare and justice models (Hazel 2008).

Welfare—highlights similar characteristics of children who transgress the law and those in need of care and protection. It understands youth crime as symptomatic of underlying need and, correspondingly, endorses treatment to address the causes of delinquency rather than punishment focused on the symptoms.

Justice—emphasises that what distinguishes youth offending from other forms of problematic behaviour (and 'young offenders' from other children in need) is precisely its criminality. But since children are less accountable for their actions than their adult counterparts, a distinct response—that systemically mitigates for age—is required. Transgressions of the law should thus be met by punishment that is proportionate, in accordance with clearly delineated safeguards, and appropriately tempered to allow for reduced culpability. Welfare need, according to justice tenets, should be addressed outside the criminal arena (Smith 2005).

Compiled from Bateman (2017)

It is a well-established and widely cited criminological fact that perpetrating crime and being a victim of crime decreases with age, often referred to as the age-crime curve/distribution. (Bows, 2016: 1)

A number of common characteristics are observed in relation to offenders; offenders tend to be young, white men who come from deprived backgrounds with low socioeconomic status and have significantly poorer mental health than their contemporaries. (Bows, 2017: 85)

The first quote from Bows above emphasises Braithwaite's (1989) second famous fact about crime: that it is perpetrated disproportionately by 15–25-year-olds (see Fig. 8.1). In Chap. 7, we explore the first fact about crime—that it is committed disproportionately by men. In this chapter we explore how, with a focus on age

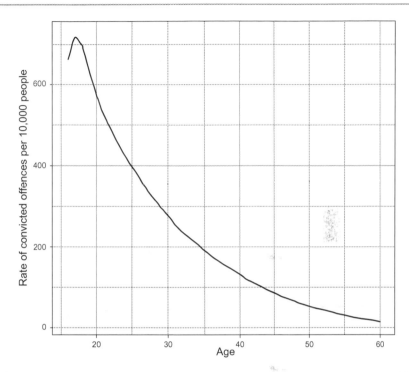

Fig. 8.1 Age-crime curve for all convicted offences in the Scottish Offenders Index 1989–2011. (Matthews and Minton 2018: 298)

and power, we can begin to make sense of this peak age of offending—particularly by young men—at the same time as we appreciate how a similar age group bear a disproportionate share of victimisation. Whilst Fig. 8.1 illustrates Matthews and Minton's (2018) findings related to age and crime in Scotland, they and others note that this pattern holds true for most countries. The majority of offences are committed by teenagers and young adults. Their graph does not show the male and female contribution as the scale of the graph tends to make this tricky in light of male offending vastly outweighing female offending. However, the shape of the curve is the same albeit with much lower amounts for women. Since it is well documented that crimes decrease with age, there has been little or no attention given to crimes committed by the elderly. There has not been the need to implement special measures for older offenders as we see in the above discussed emphasis on youth justice. However, with longer sentences meaning offenders are still in prison in their later years, there is a recognised concern about the incarceration of older offenders in UK prisons and whether their healthcare and housing needs are being adequately addressed.

The second quote from Bows above draws attention to two dimensions of young people's relationship to criminal justice: their status as offenders and, indirectly— by referring to their 'deprived backgrounds', 'low socio-economic status' and 'poor mental health'—their vulnerability. This quote introduces the idea of young offenders occupying two identity territories. They are a group or category of offenders who are typically under privileged and already marginalised. In this sense, young male offenders are both inflicting and experiencing harm—they are 'more sinned against than sinning' (Brown 1998). Their master status is neither offender nor victim, but is a complex simultaneous mix of both. Drawing on the media time-line of events, the complex status of youth is evident in Case Study 1 about the murder of James Bulger in the United Kingdom in 1993.

Case Study 1:   The Murder of James Bulger

In February 1993, James Bulger, who would have turned three that March, is in a butcher shop in Liverpool, England, with his mother (CNN 2001a). Two ten-year-old boys, Robert Thompson and Jon Venables, entice him out of the shop, walk holding his hand for over two miles before beating and stoning him to death and leaving his body on railway tracks (CNN 2001a). Two days after his abduction, James' body, which has been torn apart by a train, is found. The two boys are arrested six days later largely because of closed-circuit television footage of them leading James away.

In November 1993, both boys are tried as adults (CNN 2001a). Initially, they are sentenced to eight years, but over the next few years several judges and the UK Home Secretary increase their prison time to 10, and then to 15 years. A Judicial Review in 1997 overturns the 15 years, but does not set a minimum sentence (CNN 2001a). In 1999, the European Commission of Human Rights rules that the boys' human rights were violated due to the intimidating atmosphere of the trial. Soon afterwards, the European Court of Human Rights also rules that Thompson and Venables had their rights violated because they were tried as adults and because a minister of the United Kingdom could make this decision as well as increase their sentences (CNN 2001a). Based upon these rulings in 2000, the Lord Chief Justice of England and Wales reduces the boys' sentences back to the original eight years.

(*continued*)

> **Case Study 1:** (continued)
>
> During this time, Thompson and Venables are incarcerated in a secure unit. Even though they were tried as adults at the age of ten, they were not placed in an adult prison. In 2001, they finished serving their eight-year sentence, and despite public protests and pleas from the Bulger family, they were released. Both were given new undisclosed identities to protect them from retaliation by the public or the family and friends of James Bulger (CNN 2001a). Thompson was known to be problematic by neighbours and the police (CNN 2001b). He is thought to have initiated the crime and was the one reassuring people along the street, where he and Venables were leading a crying, bleeding Bulger that everything was all right (CNN 2001b). Thompson's family life was dysfunctional including abuse, alcoholism, unemployment and an absent father (CNN 2001b). Venables, on the other hand, had a supportive, if separated, family, and was described as a willing follower (CNN 2001b). The boys frequently skipped classes together.

The traumatic case of James Bulger raises numerous issues about youth crime and victimisation (for a more detailed account of events and unpacking of how such a crime could take place, see Smith 2005). At less than three years of age, Bulger was vulnerable to enticement as well as to physical force. In this instance, that enticement and force came from other children. It seems from the descriptions of Thompson's home life that he may well have been a victim of abuse. Being a victim of violence himself is likely to have played a role in Thompson's behaviour. This illustrates the sometimes interlocking identities of offender-victim. That Thompson and Venables were only ten years old is central to the case. They likely know right from wrong, but it is hard to say whether ten-year-olds can think through and see the consequences of their actions. For Thompson and Venables, the consequences were eight years in a secure unit with little contact with the outside world during crucial formative years. In the UK system, it is recognised that young offenders should be treated in ways different to adult offenders. Thompson and Venables took their school exams from their prison and did not interact with adults apart from the prison staff (CNN 2001b). The UK system also recognised that notorious young offenders, like Thompson and Venables, needed special treatment upon release if they ever were to have a semblance of a normal life. This meant giving them new identities and making it an offence for anyone to reveal their identities publicly. Their experience in prison and upon release highlights the vulnerability of young people even if they are offenders.

Pause for Thought

- Drawing on Case Study 1, how might we conceive young people as both victims and offenders?
- What can the James Bulger case tell us about the criminal age of responsibility?

Power, Powerlessness and Vulnerability

The notion of vulnerability is often invoked to explain not only their victimisation but also to explain why children and young people get involved in crime and offending. Criminologically, youthful offending has been explained as a show of power (in Chap. 7 we considered how young men and boys may be posturing to demonstrate their masculinity and as a response to powerlessness where young people are marginalised and strained. Vulnerability has other dimensions. Increasingly, it has been linked to risk, and the extent to which different groups are victimised can be compared using data from crime surveys. Such data show clear patterns to the types of crime that people experience at different ages. Victimologically, risks of victimisation from types of crime that people experience change with age and over the life course. The disproportionate victimisation of younger groups that we have explored above has been attributed to their vulnerability.

Other dimensions to vulnerability have been explored in relation to crime, including how vulnerability and fear are connected. Young people, but especially young men, seem to very rarely acknowledge their vulnerability, which may be explained by their efforts to accomplish manhood (again see the discussion in Chap. 7). Some attribute this lack of acknowledgement to their reluctance to admit their vulnerability especially in methods like surveys that seek to establish levels of crime and victimisation (Lees 1997, Goodey 2005). In contrast, the elderly (and women) in various parts of the world always report higher levels of fear than other cohorts. Fear and worry about crime has been the subject of significant research and various ways of measuring people's concerns about crime and victimisation tend to produce similar results that, with an uncritical reading, appear unfounded when compared with levels of risk. Unfounded fear has been discussed in the context of gender and crime in Chap. 7, and, given the scarcity and recentness of surveys that include both the young and the elderly, there is scant information on actual experiences from these traditional ways of measuring and exploring the nature and extent of crime and victimisation suffered by these populations. Mawby (1988), as discussed below, has explored how it is unjustified to identify the elderly as particularly vulnerable to crime and, as mentioned, others have at least noted how young people's vulnerability can be linked to mental health (Bows, 2017).

The concept of vulnerability is variously defined and interpreted in criminal justice contexts and across different jurisdictions. In the EU, for instance, being under the age of 18 affords such victims' special protective measures. Furthermore, the European Commission also recognises children as vulnerable suspects. As seen in Case Study 1, the European Commission ruled that the United Kingdom had violated the rights of Thompson and Venables because the boys were young suspects in an intimidating environment. Despite this treatment, the conceptualisation of vulnerability in England and Wales goes further than the European Commission. Following the Youth Justice and Criminal Evidence Act 1999, some categories of *witnesses* are afforded enhanced protection, including those that are under 18. Allowances for vulnerable witnesses can include screens in the courtroom to prevent the defendant and the witness seeing each other and allowing the defendant to give evidence via a live video link from somewhere outside the courtroom.

As of yet, elderly people's vulnerability is not recognised within most legal systems. There is increasing awareness though that older people are vulnerable to numerous crimes because of their age, which is at times linked to isolation, physical frailty and mental health issues. The abuses elderly victims are subjected to are grounded in the power relationship between the elderly person, who is to some degree powerless, and their caregiver, who is likely holding the power. As the second case study shows, such power dynamics result in a range of crimes against elderly people around the world.

Case Study 2:   Exposing Elder Abuse in Australia

The United Nations has made 15 June World Elder Abuse Awareness Day (UN n.d.). The rationale behind marking such a day is to highlight that elderly people are victims of abuse and suffering (UN n.d.). According to the UN (n.d.), one in six elderly people are estimated to be abused, and with the global population of people over the age of 60 doubling to 2 billion by 2050, the problem of elder abuse is likely to increase significantly.

In 2018, the West Australian Parliament opened an inquiry into elder abuse, and the testimonies given have uncovered varying forms of abuse and neglect (Turner 2018). The statements from elderly victims document family members tricking them into signing away their homes and finances as well

(continued)

Case Study 2:   (continued)
as being forced to move into nursing homes. Most of the victims in this inquiry are women over the age of 60, and, surprisingly compared to other
crime trends (see Chap. 7), most of the perpetrators are the women's daugh-
ters (Turner 2018). Whilst this may be particular to the Australian context,
many of the offenders are 'boomerang' children, who have moved back into
their parent's home as an adult (Turner 2018).
    The parliamentary committee has noted that elder abuse in the home is
different to domestic or family violence, since the violence involves an
abuse of trust (Turner 2018). The committee will be defining what elder
abuse is and coming up with guidelines to be used by social services. They
have acknowledged that elderly people are particularly vulnerable because
of their isolation, mental health issues, and because of ageist attitudes
(Turner 2018).

Australia is one of many Western countries uncovering and holding inquiries on elder abuse. They are also just one of many countries, which are experiencing rapid increases in the number of elderly citizens. Interestingly in the
Australian example, the elderly victims are being abused in their own homes.
There is also an inquiry in Australia into the state of conditions in aged care
homes, which has found a shocking state of neglect (Royal Commission 2019).
Similarly, cases in other countries like the United States and United Kingdom
have found abuse and neglect in nursing homes and elder care facilities. In
these situations care home workers steal and/or abuse (physically, verbally, sexually) the elderly victims. In fact, the UN (n.d.) suggests that rates of elder
abuse are probably higher in institutions than in the community. Either at home
or in an institution, isolation, which leads to vulnerability, seems to be a key
factor. This combined with possible mental health or memory concerns makes
elderly people susceptible to victimisation, though this victimisation may not
be visible or recognised by society. Thus, age—which increases for each of us
on an annual basis—is one factor which, in different combinations with other
features of our individual characteristics, combines to increase or decrease the
apparent likelihood of us being vulnerable (see the discussion on intersectionalities theorising in Part I).

Pause for Thought

- How might vulnerability explain elder abuse?
- What are the different power dynamics between elder abuse in a care home and in their own home?

Ideal Victims and Age

The late Nils Christie's (1986) seminal piece of writing on the 'ideal victim' derives from his analysis of media (and related social, political and legal) discourses around victimisation. Christie (1986: 18) noted how the ideal victim is 'a person or category of individuals, who, when hit by crime, most readily are given the complete and legitimate status of being a victim'. In this view, the ideal victim embodies a number of attributes, which confirm their victim identity: the victim should be weak, of good reputation, virtuous and worthy of compassion, whilst the offender should be big and bad, and a stranger (Duggan and Heap, 2014). As we have seen in Chap. 7, the victim attributes described above are nowhere more important than in rape cases. For the complicit victim, sympathy levels are low, access to justice restricted. In this chapter, where the focus is on crime, power and age, Christie's illustration of the 'ideal victim' is a useful analytical construct. 'Real rape' stereotypes are problematic not only for young women who fail to meet the ideal rape victim attributes, but also for older women who are sexually victimised. Rape myths and stereotypes (Burt 1980) have depicted the 'real rape' victim to be young, female and attractive and the rape is committed by a man, usually a stranger, who attacks the vulnerable woman late at night as she walks home. Decades of research has challenged these myths and stereotypes, and it is well known that the majority of rapes occur in the context of a relationship in the victim's home (ONS 2013). Despite this, the 'real rape' stereotype persists in society and is perpetuated by the media who tend to report cases of rape that are in keeping with this stereotype (Korn and Efrat, 2004; Franiuk et al., 2008). Despite the feminist effort to challenge these dominant myths, there has been very little research or activism challenging the myth around victim age. As Jones and Powell (2006) point out, feminists have largely distanced themselves from issues relating to older women. Older rape victims do not fit the 'real rape' stereotype of a young attractive woman who is attacked, late at night, because of her sexual desirability. However, when cases of rape involving older people hit the headlines, the 'ideal' victim that Christie (1986) describes is crucial in framing and conceptualising their victimisation. In particular, older people are portrayed in the media as inherently vulnerable, old and frail, making them 'ideal' victims. Data from the first national study to examine the extent of recorded rape offences involving a victim aged 60 or over challenges the depiction of the 'ideal' older rape victim that dominates the media coverage of such cases (Bows and Westmarland 2018).

Rape and other crimes against elderly people seem to get lumped into the category of 'elder abuse'. However, there are issues with this term. Penhale (2013: 170), for example, draws our attention to the use of the term 'elder abuse' and concludes that the term hides the gendered nature—or intersectionality—of much victimisation:

> [T]he term elder abuse, by virtue of its gender-neutral status, may disempower older women who are the majority of elders who experience abuse in later life. Links with the feminist movement to end violence against women may serve to empower older women and to promote their rights to full citizenship.

Popular Representations and Visibility

Perceptions of the 'credible' ideal victim on the one hand and 'non-credible' culpable victims who 'precipitated' their victimisation on the other appear firmly entrenched (especially in regard to rape). Special measures have yet to impact on the attrition rate and 'victim blaming' attitudes continue to thrive in the criminal justice system in England and Wales. Our discussion sees conceptualisations of vulnerability in the criminal justice context being called upon to act as a mitigating factor for youth. Young offenders are less accountable and should have clear safeguards that mitigate for their age to ensure proportionality in the criminal justice response. It seems that others may be treated 'as children' if they meet conditions that render them as powerless as a child, but this has not happened for elderly victims. Vulnerability can be seen as a proxy for illustrating differences in power relations:

> In popular imagery, the elderly are often associated with victimization, crime is perceived to be age war, with young offenders preying on innocent older victims. In Britain and the US, politicians have quickly, and quite unjustifiably, identified the elderly as particularly vulnerable to crime. (Mawby, 1988: 101)

The quote—from over 30 years ago—reproduced from Mawby (1988) above presents common images of both young and older people. The young continue to be presented as archetypal offenders and older people as archetypal victims in media reports of crime, crime prevention policy and government and some academic research. Both the younger and older generations are stereotyped as groups of people who are socially and economically vulnerable, likely to possess less social and financial resources to support and protect themselves. These factors have been used to bolster different ideological positions about young and older people's relationship to crime and victimisation. The simplest articulations appear uncontroversial, yet a critical reading and reaction might suggest this foregrounds young people's status as offenders and perpetrators (as seen in the quote from Bows above) and denies, or at best obscures, young people's victimhood. With respect to older people, as noted by Mawby above, assuming elderly people are vulnerable has negative impacts. The assumption that they are vulnerable is unjustified for various reasons. The 'elderly' are not a homogenous group of people, who are all passive victims. Nor are they all lacking resilience in terms of being victimised or protecting themselves. Stereotyping elderly people in this way infantilises them in such a way that collapses 'elderly' into a category equivalent to the young. This, however, fails to acknowledge both agency and autonomy as well as glossing over the different needs of young and older people.

As Mawby alludes to, much of the reason behind these perceptions of the young offender and older victim is likely linked to portrayals in the media and larger popular culture. The young person as a victim is largely invisible. Portrayals of young victims are of babies and toddlers, like James Bulger, not pre-teens suffering domestic violence and abuse behind closed doors, like Robert Thompson. News stories do not focus on the resilient independent elderly person easily living alone and not being victimised by family or friends; they, too, are invisible. Again, the point is that young and old are not groups with singular experiences or perceptions, and offenders and victims in either age range are at times rendered invisible by society at large.

Summary

In the context of 'youth justice', we have stressed the importance of politics and power. We noted a binary distinction between the contrasting approaches of welfare and justice and how historical and social contexts, political moods and key moments or signal events can be a catalyst for more punitive policies. 'Youth' are not a singular group of people. Although all of them were young people, James Bulger, Robert Thompson and Jon Venables were clearly different in terms of vulnerability, victimisation and, for the latter two, offending. For young women or young people of different races, religions or sexualities, their vulnerability, victimisation and offending are likely to be even more differently constructed. Apparent in discussions about young people and crime is that often youth sit at the intersection of offender and victim. Not only, as the age-crime curve illustrates across space and time, does criminality peak between the ages of 15 and 25, but largely so does victimisation. Young people exposed to violence may react with violence. But their exposure to violence is largely invisible and hidden. Adults (and older youth) are more powerful, bigger and stronger, and have more of a voice. The power differential between young people and adults is at the core of youth offending and victimisation.

In the context of older age and victimisation, it is similarly important to bring a critical reading to bear on the problem. At the beginning of this chapter, we problematised 'age' as a social construct. People in older age are not a homogenous group, but represent a cross-section of the population. Some will offend, some will experience criminal victimisation, and some may benefit from safeguards and protective measures as vulnerable victims, witnesses or suspects. The same is true of young people. There are other definitional and conceptual problems, too, and these can also contribute to the disempowerment of older people as we mentioned in regard to the gendered nature of elder abuse, which is not evident by the neutral label of 'elder'. Power can be wielded against people living in isolation and who may have mental health or memory problems. Thus, elderly people are vulnerable to victimisation in particular ways. The elder population can be seen as marginalised and their lesser status in many societies leads to crimes against them being hidden and invisible.

Age, as an individual characteristic linked to power, is inextricably tied to the other individual characteristics—gender, religion, race, class. According to dominant ways of measuring and documenting the problematic, elderly women are more likely to be victims than elderly men; young men are more likely to be victims and offenders than young women. Similar patterns are seen with religion, race and class depending on the offence and the harm. For both the young and old, power may manifest as vulnerability; both groups are susceptible to being taken advantage of physically, mentally and financially by people who are more powerful. That power may stem from someone's status, position or physique. To protect young people and the elderly, more must be done to understand what makes them vulnerable, to make adjustments in society for that vulnerability and to ensure their suffering, even when they are offenders, is brought to light.

Go Further

- What are the different manifestations of power in offending and victimisation of the young and the elderly?
- What crimes appear to have an age pattern to them?

References

Anderson, S., Kinsey, R., & Smith, C. G. (1994). *Cautionary Tales, Young People Crime and Policing in Edinburgh*. London: Routledge.

Bateman, T. (2017). Youth Justice. In P. Davies, J. Harding, & G. Mair (Eds.), *An Introduction to Criminal Justice* (pp. 346–367). London: Sage.

Bows, H. (2016). Age and Victimisation. In K. Corteen, S. Morley, P. Taylor, & J. Turner (Eds.), *A companion to Crime, Harm & Victimisation* (pp. 1–2). Bristol: Policy Press.

Bows, H. (2017). Characteristics of Offenders. In P. Davies, J. Harding, & G. Mair (Eds.), *An Introduction to Criminal Justice* (pp. 85–105). London: Sage.

Bows, H., & Westmarland, N. (2018). Rape of Older People in the United Kingdom: Challenging The 'Real Rape' Stereotype. *British Journal of Criminology, 57*(1), 1–17.

Braithwaite, J. (1989). *Crime, shame and reintegration*. Cambridge: Cambridge University Press.

Brown, S. (1998). *Understanding Youth and Crime: Listening to Youth?* Milton Keynes: Open University Press.

Burt, M. (1980). Cultural myths and supports for rape. *Journal of Personality and Social Psychology, 38*(2), 217–230.

Christie, N. 1986. The Ideal Victim, from Fattah, E.A. (ed.) *Crime Policy to Victim Policy: Reorienting the Justice System*. Basingstoke : Macmillan: 17-30.

CNN. (2001a). Bulger Case: Timeline of Events. Retrieved May 31, 2019, from http://edition.cnn.com/2001/WORLD/europe/06/21/bulger.timeline/.

CNN. (2001b). The Killers and the Victims. Retrieved May 31, 2019, from http://edition.cnn.com/2001/WORLD/europe/06/21/bulger.profiles/.

Duggan, M., & Heap, V. (2014). *Administrating Victimization: The Politics of Anti-Social Behaviour and Hate Crime*. London: Palgrave Macmillan.

Franiuk, R., Seefelt, J. L., Cepress, S. L., & Vandello, J. A. (2008). Prevalence and Effects of Rape Myths in Print Journalism the Kobe Bryant Case. *Violence Against Women, 14*, 287–309.

Goodey, J. (2005). *Victims and Victimology: Research, Policy and Practice*. London: Longman.

Hazel, N. (2008). *Cross-national comparison of youth justice*. Youth Justice Board.

Jones, H., & Powell, J. L. (2006). Old Age, Vulnerability and Sexual Violence: Implications for Knowledge and Practice. *International Nursing Review, 53*, 211–216.

Korn, A., & Efrat, S. (2004). The Coverage of Rape in the Israeli Popular Press. *Violence Against Women, 10*, 1056–1074.

Lees, S. (1997). *Carnal Knowledge: Rape on Trial*. Harmondsworth: Penguin.

Mair, G. (2017). Criminal Justice: A Brief History since 1945. In P. Davies, J. Harding, & G. Mair (Eds.), *An Introduction to Criminal Justice* (pp. 19–39). London: Sage.

Matthews, B., & Minton, J. (2018). Rethinking One of Criminology's 'Brute Facts': The Age–crime Curve and the Crime Drop in Scotland. *European Journal of Criminology, 15*(3), 296–320.

Mawby, R. (1988). Age Vulnerability and the Impact of Crime. In M. Maguire & J. Pointing (Eds.), *Victims of Crime: A New Deal?* (pp. 101–111). Milton Keynes: Open University Press.

Penhale, B. (2013). Older Women, Domestic Violence, and Elder Abuse: A Review of Commonalities, Differences, and Shared Approaches. *Journal of Elder Abuse & Neglect, 15*(3-4), 163–183.

Office of National Statistics. (2013). *An Overview of Sexual Offending in England and Wales.* London: Home Office.

Royal Commission. (2019). Aged Care in Australia: A Shocking Tale of Neglect. Retrieved June 1, 2020, from https://agedcare.royalcommission.gov.au/publications/Documents/interim-report/interim-report-media-release-31-october-2019.pdf.

Smith, D. J. (2005). *The Sleep of Reason: The James Bulger Case.* London: Arrow.

Turner, R. (2018). The Shocking Tales of Elder Abuse Victims. *ABC News.* Retrieved May 31, 2019, from https://www.abc.net.au/news/2018-03-04/the-shocking-tales-of-elder-abuse-victims/9504798.

UNICEF. (1990). United Nations Convention on Rights of the Child. Retrieved May 31, 2019, from https://downloads.unicef.org.uk/wp-content/uploads/2010/05/UNCRC_united_nations_convention_on_the_rights_of_the_child.pdf?_ga=2.219387929.1859118610.1559291649-1009947137.1559291649.

United Nations (UN). (n.d.). World Elder Abuse Awareness Day 15 June. Retrieved May 31, 2019, from https://www.un.org/en/events/elderabuse/.

World Health Organisation (WHO). (2019). Retrieved May 10, 2019, from http://www.searo.who.int/entity/health_situation_trends/data/chi/elderly-population/en/.

Part II

Groups, Power and Criminality

In the first part of the book, we saw how individuals can be powerful and how that power is wielded in a range of ways. Whilst individual power has similarities to collectively used power, there are differences, which we focus on in this second part. The four chapters in this half of the book explore how power is wielded and how power operates when groups of people, who share a common purpose or are part of the same organisation, work together to maintain power and/or make money. The four groups that are the focus of each of the chapters are: corporations, organised crime groups, states, and insurgents. On one hand, organised crime and insurgents are likely to be conceptualised or thought of as groups who commit crimes. In those chapters, we will provide evidence as to how both are powerful though this is expressed in different ways. In addition, organised crime groups and insurgents have different levels of visibility. In terms of organised crime groups, whilst some of their activities are actively kept hidden by the group's members (i.e. smuggling of drugs and so forth), there is obviously wider knowledge and awareness of where organised crime groups exists and what crimes they are committing (i.e. the 'mafiya' in Russia, laundering money).

On the other hand, corporations and states are possibly not who criminologists (and the general public) would think of as 'criminals', but as we will see in Chaps. 9 and 11, corporations and states regularly engage in deviant acts. Although in each of those chapters, we discuss theories as to why corporations and states commit crimes, first it is worth exploring the broader concept of organisational deviance, which applies to group deviance in general. This will help to better understand how it is that sometimes groups of people collaborate to engage in deviant behaviour. It may also clarify why it is that sometimes people in groups stop each other from acting deviantly or criminally.

In general, deviance is a behaviour or an act, which infringes or departs from an unwritten social rule (Green and Ward 2004). Of course, as Green and Ward (2004) correctly note, social rules are often debated and not necessarily agreed upon, so are frequently contested. Deviance then is determined by the combination of the actor, the rule, and very importantly, the audience (Green and Ward 2004). The latter plays an important part when exploring organisational deviance. The actors in instances of organisational deviance are individuals acting on behalf of or as a part of a corporation or a state. The rule could be a specific piece of legislation (i.e. the Health and Safety Act 1974) or something more general like treating employees well or not hurting innocent bystanders. The audience makes the difference though if the act is viewed as deviant or not. If it is other people in the actor's corporation or state agency, we suggest an act may be judged quite differently than if the audience is the general public or people outside of the corporation or agency. For example, the 2008 financial crisis was in part caused by giving subprime mortgages to 'high-risk' people, meaning the housing loans where given to people who could likely not afford to repay the loan. Whereas to the general public and those outside the mortgage and banking industries such acts seem deviant because they are harmful (it seems wrong to lend money to someone, who is not going to be able to repay it and they are then likely to go bankrupt and/or lose their home), this was standard practice. Numerous individuals from numerous mortgage lenders and banks issued subprime mortgages. People within these organisations are acting to a set of agreed upon rules. Thus, the audience—the public or the actor's peers—determines whether the act is deviant. As we will see in Chaps. 9 and 11, harmful, deviant, and criminal acts by corporations and states are fairly common place, which implies that within those cultures and organisations such acts are often standard, acceptable behaviour rather than deviant *to them*. Yet to their victims, society, and the general public, the acts may be seen as unfair and/or unjust. This makes the public, civil society, international organisations, other states, other agencies within an offending state (Green and Ward 2004), and whistle blowers, among others, crucial in combatting crimes by powerful entities as they can label such harms deviant and try to hold these groups accountable.

A critical appraisal would indicate that there has been an overall shift in most societies to a neo-liberal ethos, and with this shift fewer and fewer harmful acts are being seen as deviant. Snider (2000: 170) says that the "corporate counter-revolution [that] has legitimized every acquisitive, profit-generating act of the corporate sector, and challenged every policy that impeded this agenda". As such, very few of the harmful acts, by corporations in particular, are defined as crimes and any attempt to restrict capital comes under attack (Snider 2000). Snider (2000) links the failure of corporate deviancy to be defined as crime to a power imbalance and the power dynamics of knowledge claims. Powerful groups, like corporations, control the knowledge and the discourse around the economy, and societal concerns. For instance, reams of evidence around the supposed benefits and the ability of free markets to combat poverty and inequality are widely circulated. The counter discourse that free markets cause inequality, harm, and exploitation, is, however, squelched by powerful groups (Snider 2000). This links closely to the first of the seven features of invisibility 'no knowledge' as there is knowledge, but only from the point of view of the powerful, who support the status quo of free markets and continual growth.

In each of the forthcoming chapters, we will explore power imbalances and dynamics as they relate to knowledge, but also to the other six features of invisibility—no statistics, no research, no theory, no control, no politics, no panic. We will also, where relevant, link the discussion of powerful groups back to the dimensions of power investigated in the first part of the book—race/ethnicity, religion, age, and gender. As in the first part of the book, each chapter contains case studies highlighting different aspects and elements of power. In this second part of the book, because of the nature and reach of groups who are powerful, this means looking at victimisation and harm on large scales with disturbing consequences.

Questions to Ponder
• What would the role of a whistle blower be in each of the chapters?
How has neo-liberalism contributed to these crimes of the powerful?
How do individual and group power interact?

References
• Green, P., & Ward, T. (2004). *State Crime: Governments, Violence and Corruption*. London: Pluto Press.
Snider, L. (2000). The Sociology of Corporate Crime: An Obituary (or: Whose Knowledge Claims has Legs?). *Theoretical Criminology*, *4*(2), 169–206.

Corporations

9

Introduction

Whereas individuals who work for corporations commit crimes, as explored in Chap. 4 of Part I, in addition to occupational crimes by elites, entire corporations can operate outside of the law. This chapter unpicks the neoliberal and business ethos that several argue underpin the criminogenic nature of corporations (Box 1983; Pearce and Tombs 1998; Croall 2001, 2007). This leads to an examination of the types of offences committed by corporations—financial crimes, crimes against consumers, crimes against employees and environmental crimes—in the examples given and the two case studies explored (Beirne and South 2007; Levi 2014; Tombs 2014; White, 2008, 2009, White and Heckenberg 2014). The latter detail the Volkswagen Defeat Device and the actions of Carbofin, an Italian shipping company. We also investigate the challenges for law enforcement and regulatory agencies to prove corporate guilt and to prosecute entities or individual employees (Braithwaite 1989; Croall 2007; Pearce and Tombs 1998). Underlying this chapter is an analysis of the power wielded by corporations to evade justice and remain hidden from media and public scrutiny.

© The Author(s) 2021
P. Davies, T. Wyatt, *Crime and Power*,
https://doi.org/10.1007/978-3-030-57314-0_9

What Is a Corporation and What Is Corporate Crime?

Unlike other concepts, what a 'corporation' is or is not does not seem to be a controversial concept that has engendered a lot of scholarly debate. For the most part, corporations are all companies registered within their own or another countries' territory. In the United Kingdom, for instance, this means registering under the Companies Act. Size also does not matter, as small companies as well as multinationals must register. The diversity of corporations is one factor that we will return to in regard to challenges for regulating and monitoring their actions.

Corporate Crime

If a corporation is then any registered small business all the way to a transnational company, what is a corporate crime? One definition is as follows:

> [I]llegal acts or omissions, punishable by the State under administrative, civil or criminal law, which are the result of deliberate decision making or culpable negligence within a legitimate formal organisation. These acts or omissions are based in legitimate, formal, business organisations, made in accordance with the normative goals, standard operating procedures, and/or cultural norms of the organisation, and are intended to benefit the corporation itself. (Pearce and Tombs 1998: 107–10)

For Box (1983: 20) corporate crime are acts of 'omission or commission by an individual or group of individuals in a legitimate formal organization—which have serious physical or economic impacts on employees, consumers or the general public'.

These definitions of corporate crime raise a number of issues to explore regarding how corporations are punished and the basis for their acts and/or omissions. First, regarding how corporations are punished, Sutherland (1983 [1949]) argued that the distinctions between different illegalities—criminal, civil, administrative—are significant. Having an act or omission categorised as a civil violation rather than a criminal one often reflects the ability of the powerful, especially corporations, to define their activities as less serious. At the other side of the spectrum, protest against injustices (as we saw in Chap. 5 in terms of race and Black Lives Matters) is often criminalised. In his classic text *Crimes of the Powerful*, Pearce (1976) demonstrated this when highlighting how supposed troublesome activity of labour unions was made a criminal offence in the United States. In this particular instance, corporations colluded with organised crime groups to suppress the labour unions. The powerless (the workers) were thus kept in check through brute force of the powerful (corporations and organised crime groups). Furthermore, the powerful's ability to manipulate the legal system and the definition of crime leads to the minimisation of the powerful's own criminality and also to the exaggeration of the criminality of the powerless (Pearce 1976).

The second aspect worth expanding upon is the basis for these acts and omissions. Again drawing on Pearce's (1976) investigation of the US state, he describes how American corporations (with the connivance of the state—which we return to in Chap. 11) act systematically to control the markets within which they operate. That is to say manipulation, control, lobbying and so forth are not one-off occurrences to gain a single outcome in a single instance. Such acts are repeatedly engaged in. The primary goal of corporations is to make profits for their shareholders (Snider 2000). To achieve this, corporations habitually engage in anti-social, illegal and criminal conduct (Pearce 1976), which brings us to why corporations can be considered criminogenic.

Why Are Corporations Criminogenic?

Slapper and Tombs (1999) have made the case that there are not just some 'bad apples' or as Snider (2000) points out it is not just 'rogue traders'; if one were to look, even briefly, into the activities of big businesses, a pattern emerges across the spectrum of companies of routine and pervasive violations of regulations and laws (Slapper and Tombs 1999; Snider 2000). The range of these offences are vast as we will explore in the next section. They vary from financial irregularities to pollution from mistreating their employees to defrauding consumers. Adding to the complexity of corporate crime is that whereas sometimes the violations are intentional and well planned (see the Volkswagen emissions case study below), other times the harm and/or crime may be the consequence of a shortcut taken and therefore lacks intention (i.e. the lack of maintenance on the oil rig responsible for the Deep Water Horizon Oil Spill in the Gulf of Mexico). The intention is not to cause death, injury or illness; these are unintended consequences of the prioritisation of profits and the often drastic measures that are taken to maintain and/or increase profits.

It is not enough to simply say though that corporate crimes are explained by greed. This explanation does not account for corporate crimes pervasiveness or how it is that numerous people, who have possibly not committed crimes before, then commit corporate crime. To try to unpack corporations' criminogenic nature more fully, we turn to traditional criminological theory. For some, the classic theory of rational choice explains corporations being criminogenic (Paternoster and

Simpson 1993). If employees and companies were to weigh up the costs and benefits of violating regulations and breaking laws, they may well determine it is in
their interest to do so since the chances of getting caught are slim, and the punishment if caught is minimal. Set these factors within the context that corporations are
very weakly regulated in general and you have a situation that is ripe for criminality (Tombs 2005).

In addition to traditional classicism providing possible explanations of corporate crime, positivism, both individual and sociological, also provide some theories. In terms of individual positivism, there is speculation that some corporate
employees, at least those in the higher levels of management, may have personality
traits that contribute to their and the corporation's criminality. We rarely talk about
corporate offenders as 'pathological' or as suffering from other mental health issues, but that is not to say that it is not possible that individual personality characteristics are not relevant to discussions of corporate criminality. Yet, the imagery of
pathology is hard to accept when it is the well-respected, educated and so forth who
are harming people more than others, but maybe they are rational and not abnormal
(Box 1983).

A number of sociological positivist theories seem poignant to corporate offending. Differential association posits that attitudes, techniques and motives for committing crime are learned (Sutherland 1939). In the corporate context, new employees are indoctrinated into a culture accepting and/or supportive of law violations.
Foucault (1975 [1977]: 253) suggests that 'one type of offender is the one perver-
ted by the tendencies of their organisation'. Criminality is thus perpetuated in businesses. Merton's (1938) strain theory can also apply to corporations. Whereas
strain theory originally proposed that individuals feel the tension to succeed in
specific ways in society and if they are unable to meet these expectations through
legitimate means then people might turn to crime, this is relevant to corporations as
well. Strains are also felt by corporate entities in whichever industry they are trying
to compete. Similarly, if they are unable to reach their goals legitimately, they may
pursue criminal means of achieving the same goals.

Of course, the composition or structure of corporations and the market context
vary widely and affect whether or not a corporation offends or not (Tombs 2005).
As mentioned above, there is the possibility that the characteristics or personalities
of individual employees—from line workers all the way up to chief executive officers and board members—play a part in whether or not a corporation violates
regulations and/or breaks laws (Tombs 2005). The place or department where that
person works within the company and who that person works with may determine
criminal behaviour. First, there is the immediate work group or sub-unit within
which a person works. Who is in that sub-unit influences criminality through those

employees' interpersonal dynamics as well as the corporate culture into which they all have been socialised. In addition, the location of that work group in the hierarchy may be relevant to criminality. A work group with high levels of autonomy and low levels of accountability may be more likely to cut corners as their actions are less scrutinised. Furthermore, the physical location of the group may play a part in criminality. For instance, the Deep Water Horizon oil rig that explodes and leaks into the Gulf of Mexico is in an isolated location with limited people visiting and observing the location, whereas typical office work spaces have numerous people coming and going providing an element of informal social control.

Furthermore in terms of organisation, the overall structure of the company impacts upon the work groups discussed above, but also on the accountability mechanisms that are in place and thus the ability to hide crimes (Tombs 2005). Organisational culture features at the structural level, too, since, as mentioned above in discussing differential association, the learning of attitudes, techniques and motivations of offending, are taught at the organisational level. A business or company as an entity has an overall culture that includes acceptance or not of rule-breaking behaviour. Also important at the organisational or structural level is the overall economic health of the company. If a company is performing well, there may be less motivation to commit crime. But, if the company is struggling, there may be the motivation to commit crimes to become more profitable. In addition, whether the company is operating in a single part of a country, in a single state or transnationally will impact upon its criminality. This is not only due to the fact that there are different strains, but also there are different regulations. The complexity of registering companies and jurisdictions across borders may well lend itself to those corporations committing crimes if it enables them to be less likely to be caught. Finally, the nature of the market or the industry plays a part in all of the above, but also is a factor on its own (Tombs 2005). The size and scope of industries differ greatly. For instance, the pharmaceutical industry is much different to the jewellery industry. Furthermore, different industries have different relationships to the state. Pharmaceutical companies have to go through different inspections to comply with different regulations than companies making jewellery. In addition, each state will have its own perspective and approach to the oversight of all these different markets. Those states with weak enforcement and lax regulation may well attract corporations as they are able to commit crimes without getting caught. Lastly, the entire economy's health and that of the industry plays a role in whether or not the corporations in that industry turn to crime. If the economy is suffering, corporations could be tempted to break rules to maintain their profits.

Overall though, it should be evident that corporate crime is complex and varied for numerous reasons. As we turn to our case studies, we will explore from a critical criminological perspective the criminogenic nature of different corporations within different industries with the aim of shedding more light on corporations as powerful criminals.

Financial Crimes

We propose there are four types of corporate crime ((i) financial crimes, (ii) crimes against consumers, (iii) crimes against employees and (iv) environmental crimes). One of the main types are financial crimes (see Snider 2000, among others, for a debate about categorisations). These tend to align with organisational systematic deviance and criminogenity. They are not one-time occurrences but patterns of behaviours engaged in by corporations to maximise profit and outcompete other corporations. Offences include (i) illegal share dealings and mergers, (ii) various forms of tax evasion, (iii) forms of illegal accounting and (iv) bribery.

Illegal Share Dealings and Mergers

Illegal share dealings are more commonly referred to as 'insider trading'. This is when a person with information not available publicly about a company's stocks or securities shares this information with people, who then make profitable transactions based upon the information that they should not have known. Martha Stewart, the American celebrity, is a somewhat well-known example of this. She was given non-public information by her stock broker that one of the stocks that she owned in 2002 was soon going to lose value. Stewart sold the stock and avoided losing $45,000 (Carlin and Rashkover 2003). Stewart was convicted and served five months in a US federal prison. Illegal mergers are when corporations combine to form a monopoly that then controls most, if not all, of an industry. For instance, there are relatively few supermarkets or cable TV providers in the United Kingdom. If these started to merge, then there would be no competition in the market. This type of total control has been deemed to be illegal.

Tax Evasion

A second type of financial crime is tax evasion. Tax evasion may be criminal when corporations act in ways to not pay taxes by hiding activities or making false reports. In Chap. 10 where we discuss organised crime groups, the case study about illegal waste dumping highlights how corporations pay organised crime groups to illegally dump their waste. By hiding the amount of waste generated, the true amount of the corporation's production, and thus the amount of taxes they should pay, is not known and does not have to be reported to the state. In this example, a criminal activity enables the corporation to avoid taxes. A common occurrence seen throughout the West is corporations registering their companies in other countries that are 'tax havens', which do not require corporations to pay taxes. Corporations then do not have to pay the taxes of the countries in which they operate. Starbucks, the major coffee house, is a prime example. In 2012, UK sales for Starbucks were £400 million, but they paid no corporation taxes in the United Kingdom as they are registered as a corporation in a different country (Barford and Holt 2013). Whilst technically not criminal or illegal, it certainly appears unethical.

Illegal Accounting

Corporations sometimes utilise illegal accounting practices that make it appear as if the company is always doing well. The company Enron in the United States was at the centre of an illegal accounting scandal in 2000. Projected profits were immediately claimed on their books, though no actual money had yet been made on their asset building or investment (Segal 2018). If a loss was anticipated, the asset was transferred to an off-the-books corporation, so that the loss would go unreported. This type of mark-to-marketing accounting deliberately hides the true financial health and status of a corporation (Segal 2018). Similarly in the United Kingdom, derivatives broker, Nick Leeson, used an error account to hide losses from speculative sales he had been making. In this case though, Leeson hid £800 million of losses! He was able to hide the losses because Barings Bank, his employer, let him approve his own trades. When he was finally caught, Barings Bank, the oldest Merchant bank in the United Kingdom at the time, was declared insolvent because the government could not cover their losses. Leeson served six and half years in a jail in Singapore, where he was based at the time of his fraudulent activities (watch interviews with Leeson in the *25 Million Pounds* documentary—https://topdocumentaryfilms.com/25-million-pounds/).

Bribery

Corporations are also guilty of bribing states and other companies to gain access to new markets and to new places. In the United States, there is a federal law, the

Foreign Corrupt Practices Act (FCPA), prohibiting US companies from making payments to foreign officials in order to win or keep business (McCoy 2015). The US agency that is tasked with investigating violations of this act is the Securities and Exchange Commission (SEC). In 2015, they found that the Goodyear Tire and Rubber Company had failed to institute proper oversight of the actions of its subsidiaries in Kenya and Angola (SEC 2015). In Kenya, Goodyear's subsidiary bribed employees at eight different government agencies or corporations (SEC 2015). Similarly in Angola, Goodyear's subsidiary bribed employees of six government agencies or corporations. Under the FCPA, the corporation must pay back all the illicit profits as well as the fees for the investigation. Thus in this instance, Goodyear agreed to pay over $16 million. The SEC (2015) reported that the subsidiaries had recorded the payments as legitimate business expenses. This example demonstrates that corruption intersects with public officials—the Kenyan Port Authority—but also with private entities, the Nzoia Sugar Company (SEC 2015). Interestingly, by paying the settlement, Goodyear neither denied nor admitted to the bribery. Thus, even though there is a press release of the wrongdoing, there is no record of a civil or criminal violation of any kind.

Offences Against Consumers

Whereas financial crimes discussed above may indirectly affect consumers who buy products from corporations, corporate crimes can also directly affect consumers in the corporations' efforts to cut costs and/or maximise profits. There are five categories of such offences. First, there are illegal sales and marketing practices, where unsafe products are sold or where false and/or misleading information is given about the product. Marketing needs to be honest and socially responsible. Furthermore, no information can be left out and comparisons between different corporations' products need to be accurate and like-for-like in regard to what is being compared. Second, there is the sale of unfit goods or sale for improper use. Products or goods, whether physical or digital, must meet standards set by law. Products should not be damaged or faulty when a consumer purchases them. In addition, goods should fit the purpose that they are advertised for as well as match the descriptions given. Most countries have protections against violations of these standards, such as in the United Kingdom with the Consumer Rights Act 2015.

Third, corporations have been known to engage in conspiracies to fix prices and/or carve up market share amongst different companies. Corporations should not be collaborating or making agreements about how much to charge consumers. For example, in 2018 the European Commission fined a number of companies in the technology industry for price fixing (Mills 2018). Asus, Denon & Marantz, Philips and Pioneer were found by the European Commission to be leveraging online resellers of their products to keep prices of their products high. If the online resellers refused, the corporations would block purchase of their products by the online resellers in violation of EU anti-trust laws (Mills 2018). As a result, the corporations have collectively been fined $130 million (Mills 2018). Fourth, there is false and/or illegal labelling or information. For instance, use of the terms 'environmentally-friendly', 'natural' and 'organic' have specific meanings that cannot be used on products that do not meet the strict definitions associated with these terms. Using them when the term does not apply is false or illegal labelling. The final category is fraudulent safety or environmental testing of products and will be detailed in the next case study.

Case Study 1: Volkswagen's Defeat Device

In 2015, Volkswagen—the German automotive company—admitted to using software or a 'defeat device' to mask the actual amount of emissions produced by their diesel vehicles (Krall and Peng 2015; Blackwelder et al. 2016). Initially, 500,000 vehicles were recalled (at first because of a 'glitch'), but eventually more than 11 million cars were thought to contain the software and not just Volkswagens (Mays 2015). The so-called scandal broke because the International Council on Clean Transportation (ICCT) was conducting research in 2014 to confirm that there was such a thing as clean diesel (Blackwelder et al. 2016). ICCT had researchers at West Virginia University's Center for Alternative Fuels, Engines and Emissions road test various Volkswagen models. Concurrently, the California Air Resources Board (CARB) was testing Volkswagen emissions in a laboratory (Blackwelder et al. 2016). Whereas CARB's results matched Volkswagen's claims and the allowable levels of emissions, the ICCT research found that two models in particular, the Jetta and the Passat, were 5–35 times above US emission standards (Blackwelder et al. 2016). In 2015 when CARB and the United States Environmental Protection Agency (EPA) informed Volkswagen that they would not certify Volkswagen's 2016 vehicles unless they met emission standards, the Chief Executive Officer (Martin Winterkorn) released a statement that their cars had been engineered to give inaccurate emission test results that appeared to comply with emissions regulations (Blackwelder et al. 2016). He is still facing criminal charges in 2020; the lead engineer has already been convicted of a crime. The lawsuits to compensate consumers are ongoing in Europe and the United States.

As Crete (2016) points out, the media coverage has largely focused on the negative impacts on Volkswagen, their stakeholders (including employees, directors, investor, suppliers and consumers) and on the automobile industry. This indicates the concern is mainly an economic one, and there are undoubtedly numerous economic fallouts from the nature and scale of this crime. And it is certainly a *crime* rather than a scandal, as Volkswagen was purposefully altering its vehicles to not be detected whilst polluting. Jobs were lost, car sales dropped, stock values dropped, and Volkswagen is the target of numerous investigations and civil, administrative and criminal lawsuits (Crete 2016). Of utmost importance though are the environmental and human health implications of millions of vehicles producing excessive emissions. Combining the data and estimates of other researchers, Krall and Peng (2015) estimate that Volkswagen's actions are responsible for between 72 and 361 premature deaths due to nitrogen oxide pollutants. These are the human victims; later it emerged that Volkswagen locked ten Java monkeys into small rooms with the exhaust pipe of a vehicle piped in (Connolly 2018). The corporation was testing whether the amount of pollutants had decreased with the addition of modern cleaning technology.

It seems the reasons for Volkswagen's blatant criminal behaviour lie in the above discussion as to why corporations are criminogenic. 'The corporate strategy and pressures exerted on VW's employees may have led them to give preference to the performance priorities set by the company rather than compliance with the applicable legal and ethical standards' (Crete 2016: 25). Crewe goes on to note that this went undetected because of a lack of compliance monitoring systems, particularly within Volkswagen. At first the tactic in assigning blame was for the senior management in Volkswagen to single out a few software engineers who were responsible (Crete 2016). Later though, the corporation has admitted that 'organizational problems had also encouraged or facilitated the unlawful corporate behaviour' (Crete 2016: 26). Crete (2016) refers to such actions as the unwanted side effects that come with setting ambitious objectives; a crime then—the installation of the illegal software to avoid regulations—is a by-product of fierce competition.

Pause for Thought

- What factors, internally and externally, contributed to Volkswagen's organisational deviance?
- Who are the victims of the defeat device?

Crimes Against Employees

Consumers are not the only victims of corporate power. Employees of corporations are often subjected to unsafe, unstable and/or unethical practices, again as a way for the corporation to maximise profits or maintain power. There are five categories of crimes against employees: discrimination, violations of employment law, violations of wage laws, violations of employees' right to organise and health and safety crimes. Discrimination is the first of these crimes. This could be gender or racial discrimination but also discrimination based on religion, sexual orientation or age. In these instances, employees of these particular demographics are treated unfairly because they are a woman, an ethnic minority and so forth. It is illegal to discriminate on this basis as it violates employment law in most countries. There are other ways to violate employment law, the second category of offences against employees. To not offer a woman a job because she is pregnant, for instance, is also a violation. Not making adjustments for disabled employees is likely also a violation of employment law. The third category of crimes against employees is violations of wage laws. In these cases, employees are not paid properly for the work they have done. This could be to do with not paying minimum wage, when it is required; not paying overtime, when it has been earned; or not giving cost of living increases on employees' wages. Further crimes against employees may come in the form of the fourth category—not allowing employees to organise or to take industrial action. Workers are entitled to form and/or join a trade union and corporations should in no way infringe upon this (again in most Western countries). Likewise, those employees who belong to trade unions (though there are some exceptions like police unions) are entitled to take industrial action or go on strike when the members of the trade union have voted to do so. Companies like Walmart actively discourage their employees from unionising (Berfield 2015). This purportedly saves the company millions of dollars as they can keep wages low and employ most people part-time, so as to avoid paying benefits. Walmart has been accused of retaliating against employees who try to unionise or who protest how they are treated (Berfield 2015).

Discrimination and violations of employment law, wage law and the right to organise are all difficult to prove. The fifth category of crimes against employees—occupational health and safety violations—is also difficult to uncover and to prove because of their complexity and because they are hidden behind the closed doors of private factories and workplaces (Tombs and Whyte 2007; Tombs 2014). Health crimes and safety crimes are two separate types of violations. Health crimes violate occupational health law, which pertains to requirements for work environments to be free of substances that can damage people's health or not providing the correct equipment for people to protect themselves. Violations of health law are likely continual or persistent rather than a one-off incident or single event. There are likely numerous codes in regulations that govern health law, which adds to the complexity of health crimes. An example of a health crime is employee exposure to asbestos. Exposure to asbestos is linked to mesothelioma and to lung cancer. Proving though that employees in industries that work(ed) with asbestos, like construction and demolition, is complex and contestable. Finding evidence and a causal chain from asbestos exposure to cancer or other diseases 10–40 years later is clearly very challenging. The burden of proof is very high and the data needed is very technical. As such, we know very little about health crimes. The International Labour Organization (ILO—the United Nations agency tasked with dealing with labour issues, such as international labour standards and social protection) (Ryder 2018) estimates that there are 2.4 million deaths annually worldwide from work-related diseases. In addition, because ill-health is not always visible, the links to unhealthy workplaces may not be suspected. Therefore, there is a very large dark figure of health crime.

Similarly, there is very little known about safety crimes. These differ to health crimes in that occupational safety violations cause, or have the potential to cause, immediate injury or death due to tasks at work (Tombs and Whyte 2007) rather than illness or death because of prolonged exposure. Again, safety crimes are regulated through a multitude of legislation, and regulatory mechanisms, that are likely administrative or civil rather than criminal. This does of course depend on the state. Some states have very weak safety (and health) standards for their workers. For instance, data about safety crimes indicate workers in China and India as well as Russia and Ukraine are more likely to be killed at work than workers in the European Union (Tombs and Whyte 2007). The ILO (Ryder 2018) estimates around 380,000 worker deaths each year. The annual death toll caused by work is greater than that by war or terrorism (Tombs and Whyte 2007). Fatalities are just one part of safety crimes. Even though we mentioned little is known about safety crimes, what data are available in the United Kingdom through the Health and Safety Executive (the agency that oversees compliance with occupational health and safety legislation and regulation) and through a self-report Labour Force Survey uncovers worrying patterns of underreporting and victimisation. Through the Health and Safety Executive, major injuries and injuries requiring over three days off of work are also required to be reported. Yet through comparison to the self-report survey, it is evident non-fatal data is severely underreported, particularly for people who are self-employed (Tombs ad Whyte 2007). Furthermore, small companies are more likely to underreport or not report at all, raising concerns about the ability of some small businesses to safeguard their employees. In addition, in the United Kingdom, 95% of reported fatalities are men and men are far more likely to suffer a non-fatal injury than women (Tombs and Whyte 2007). The gendered nature of this victimisation is probably due to the research being focused on men, but also that men are most likely working in more dangerous industries (i.e. construction, mining, etc.).

Gender is just one of the victimisation patterns evident. Those dying or getting injured at work are also more likely to be unorganised workers (not part of a union), traditionally class-divided work such as construction and manufacturing, temporary and/or part-time employees, 'invisible' employees (people working at home, children and undocumented immigrants) and workers in developing countries or marginalised groups (Tombs and Whyte 2007; Tombs 2014). It is important to note that safety violations may not just negatively impact workers; there is also the possibility that the surrounding areas of the factory or industrial site may be affected as well. The Bhopal, India chemical plant explosion in 1984 and the Deep Water Horizon oil rig disaster in the United States in 2010 are both examples of this. Not only did employees in both instances lose their lives because of safety violations from lack of proper maintenance, but also people in the surrounding areas were injured and/or the environment damaged because of the safety crime.

Although the numbers of victims of health and safety crimes are quite shocking, they are probably at an historic low (Nichols 1990). There have been significant advances in medical care, which means workers are now surviving accidents and diseases that are a result of their work where in the past this would have not been the case. Corporations have also invested in technology that has improved the safety of their workforces. There is also much greater knowledge and awareness of safe practices as well as knowledge and awareness of the contributors to chronic illnesses, like cancer. Improvements in communication and transport mean that medical help can be contacted and arrive much more quickly, which also increases survival rates. In general, there has been a shift from manufacturing to service jobs, which has led to work overall being physically safer (Nichols 1990), though seemingly there are now other stress-related health issues on the rise.

Environmental Offences

As with the above three types of corporate crimes, environmental offences consist of several various categories. These are illegal emissions to air, water and land; failure to provide or provision of false information; waste dumping; and illegal manufacturing practices. Pollution to air, water and land is allowed in a majority of places within set limits. This becomes illegal when the pollution exceeds the limits set within the regulations. Corporations frequently violate these limits and pay the fines if caught as this is still likely cheaper than abiding by the law. The second category, failure to provide or provision of false information, can be linked to the first (pollution), as will be seen in Case Study 2. For instance, not disclosing pollution or lying about the amount of pollution would fall under this category. It could also be related to other environmental offences, such as incorrectly listing species of timber during transport. Logging companies have been known to declare a non-protected common species of tree on customs and tax documents to either avoid paying high duties on protected timber or to smuggle species that are not allowed to be traded (Wyatt 2014). For category three, as the second case study in Chap. 10 documents, corporations are also guilty of dumping waste. They may do this themselves, or, as we will see, hire organised crime groups to do it for them. Again, from a critical criminological perspective, the motivation is profit. It is cheaper to illegally dispose of waste rather to pay the full costs to dispose of waste responsibly. Finally, corporations are implicated in manufacturing products illegally. In 2018, the Environmental Investigation Agency (EIA—a non-governmental organisation headquartered in London) uncovered that the unexplained high levels of chlorofluorocarbons (CFCs), particularly CFC 11, detected in the atmosphere over East Asia came from factories in China ignoring the ban on CFC production and using the ozone-depleting and greenhouse gas to make foam (EIA 2018). This is in clear violation of an international convention, the Montreal Protocol, to which China is a signatory. The Protocol, starting in 1989, implemented the phasing out of ozone-depleting gasses.

Case Study 2:   Carbofin, the Italian Shipping Company
In April 2014, one of the Carbofin's (an Italian shipping company) ships docked in the Port of Tampa in the US state of Florida (Department of Justice 2014). Two of the ship's crewmembers gave the inspectors a mobile phone video of a hose being used to bypass the proper disposal of the ship's engine room waste (Department of Justice 2014). Normal ship operation produces an oily waste from the running of the engines that is required to be disposed of in specific ways, and the disposal and transfer of this waste must be recorded in a ship's oil record book (Montgomery McCracken 2015). The inspectors determined after speaking with the crew that the hose had been used on at least two occasions to dump sludge, waste oil and machinery space bilge water from the engine room directly into the sea (Department of Justice 2014). This had been at the direction of the ship's chief engineer, who was also responsible for maintaining the ship's oil record book.

(*continued*)

Case Study 2:   (continued)
    The chief engineer and the second engineer both pled guilty to a violation of the Act to Prevent Pollution from Ships. As a result, Carbofin paid a criminal penalty of $2,750,000. Six hundred thousand dollars of that penalty went to Florida National Keys Marine Sanctuary (Department of Justice 2014).

This may at first appear to be individual criminality—the two engineers cutting corners in relation to waste disposal. Their actions though would not have served to benefit them personally. The reason for dumping the waste is to save the corporation the fees for incinerating the waste or transferring it to the proper place for disposal. Interestingly, the only way that this corporate crime was uncovered was by whistle blowers. For whatever reasons—uncomfortable with breaking the law, concerned about the environmental harm or some other reason—the crew felt compelled to record the crime and then to share it with the authorities. If it were not for the wider crew's actions, this environmental offence in international waters would have remained hidden due to its remote location and the actions of the chief engineer to hide it by not properly keeping records.

Pause for Thought

- Are fines an effective way to control corporations like Carbofin?
- What factors, internally and externally, contributed to the waste dumping?
- Who are the victims of the dumping waste at sea?

The Consequences of Corporate Power

The negative impacts of corporate power and crime are far-reaching. There are economic, physical, environmental and social consequences that stem from their pursuit of profit. Although not discussed widely and seldom part of mainstream criminological discussions, these negative consequences in terms of prevalence, cost, victims—nearly any metric—are greater than that of street crime. Economic consequences of crimes by corporations are born by governments, taxpayers, consumers, workers and other companies. Some states spend millions trying to regulate corporations, but then must also spend millions investigating concerns.

For instance, numerous government agencies around the world have had to investigate and gather evidence related to Volkswagen's and other automotive companies' defeat software that was detailed in Case Study 1 in this chapter. States also have to incur the costs of the pollution and related health issues from such crimes. Similarly, costs of pollution and healthcare are shouldered by taxpayers. Consumers bear the brunt of increased prices, when corporations are caught and transfer their fines to the price of their products. Workers at corporations have stagnant wages or take pay cuts to maintain or maximise corporate profits or, like consumers, because the corporation passes the costs of fines to other areas. Crime destabilises industries and gives criminal corporations an unfair competitive advantage. Honest, ethical, law-abiding corporations may struggle to survive because they are, for instance, paying proper taxes and/or not cutting corners.

Then, there are the physical consequences of corporate crime. Many of the examples provided in this chapter document the deaths, injuries and ill-health that arise from violations of health and safety regulations as well as environmental laws. The victims of these crimes are employees, bystanders, consumers, other species and the environment. The social consequences show a pattern of discrimination, which link to the intersectionalities of power discussed in the first part of this book. It is low-paid, temporary, part-time workers, who tend to work in the dangerous places. It is poorer people (which overlaps with race and ethnicity), who are unable to get away from pollution. The most impoverished people may have less of choice to buy the cheapest goods, which may be unsafe. Throughout society, corporate crime and ongoing corporate 'scandals' decrease the trust in corporations, which has larger impacts on the function of society as a whole in terms of citizen engagement and wellbeing. With so many different and important impacts, it is crucial to explore how corporations and corporate power can be made accountable and brought under control.

Control

Regulating and controlling corporations raises many challenges for states. This is due to a variety of factors including, but not limited to size, transnational scope, power and status. In regard to status, this is key to how corporations are treated by the legal system. Are corporations 'legal persons' and if so how does that translate into reality when holding an entire corporation accountable as a person would be? And if they are not legal persons, what are they? States tend then to either have legislation that differentiates how corporations are dealt with or they have legislation that assimilates corporations into the main legal system (Pearce and Tombs 1998). In the differentiation model, there is a separate legal sphere segregated from other crimes. This has mostly led to decriminalisation of corporate behaviour. The assimilation model is blending treatment of corporations into existing structures. This entails re-shaping corporate liability into the mainstream. Yet, liability presents the challenge just mentioned—how to attribute and prove liability—individually or on some new basis? Further challenges arise when corporate structure allows for limited liability, which may curtail the amount of financial compensation that may be sought (Croall 2007). The balanced blend of corporate and individual liability and the impact of this for controlling corporations continues to be hotly contested as the seemingly inherent duality of corporate and individual criminal liability coexist (Fisse and Braithwaite 1993).

Trends in Control

Control of corporate crime can be categorised as either enforcement or regulation. Enforcement means that corporate violations are likely defined as criminal and are therefore enforced through a state's penal code. What is evident though is that in actuality, non-enforcement is the most frequent response to corporate crime. When criminal charges are brought against companies, the trend is that it is the smallest and weakest people or companies, who/which are charged. So bigger companies and multinational or transnational corporations are not likely to have criminal charges brought against them for the range of crimes that were detailed above. When criminal charges are brought against these small and weak people or companies, the sanctions that are imposed are usually light. By and large, they consist of monetary fines and that quite low. For instance, a £15 million health and safety violation by a company called Transco resulted in a fine of only 2% of their after tax profits. Thus, sanctions (particularly fines) do not act as a deterrent as they rarely impact upon the financial benefits that come from committing the crime. The danger though of high fines is that they might result in lower pay for workers and higher prices for consumers as the corporations displace fines away from their profit margins.

Since enforcement is not used or not effective, regulation—administrative or civil violations—may be better at ensuring corporations comply with the law. This is evident in the United Kingdom where the Environment Agency of England starts with regulatory measures before moving through a range of actions to gain compliance from environmental offenders, including moving to criminal charges as one of the final approaches (Brosnan 2017). The first tactic to gain compliance is one of cooperation, using persuasion, negotiation and/or compromise to get corporations to not (re-)offend (Brosnan 2017; Pearce and Tombs 1998). Other trends in terms of regulation have been to prioritise violations, when inspectors have uncovered multiple offences (Pearce and Tombs 1998). In these instances, those violations that are the most dangerous would be targeted to be fixed and less urgent violations would be the subject of discussions and negotiations. In Australia and New Zealand, a newer regulatory approach is the Enforceable Undertaking (EU). These legally binding agreements in lieu of a court trial set out what the alleged offender will do to improve the workplace health and safety arrangements and thus provide benefits for employees, the industry and the wider community (HRD 2020). The EU is published online outlining the trainings, improved equipment and so forth that has been agreed to (HRD 2020).

The main trend though is self-regulation (Braithwaite 1989), where corporations are deregulated and enter into voluntary compliance schemes. In this approach, corporations oversee their own reporting in regard to health and safety and environmental regulations as well as financial and employment reports. Snider (2000) goes so far as to propose that there is no such thing as corporate crime, because all regulation and enforcement has been done away with under neoliberal policies.

Alternatives to Current Approaches

Since corporations re-offend repeatedly, the enforcement and regulatory oversight needs to be reconsidered. As Pearce and Tombs (1998) suggested, over 20 years ago, why not consider a more adversarial and interventionist strategy to bring corporations into compliance with legislation. In addition, a more punitive approach should also be considered so as to remove the lack of deterrence that currently seems to be the norm. Furthermore, law enforcement agencies and the criminal justice system in general need to treat corporate crime as 'real' crime rather than avoiding or ignoring it. This is true of legislative and political spheres as well, where corporate offences are regulated leniently, if at all, and are not part of political platforms or manifestos is a concern that needs to be addressed in society. Overall, differentiation or assimilation seems to not work in isolation. It is likely better to combine approaches rather than have an either or tactic. This fits with proposals for regulatory continuums, like that used by England's Environment Agency, where when corporations prove to be non-compliant the approach becomes stricter and more forceful. This is in line with Ayres and Braithwaite's (1992) enforcement pyramid, which illustrates that persuasion should be used first and the most often and then each approach included in the pyramid (warning letter, civil penalty, criminal penalty, licence suspension and licence revocation) should be used less frequently (Fig. 9.1: 35).

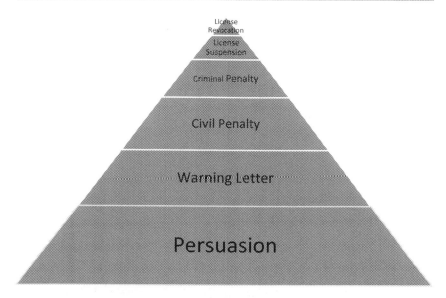

Fig. 9.1 Ayers and Braithwaite's (1992) enforcement pyramid

Finally, as evident from the first case study, we cannot overlook the corrupt behaviour of corporations, and definitions of corruption in legal statutes should consider corruption to consist of not only public officials, but also private individuals acting on their own behalf or for a corporation (Wyatt et al. 2017).

Power Through Invisibility

Corporations utilise a mixture of tactics to hide their crimes and to avoid being held responsible. They also employ language and rationale to make it seem like there are legitimate and/or necessary reasons for them to offend. Using the seven features of invisibility in relation to corporations, it is evident that corporations are able to manipulate all seven features.

No Knowledge

Corporations can control the flow of knowledge largely because of being private entities behind closed doors with security. What happens in factories, offices and corporate suites then can mostly be kept hidden. Knowledge of corporate crime is also hidden in certain circumstances because it is difficult to link the causality of corporate action to victimisation. As we saw in health and safety violations, in cases of chronic illness or failure of the corporation to undertake maintenance, it is very hard to prove the conditions of the workplace are/were the cause of the disease or injury.

No Statistics

The statistics about ill health and safety violations are minimal with many incidents going unreported by corporations and by individuals. This is the case with all of the crime types discussed in this chapter. Since corporations are largely self-regulated, there is little sharing of the number or nature of violations even if they are uncovered.

No Control

In regard to self-regulation, corporations tend to be treated differently to individual offenders. Whereas this is somewhat a practical issue of how you hold a collective entity responsible for a crime (Croall 2007), it is also down to the power of corporations to lobby states so that corporations continue to be treated differently. Therefore, 'no control' is a core aspect of corporate invisibility.

No Politics

In policy decisions and in political rhetoric, corporate crime is marginalised. This is clear since after the 2008 economic recession no significant changes were made to banking regulations after the collapse of the mortgage industry. Again, this is in part due to the power of corporations over politicians. Corporations would likely withdraw campaign funding from parties or candidates who advocated for being tough on corporate crime.

No Panic!

The media clearly have a part to play in all of this in their portrayal of corporations. Yet they do not talk about corporations as criminals or their crimes as crimes. Instead, the media talk about scandals and accidents. 'Accident prone workers' get blamed for 'disasters' (Tombs and Whyte 2007). All of these incidents are framed as the fault of individuals, whose behaviour can be improved, rather than a call to action to change the criminogenic nature of boardrooms and suites. As Tombs (2005) rightly says, each of these features on their own would not be enough to render corporate crimes and criminality invisible, but when combined they mutually reinforce one another, thus hiding corporate crime and keeping it off the agenda.

No Theory and No Research

There are two additional features of invisibility, which are mentioned separately because to some degree there are efforts in these areas. As evident from the above, scholars have developed theories to explain corporate crime, and there is research into the various aspects of corporate deviance and power. This is though still just the tip of the iceberg, and much more can and should be done to highlight the full spectrum of corporate criminality. We agree with Tombs and Whyte (2007) that part of the battle to change the perceptions of corporations and corporate crime is the resilient steadfast understanding of violence as both interpersonal and an act committed with intent. The long list of victimisation that this chapter has outlined is, we believe, a catalogue of violent acts, and they need to be recognised as such and treated accordingly. In conceptualising corporate behaviour that causes injury as violence, this may help to bring corporate crime from the margins to the mainstream.

Summary

Corporations may be the epitome of power. From their suites (one of the typologies of invisible crimes that we introduced in Chap. 3), they are able to influence: what a legal person is, what is criminal, what is regulated and/or enforced, what is (in)visible about their business and so forth. Their crimes are numerous ranging from financial crimes, to crimes against consumers, to crimes against their employees and to environmental crimes. Within these four categories, there are a diversity of crimes, but they have similarities—corporate crimes have many victims (humans, non-humans and the environment), cost governments, consumers, tax payers and employees a lot of money, and are not taken seriously enough, so remain underreported and largely unexamined. It is difficult to picture with the current neoliberal system how the power of corporations can be challenged and curbed. As criminologists, it is our task to expose their wrongdoing and continue to advocate for the powerful to be held accountable.

Go Further

- How is corporate crime violent?
- What is the relationship between corporations, the state and politics?
- Are there examples of corporations, which are not criminogenic?

References

Ayres, I. & Braithwaite, J. (1992). *Responsive Regulation: Transcending the deregulation debate*. New York: Oxford University Press.

Barford, V., & Holt, G. (2013). Google, Amazon, Starbucks: The Rise of Tax Shaming. *BBC News*. Retrieved July 24, 2018, from https://www.bbc.co.uk/news/magazine-20560359.

Beirne, P., & South, N. (2007). Introduction: Approaching Green Criminology. In P. Beirne & N. South (Eds.), *Issues in Green Criminology: Confronting Harms against Environments, Humanity and Other Animals* (pp. xiii–xxii). Cullompton, UK: Willan Publishing.

Berfield, S. (2015). How Walmart Keeps on Eye on its Massive Workforce: The Retail Giant is Always Watching. *Bloomberg Business News*. Retrieved July 27, 2018, from https://www.bloomberg.com/features/2015-walmart-union-surveillance/.

Blackwelder, B., Coleman, K., Colunga-Santoyo, S., Harrison, J. S., & Wozniak, D. (2016). *The Volkswagen Scandal. Case Study*. University of Richmond: Robins School of Business. Retrieved July 26, 2018, from https://scholarship.richmond.edu/cgi/viewcontent.cgi?referer=&httpsredir=1&article=1016&context=robins-case-network.

Box, S. (1983). *Power, Crime and Mystification*. London: Tavistock.

Braithwaite, J. (1989). *Crime, Shame and Reintegration*. Cambridge, UK: Cambridge University Press.

Brosnan, A. (2017). Determining the public interest in environmental enforcement, sanctioning and prosecution. In Bergin, T, & Orlando, E. (Eds.). *Forging a Social-legal Approach to Environmental Harms* (185–204). London: Routledge.

Carlin, W., & Rashkover, B. (2003). SEC Charges Martha Stewart, Broker Peter Bacanovic with Illegal Insider Trading. (June 4 Press Release). U.S. Securities and Exchange Commission.

Connolly, K. (2018). VW Suspends Media Chief Amid Scandal Over Fume Tests on Monkeys. *The Guardian*. Retrieved July 26, 2018, from https://www.theguardian.com/business/2018/jan/30/vw-suspends-media-chief-monkey-exhaust-tests-diesel-emissions.

Crete, R. (2016). The Volkswagen Scandal from the Viewpoint of Corporate Governance. *European Journal of Risk Regulation, 1*, 25–31.

Croall, H. (2001). *Understanding White Collar Crime*. Buckingham, UK: Open University Press.

Croall, H. (2007). Victims of White-Collar and Corporate Crime. In P. Davies, P. Francis, & C. Greer (Eds.), *Victims, Crime and Society* (pp. 78–108). London: Sage.

Department of Justice. (2014). Italian Shipping Company Pleads Guilty to Environmental Crimes for Concealing Vessel Pollution. Retrieved July 27, 2018, from https://www.justice.gov/opa/pr/italian-shipping-company-plead-guilty-environmental-crimes-concealing-vessel-pollution.

Environmental Investigation Agency (EIA). (2018). *Blowing It: Illegal Production and Use of Banned CFC-11 in China's Foam Blowing Industry*. Retrieved July 27, 2018, from https://drive.google.com/viewerng/viewer?url=https://eia-international.org/wp-content/uploads/Blowing-It-final.pdf.

Fisse, B., & Braithwaite, J. (1993). *Corporations, Crime and Responsibility*. Cambridge: Cambridge University Press.

Foucault, M. (1975 [1977]). *Discipline and Punish: The Birth of the Prison*. Trans. Sheridan, A. London: Penguin.

Human Resources Director (HRD). (2020). What is an Enforceable Undertaking and How Does it Work? Retrieved June 1, 2020, from https://www.hcamag.com/au/specialisation/employment-law/what-is-an-enforceable-undertaking-and-how-does-it-work/145289.

Krall, J., & Peng, R. (2015). The Volkswagen Scandal: Deception, Driving and Deaths. *The Royal Statistical Society*. Retrieved July 26, 2018, from https://rss.onlinelibrary.wiley.com/doi/full/10.1111/j.1740-9713.2015.00861.x.

Levi, M. (2014). Regulating Fraud Revisited. In P. Davies, P. Francis, & T. Wyatt (Eds.), *Invisible Crimes and Social Harms* (pp. 221–243). Basingstoke: Palgrave Macmillan.

Mays, K. (2015). VW Diesel Crisis: Timeline of Events. Cars.com. Retrieved November 16, 2015, from https://www.cars.com/articles/vw-diesel-crisis-timeline-of-events-1420681251993/.

McCoy, K. (2015). Goodyear Agrees to $16M Bribery Settlement. *USA Today*. Retrieved July 24, 2018, from https://eu.usatoday.com/story/money/2015/02/24/goodyear-fined-16-million/23935581/.

Merton, R. (1938). Social Structure and Anomie. *American Sociological Review, 3*(5), 672–682.

Mills, C. (2018). European Commission Fines Big-name Electronics Companies for Price Fixing. *BGR*. Retrieved July 26, 2018, from https://bgr.com/2018/07/24/european-commission-fine-price-fixing-asus-philips/.

Montgomery McCracken. (2015). Two Wrongs Don't Make It Right—False Record Keeping of Illegal Overboard Discharges Lead to Criminal Penalties. Retrieved July 27, 2018, from https://www.lexology.com/library/detail.aspx?g=e2e2316d-8ff2-4dbc-8c7b-27963081c4e1.

Nichols, T. (1990). Industrial Safety in Britain and the 1974 Health and Safety at Work Act: The Case of Manufacturing. *International Journal of the Sociology of Law, 18*(2), 317–342.

Paternoster, R., & Simpson, S. (1993). A Rational Choice Theory of Corporate Crime. In R. Clarke & M. Felson (Eds.), *Advances in Criminological Theory, Vol. 5. Routine Activity and Rational Choice* (pp. 37–58). Piscataway, NJ: Transaction Publishers.

Pearce, F. (1976). *Crimes of the Powerful: Marxism, Crime and Deviance*. London: Pluto Press.

Pearce, F., & Tombs, S. (1998). *Toxic Capitalism: Corporate Crime and the Chemical Industry*. Aldershot: Ashgate/Dartmouth.

Ryder, G. (2018). Editorial. In Lehtinen, S. (Ed.), *International Newsletter on Occupational Health and Safety*. Retrieved July 27, 2018, from https://www.ilo.org/wcmsp5/groups/public/%2D%2D-ed_protect/%2D%2D-protrav/%2D%2D-safework/documents/publication/wcms_616129.pdf.

Securities and Exchange Commission (SEC). (2015). SEC Charges Goodyear with FCPA Violations. *Press Release*. Retrieved July 24, 2018, from https://www.sec.gov/news/pressrelease/2015-38.html.

Segal, T. (2018). Enron Scandal: The Fall of a Wall Street Darling. *Investopedia*. Retrieved July 24, 2018, from https://www.investopedia.com/updates/enron-scandal-summary/.

Slapper, G., & Tombs, S. (1999). *Corporate Crime*. London: Pearson Longman Publishing.

Snider, L. (2000). The Sociology of Corporate Crime: An Obituary (or: Whose Knowledge Claims has Legs?). *Theoretical Criminology, 4*(2), 169–206.

Sutherland, E. (1939). *Principles of Criminology* (3rd ed.). Philadelphia: J. B. Lippincott.

Sutherland, E. (1983 [1949]). *White Collar Crime: The Uncut Version*. New Haven, US: Yale University Press.

Tombs, S. (2005). Corporate Crime. In C. Hale, K. Hayward, A. Wahidin, & E. Wincup (Eds.), *Criminology* (3rd ed., pp. 267–288). Oxford: Oxford University Press.

Tombs, S. (2014). Health and Safety Crime in Britain: The Great Disappearing Act. In P. Davies, P. Francis, & T. Wyatt (Eds.), *Invisible Crimes and Social Harms* (pp. 199–220). Basingstoke: Palgrave Macmillan.

Tombs, S., & Whyte, D. (2007). *Safety Crimes*. London: Routledge.

White, R. (2008). *Crimes Against Nature: Environmental Criminology and Ecological Justice*. Cullompton, UK: Willan Publishing.

White, R. (2009). Introduction: Environmental Crime and Eco-global Criminology. In R. White (Ed.), *Environmental Crime: A Reader*. Cullompton, UK: Willan Publishing.

White, R., & Heckenberg, D. (2014). *Green Criminology: An Introduction to the Study of Environmental Harm*. London: Routledge.

Wyatt, T. (2014). The Illegal Timber Trade in the Russian Far East: An Organized Crime? *Crime, Law and Social Change, 61*, 15–35.

Wyatt, T., Johnson, K., Hunter, L., George, R., & Gunter, R. (2017). Corruption and Wildlife: Three Case Studies Involving Asia. *Asian Journal of Criminology*. https://doi.org/10.1007/s11417-017-9255-8.

Organised Crime

10

Introduction

Corporate entities have, for the most part, been obscured from the criminological gaze, as seen in the previous chapter. Yet, other criminal groups have received a fair amount of criminological attention. This chapter begins with a theoretical and conceptual exploration about the nature and extent of one such group—organised crime. We analyse historical and contemporary stereotypes of organised crime groups and test the utility of criminological theorising that ignores the often invisible nature of organised criminality and victimisation as well as the power dynamics that contribute to its emergence and persistence. In particular, we explore the evolution of the power of organised crime groups in a globalised world and investigate the varying forms of victimisation for which they are responsible. This includes case studies of drug cartels challenging the rule of law in Mexico and organised crime groups in Italy destroying the environment and thus harming the local people. Foregrounded in the discussion of power is the use of violence and profit motives of these groups. We end the chapter by unpicking the difficulties for law enforcement and states in controlling organised crime especially when the group becomes powerful enough to challenge the state itself.

© The Author(s) 2021
P. Davies, T. Wyatt, *Crime and Power*,
https://doi.org/10.1007/978-3-030-57314-0_10

What Is Organised Crime and What Are Organised Crime Groups?

There is much debate about what crimes and crime groups constitute organised crime (which is used to mean the group as well as the activity) and what amounts to organisation. For instance, the Italian mafia and Chinese triads are typically thought of as organised crime (groups), whereas groups of pickpockets are not, or that human trafficking is seen as an organised crime, but cybercrime is not (Siegel 2008). In the different conceptualisations that exist, it seems to be agreed that for crime to be classified as 'organised crime', there are other elements beyond simply the fact that the commission of the crime has been organised (Schelling 1971). Many proposed definitions include that organised crime groups are motivated by profit. Cressey (1969: 72) in detailing the Cosa Nostra Model[1] of organised crime stated: 'The organised criminal, by definition, occupies a position in a social system, an "organisation" which has been rationally designed to maximise profits by performing illegal services and providing legally forbidden products demanded by the broader society within which he lives'. Fijnaut et al. (1996) define organised crime as a group whose primary focus is illegal profits, and they commit crimes systematically in order to meet this objective. This may be out of individual self-interest (Albini 1971). Others, too, have included the rational nature of organised crime as a key element, which makes it calculated or business-like (Carter, 1999; Fijnaut and Paoli 2004; Spapens 2010).

Although not specifically highlighted in the proposed definitions as an agreed element, we suggest power is another of the characteristics of these groups that make them 'organised crime'. The agreed-upon elements that we include within power are organised crime groups use of violence and corruption to maintain their profits as well as to hide their activities and avoid the criminal justice system (Hagan 1983; Fijnaut et al. 1996). The violence is multifaceted. It may be individual violence between rival organised crime group members or against criminal targets, but it may also be structural, such as committing a violent act in order to gain membership to the group. Rarely is the violence committed gratuitous. As a rational group, the violence, too, has a purpose, which may be to secure profits, or maintain power. In regard to corruption, bribery is a common tactic of organised crime groups to gain access to closed spaces or to have authorities turn a blind eye. The power that comes from having large amounts of money enables organised crime to use corrupt tactics as a means to further their criminal activities.

---

[1] Cosa Nostra are a Sicilian organised crime group sometimes just referred to as the Mafia.

In addition to violence and corruption as core aspects of organised crime (Maltz 1976; Abadinsky 1997), these groups also are sophisticated in terms of managing multiple criminal enterprises as well as existing over longer periods of time (Maltz 1976). Furthermore, Abadinsky (2007) suggests that organised crime groups are non-ideological with limited or exclusive membership. The different members have specialised roles within a monopolistic organisation, which has set rules. He also proposed that organised crime was structured hierarchically, but other evidence suggests this is not always the case. Rather, some organised crime groups have network structures or are formed of loosely structured relationships (Albini 1971). Van Duyne (1996) argues organised crime is less well organised than thought and quite diverse. He suggests it might be better to conceptualise as 'criminal enterprises' (Van Duyne 1996: 53).

In short (see Holmes 2016, among others, for a more detailed discussion), organised crime is a structured profit-orientated group that has existed over a long period of time by using violence and corruption to survive. The combination of these elements results in powerful groups that control aspects of some societies and can challenge the state and the rule of law. Organised crime groups and the efforts to combat them continue to be an emotive subject that typically garners strong reactions. It is clear though that overall, organised crime is characterised by having an adverse impact on society (Fijnaut et al. 1996) as we will explore in more detail in the case studies.

How Is Organised Crime Explained?

We saw in Chap. 9 that corporate crime arises from economic explanations of crime (rational choice, strain/relative deprivation) as well as cultural or organisational explanations (corporations as criminogenic and employees are indoctrinated into deviancy). Explanations for organised crime groups have similar economic and cultural aspects in addition to suggestions that organised crime arises out of a prohibitive socio-legal system. There is the argument that societies create their own organised crime problem by legally banning certain activities and services that are in demand. A common example used to support this theory is the prohibition of alcohol in the 1920s in the United States. Largely as a result of a Christian Puritan belief of what constituted appropriate devout behaviour, alcohol was made illegal, yet clearly it was still in demand. The argument goes that by making it illegal this led to the birth of organised crime groups to meet that demand through illegally making, transporting and selling alcohol. The organised crime groups' motivation was profit, which sits firmly within the definitions of organised crime outlined earlier. They also had the power to subvert the law because of being wealthy and having connections to establish the substantial infrastructure for 'boot-legged' alcohol across thousands of miles. Whereas prohibition like this is clearly part of the equation in terms of the creation of organised crime, other explanations are plausible as well.

The existence of organised crime groups could be due to the tensions outlined in strain theory. People, particularly men, who cannot earn a living in socially accepted ways may turn to membership in organised crime groups in order to achieve success. During the twentieth century in the United States, there were waves of migrants coming from Europe. Many of these groups, like Irish and Italian migrants, were subjected to widespread discrimination that meant they were denied a legitimate means to success. The theory is one of 'ethnic succession', whereby newly arrived migrants moved into communities with other immigrants. They formed organised crime groups as a means of achieving success or, as Bell (1953) referred to it, organised crime provided immigrants with social mobility. Membership was along ethnic lines in part due to the shared discrimination but also due to trust and familial ties. Language likely also played a part in group affiliation. In this context, there is also an element of rational choice. Organised crime affords those who commit it reward for relatively little risk.

Furthermore, it has been suggested that organised crime groups persist for cultural or socialisation reasons. Evidence shows that many organised crime group members live in neighbourhoods where they were constantly surrounded by criminals and criminal values. Crime then becomes normalised and accepted as well as expected. If we look again at the United States in the twentieth century, and to some European organised crime groups, the organised crime groups there seemingly had cultural or social elements. Some argue that the acceptance and structure of organised crime was brought with immigrants to their new homes, particularly from Sicily (Lyman and Potter 1998). This is called the 'alien conspiracy theory' whereby organised crime groups are direct branches of the 'Mafia' secret society (Lyman and Potter 1998). Whereas historically, organised crime groups were made up of members of single ethnicities, this is not always the case of current organised crime groups (i.e. youth gangs), but may still be a factor.

As mentioned, most members of organised crime groups, or at least those actively involved in the criminal activities, are men. Organised crime group membership may then link to masculinities theories around men committing crime and violent acts. Crime and violence are ways of proving manliness and displaying power (Connell 2002; Connell and Messerschmidt 2005; Hatty 2000). This means that organised crime group members are no different to other criminals. Yet others suggest that with the level of violence and criminality that it should not be discounted that men attracted to this outlaw lifestyle may well be predatory psychopaths and sociopaths (Hakkanen-Nyholm and Nyholm 2012).

The media and popular culture may play a role as well. Organised crime groups are valorised in Western popular culture, on some level making them seem glamorous with luxurious life styles. For instance, television series like HBO's 'The Sopranos' or Netflix's 'Narcos' depict powerful men committing crimes with impunity, living in mansions and indulging in expensive vices. Whilst, as we mentioned in Chap. 3, media is not directly or completely responsible for people's understanding or response to crime, the valorisation of organised crime is enduring in Western popular culture and likely has some effect on people's perceptions and interest in these powerful groups. There are then a range of psychological and sociological theories as to why organised crime exists. Regardless of how these groups come about, since their main purpose is to make money, this means there tends to be a clear set of crimes that they commit.

What Crimes Are Committed by Organised Groups?

Many of the crimes that are committed by organised crime groups revolve around illicit markets. This makes sense considering the profit motivations at the core of their existence. Illicit markets are diverse, but it is thought that the ability to smuggle one black market commodity likely lends itself to having the power, expertise and capacity to smuggle a variety of illegal goods. The illicit markets include, but are not limited to, weapons, nuclear materials, drugs, pharmaceuticals, people, body parts, stolen vehicles, wildlife, domestic pets and cultural objects and art. Another large area of illegal profits for organised crime groups come from illegal vice: gambling, prostitution and loan-sharking.

In the last approximately 20 years, crime in general, but organised crime groups possibly in particular, have benefited from new technologies. Since illicit markets and illegal vice industries can be either facilitated or exist online, this has meant a boon in these areas. Illegal products can be easily advertised online, and with the scale and nature of the internet, it is difficult for law enforcement and internet companies to tackle this element. Furthermore, technological advancements in communications means that organised crime groups have an improved capacity to organise and arrange activities. With instantaneous encrypted communications, criminals—organised and otherwise—are able to adapt to and evade law enforcement efforts to catch them.

Organised crime groups' links to the so-called upperworld (Passas 2002) means they also make illegal profits from labour racketeering, fraud and corporate and white-collar crime. These links also contribute to organised crime groups' power, since it gives them the capacity to affect civil society and the rule of law. Other moneymaking enterprises are counterfeiting, extortion and protection rackets, marine piracy, theft, robbery, hijacking and kidnapping. It is also believed that there are some links between organised crime and terrorism if money is to be made (Reitano et al. 2017). The following case studies highlight the quantities of money that organised crime groups make and how that connects to them at times being powerful enough to challenge the rule of law and endanger entire communities.

Case Study 1:   The Sinaloa Drug Cartel in Mexico

If we take real-life organised crime groups and map them on to proposed definitions of organised crime, all of the elements that scholars suggest make up organised crime are evident. In particular, this case study highlights the role of violence for the Sinaloa drug cartel in Mexico. What this case study also highlights is, that at times, organised crime colludes and collides with the state, which can exacerbate the violence. The Mexican government and the drug cartels there have a long history. 'Collusion between the Sinaloa Cartel and the Mexican government goes back a long way. The Mexican drug trade, after all, began in Sinaloa (where the Chinese had originally introduced the opium poppy in the nineteenth century) under the watch of the Institutional Revolutionary Party (PRI)' (Beith 2011: 790). The PRI ruled Mexico for over 70 years, so the link between the ruling government and the Sinaloa is long-standing. The Sinaloa Cartel is Mexico's largest organised crime group based on the volume of drugs the group moves. The Sinaloa Cartel, named after the Western Mexican state in which it originated and from which it still operates, runs drugs up and down Mexico's Pacific coast and along the nearby US border. The latter operates from Tijuana in the west in the state of Baja Norte bordering California to Ciudad Juárez and Nuevo Laredo in the east bordering Texas (Kellner and Pipitone 2010).

As the largest cartel, the Sinaloa are also responsible for many of the murders throughout their territory. From 'December 2006 to June 2010, 41,648 killings have been officially linked to drug trafficking organizations a dramatic increase from previous years (2001–2006) when only 8,901 killings were linked to organized crime' (Rios and Shirk 2011). As a comparison, the United Kingdom in the same three-and-half-year timeframe had approximately 2300 murders (ONS 2016). Valdés (2011) estimates that during that time the Sinaloa Cartel and Beltran Leyva Brothers Cartel together

(continued)

Case Study 1: (continued)

were responsible for 7813 of the casualties and a further 12,174 murders were committed between the Sinaloa Cartel and the Juárez Cartel (Valdés 2011). The murders are thought to happen because the cartels are battling for territory, which is linked to being able to control a highly competitive and profitable drug market (Rios 2013). Rios (2013) also proposes that the violence and murders are a response to government efforts to crack down on the drug trafficking and the violence. The surviving members of the cartels (some members have been killed by other cartels or law enforcement) battle for power both within individual cartels, but also between drug cartels after leaders have been killed.

Although there has always been some element of violence related to Mexican drug cartels, it is clear that the violence has increased in the last ten years. For instance in 2008, the Sinaloa Cartel was in an alliance with another cartel called *La Familia* (Rios 2013). During their collaboration, the related homicides in the states of Guerrero and Guanajuato, where they were trafficking drugs, were low. This ended when a Sinaloa lieutenant, Alfredo Beltrán Leyva, was arrested. Alfredo's brothers believed that the top leader of the Sinaloa criminal organisation, Joaquín Guzmán (alias 'El Chapo'), made a deal with the authorities to have El Chapo's son released from prison in exchange for the capture of Alfredo (Rios 2013). The Beltran Leyva brothers and El Chapo went to war, with various other lieutenants choosing sides. This supports Rios' proposal that enforcement (in this case the arrest of Alfredo) and battles over territory combine and result in an escalation of violence. In this instance, the retaliatory violence between the Sinaloa and the Beltran Leyva cartels continued until 2011 (Rios 2013). The violence also spread to other areas and other groups as the Sinaloa and El Chapo tried to maintain power.

After years of effort to arrest El Chapo, on 22 February 2014, Mexican authorities captured him (TendersInfo 2014). After 16 months in prison, El Chapo escaped through a mile-long tunnel that had been dug directly into his cell (Vulliamy 2015). Corruption of the prison guards at the most secure prison in the country was more than likely how the tunnel was able to be dug (Vulliamy 2015). El Chapo was caught again though in early 2016 at one of his many homes in the state of Sinaloa (Ahmed 2016). Not unlike Pablo Escobar was in Colombia, El Chapo is one of the richest men in the world and at once hated by the authorities and his rivals, but revered by the local people for his generosity (Ahmed 2016). The latter is partly why he can avoid arrest after his prison escapes.

In terms of the other elements of organised crime groups in our proposed definition, it seems clear that the main motivation of the Sinaloa Cartel is profit. The criminal activities the Sinaloa are involved in all revolve around making money or maintaining the means to make money—stealing and selling crude oil from the government pipeline, human trafficking, kidnapping, extortion, drug trafficking ($5–10 billion annually) and murders (mostly between cartels, but also of incorruptible politicians and police officials as well as journalists—115 in total were murdered between 2007 and 2012) (Bonner 2012). The Sinaloa's power extends to protecting and hiding their tremendous illegal profits. For instance, HSBC, Britain's biggest bank, admitted to laundering El Chapo's billions in drug profit (Vulliamy 2015).

The power to protect and hide, not only their illegal profits, but their activities in general, links to another element of organised crime—corruption. There is the well-known motto of the Mexican cartels: *plata o plombo*—silver or lead—meaning take the bribe/money or die by a lead bullet. The Sinaloa's and other cartels' ability to corrupt goes to the highest levels and demonstrates a level of power that is difficult to challenge. Their infiltration and/or control of portions of or individuals in the government extends to local municipalities and entire states (Bonner 2012). Their power to control these institutions largely stems from the fact that they have amassed billions of dollars, which has afforded them the ability to operate with impunity by using the illegal profit to penetrate and corrupt the government (Bonner 2012).

Although presidents in Mexico have tried to tackle the drug cartels in general, this has met with little success because of the corrupt law enforcement. In regard to the Sinaloa Cartel, there is suspicion as to why they have continued to grow while other cartels were noticeably reduced during President Calderon's offensive against all the cartels in the mid-2000s (Beith 2011). The accusation is that the state has colluded with the Sinaloa, particularly since their leaders are the only ones to evade the police and the military (Beith 2011). It was suspected that President Calderon's right-hand man—a former police chief—was corrupt (Beith 2011) and, in early 2008, the second highest-ranking officer of the Mexican federal police was arrested for accepting a bribe of several hundred thousand dollars from the Sinaloa Cartel. As mentioned, the prison guards in the most secure prison in the country were thought to have assisted El Chapo in his 2015 escape. This was not the first time. In 2001, El Chapo also escaped from prison. Furthermore, his living arrangements in the prison were luxurious and he was known to be running illegal enterprises from the prison (Bonner 2012). The latter was alleged to have been made possible by the president at the time, Vicente Fox for a $20 million payment (Bonner 2012). The Sinaloa's power is not confined to Mexico. They are operating on every continent and in 75 US cities according to intelligence (Beith 2011).

Because the Sinaloa have become so powerful, there is speculation that the collusion by the state is more a pragmatic tactic rather than corruption. The state may reason that it is better to deal with one super cartel that might be accommodating and agree to less violence than to fight loads of battles with smaller unpredictable groups (Vulliamy 2015). Regardless, the effects on the public are extensive. Whereas much of the violence perpetrated by the Sinaloa and rival cartels is against each other, the general public are caught up in the violence and forced to live in fear due to that violence. The threat of violence for the public also stems from the government response to the cartels. In this instance, the power of the organised crime groups is expressed, in part, by open violence that disrupts the normal lives of many Mexican citizens.

Pause for Thought

- What is the relationship between the state and the Sinaloa drug cartel?
- How does the Sinaloa Cartel fit definitions of organised crime (i.e. rationality, longevity)?

Case Study 2:   The Camorra in Italy
There is an area in southern Italy known as the 'Triangle of Death' (Euronews 2015; Day 2015). The triangular space between the cities of Acerra, Nola and Marigliano has cancer rates well above average levels (two to three times higher and much younger patients) due to the fact that this area is the largest illegal waste dumping area in Europe (Day 2015; Senior and Mazza 2004). Chemicals, heavy metals, solvents, plastics and discarded construction equipment are just some of the waste buried throughout the region over the last four decades (Birrell 2016; Day 2015; Euronews 2015). The area was partly discovered because some of the waste was leaking back up to the surface from the containers; some of the waste was flammable and all of it very hazardous (Euronews 2015). In addition, an Italian organised crime group member told the police of the dumping practices because he was concerned about the environmental damage (Birrell 2016). Also, the area became so full of waste; the organised crime groups began burning it because it was becoming too difficult to hide (Birrell 2016). There are substantial fears that this once prized agricultural land has become contaminated for the foreseeable future (Slaybaugh 2017).

(continued)

Case Study 2:   (continued)

The Italian organised crime group—the Camorra—is one of the main perpetrators of the long-running practice to dump illegal waste in out of the way places near Naples (Calderoni 2014; Euronews 2015; Slaybaugh 2017). The waste is coming from all over Europe as is evident in part by the French industrial waste found at one location (Day 2015) and the suspicion that German nuclear waste had been dumped in the region (Birrell 2016). The Camorra makes hundreds of millions of Euro from illegally disposing of the waste rather than properly handling it (Day 2015). Calderoni (2014) estimates that waste is only 1% of all organised crime groups' profits in Italy, which still means it is worth around €100 billion each year. The Camorra purposefully covers the buried waste with good soil to hide the dumping (Day 2015). They are actively involved in lobbying for the closure of incinerator sites, so that they can be hired to dispose of the waste (Day 2015).

There is a clear link in this case study to legal businesses and states. Experts are certain that some landowners are likely paid for the use of their land for the dumping. Furthermore, it is likely that the companies and governments wanting to dispose of the waste are aware when they hire Camorra-affiliated firms. These companies and governments, who hire the organised crime group, must then know what will happen to the waste (Day 2015). It has been documented that richer northern Italian companies have paid the Camorra to take away the waste rather than the company paying the higher fees for safe and proper disposal (Birrell 2016). Furthermore, not documenting the amount of waste that was produced was part of some companies' tax avoidance—they needed to dispose of some or all of the hazardous waste to hide the actual amount of production that was taking place (Birrell 2016). In regard to states, the Italian government appears to be complicit, with cover-ups by police, politicians and prosecutors coming to light (Birrell 2016). Doctors who have spoken out about the alarming cancer rates and the young age of those afflicted have been ignored or demoted (Birrell 2016).

Police investigating one of the sites planned on identifying the origin of the products and try to hold the companies whose waste it originally was accountable for the improper disposal (Day 2015). Yet, no one has been held accountable and it is thought no one will be (Birrell 2016). So, potentially thousands of people will continue to fall ill with cancer because they live in a polluted environment and a rich agricultural area that should be financially and nutritionally supporting the local communities is instead contaminated and on fire. We turn now to discuss what can be done to try to tackle organised crime.

Pause for Thought

- Considering the level of human victimisation in the 'Triangle of Death', why does the Italian government not do more to tackle this problem?
- What criminological theories explain the Camorra's disregard for the environment and human life?
- How does the Camorra fit a traditional definition of organised crime?

Control

Clearly, challenging this sort of power is a difficult task for governments, civil society and the international community. Key to combatting organised crime is to try to tackle the associated corruption, so that the groups' power over the state is reduced or stopped. In part, Mexico's approach to combatting corruption was successful. President Calderon abolished the federal police and started over (Bonner 2012). He did so by vetting new police graduates before they entered the police academy. The agency then had higher salaries than previously as well as a clear set of high ethical standards (Bonner 2012). Furthermore, the new police agency partnered with the military to stop the organised crime groups. Whereas corruption has not been completely eradicated (clearly, the prison service and local and state police are still an issue), this approach has been lauded as having worked to some degree.

In the case of the Camorra and the 'Triangle of Death' in Italy, civil society has been the driving force behind stopping the devastation the organised crime group has brought to the people and the environment. *Legambiente* (League for the Environment) is the largest environmental organisation in Italy and has been instrumental in documenting the environmental and human victimisation and lobbying to the authorities for change. Having a non-governmental organisation advocating against organised crime also addresses or circumvents corrupt governments.

In terms of the international community, there are two conventions that are integral to combatting organised crime. These are the United Nations Convention

Against Corruption (UNCAC)[2] and the United Nations Convention on Transnational
Organised Crime (UNTOC).[3] In both, signatory nations are given guidance on how
to criminalise corruption and transnational organised crime. In terms of UNCAC,
there are a set of standards, measures and rules nations can implement to strengthen their legal and regulatory structures against corruption (UNODC 2004). In the
UNTOC, organised crime is specifically defined and ways to combat it are outlined. The definition is as follows:

> [A] structured group of three or more persons, existing for a period of time and acting
> in concert with the aim of committing one or more serious crimes or offences estab-
> lished in accordance with this Convention, in order to obtain, directly or indirectly, a
> financial or other material benefit. (UNODC 2000: 5)

The profit motive is clear in this definition, though it lacks elements of violence
and corruption. Ways to combat organised crime groups are to make acts committed by them 'serious crimes', which means the crime warrants a maximum of four
years in prison. Furthermore, the UN suggests making organised crime groups'
offences 'predicate offence', which allows law enforcement and prosecutors to investigate the other crimes linked to the original offence, like money laundering and
financial crimes. 'Controlled deliveries', which allow the flow of illicit goods between places so that they can be followed, are particularly mentioned as a way to
disrupt and investigate organised crime groups. Asset seizure is also thought to be
one of the better methods of investigating these crimes. The UNTOC is also accompanied by three protocols, which directly address human trafficking, smuggling of migrants and illicit manufacturing and trafficking of firearms as these are
thought to be some of the most serious offences committed by organised crime
groups. Of course, the downside is that international conventions, like the UNCAC
and UNTOC, are voluntary, so even when members sign up there is no means to
force them to properly implement the convention or to comply with it. They do,
however, have symbolic meaning and provide useful guidance for those nations
serious about tackling corruption and organised crime.

---

[2] https://www.unodc.org/unodc/en/treaties/CAC/.

[3] https://www.unodc.org/unodc/en/organized-crime/intro/UNTOC.html.

Power in Plain Sight

Organised crime groups (may be more than the other groups in the second part of this book) often display their power openly by breaking the law in visible ways. Certainly, in Mexico and Italy, the Sinaloa and the Camorra blatantly engage in violence and burning of waste. Both are obviously illegal, but because of the power of organised crime groups like these, they seem to have little or no fear of repercussions. Some organised crime activities are hidden—many of the illegal acts are associated with smuggling of illicit commodities—but this might be to hide the profits and not be bothered by the police, rather than the need to hide their actions for fear of punishment. Part of this impunity is tied to organised crime groups use of corruption and their ability to corrupt politicians and law enforcement at every level of society. With those who hold people to account in the pocket of organised crime groups, it comes as no surprise that the organised crime groups are able to act as they wish.

That is not to say that everything organised crime does is out in the open. Gambling and prostitution, which in most places are illegal, are often hidden. Power from the use or threat of violence and from having wealth means that even when illegal vices are discovered that they are swept under the rug or there is little punishment. Money obtained illegally cannot be openly used, so money laundering—even with the cooperation of the biggest legitimate banks in the world—is essential to organised crime. Intertwined within the power of organised crime groups is the fact that the groups are incredibly masculine in terms of who is involved as well as in relation to the use and threat of violence. This reiterates that power is a complex phenomenon, which is expressed at the individual level as we have seen in Part I of the book, but that this interacts with group power as we see here in the case of organised crime groups.

Summary

It should be noted that the case studies detailed here could be considered at the extremes of organised crime. There are many groups around the world that are not as powerful or visible as the Sinaloa Cartel or the Camorra. They are though powerful in their respective contexts, particularly in regard to avoiding the criminal justice system. However, the two case studies chosen are important reminders of what powerful groups are capable of. They are able to challenge the rule of law because they have usurped the state's monopoly on violence (see Chap. 11 for a more complete discussion) and because they are not always able to be held to account for the harm they cause and the crimes they commit. The impact of thwarting the rule of law is significant. People of these municipalities likely do not trust their government, thus eroding civil society. Essential funds for social services may be directed elsewhere either because of efforts to combat organised crime groups or because organised crime groups are pulling the strings behind the scenes to have money funnelled in particular directions that benefit them. People are, of course, the direct victims of organised crime. They can be caught in the crossfire of fighting between organised crime groups or of fighting between organised crime and law enforcement. In the case of Italy, people may suffer directly from illegal actions like waste dumping that damages people's health and that of their environment.

Whereas this can create impossible situations for states, which may have little willpower or capacity to tackle organised crime groups, it is essential that such harmful authoritarian entities are reduced. The international conventions of the last 20 or so years highlight that the international community and most states recognise that organised crime is a problem. It is encouraging that suggestions and efforts to tackle organised crime groups are reaching that level of importance. It seems now that steps need to be taken for some sort of organisation or support mechanism to be created that can assist states lacking the power to do so, but which want to take on organised crime in their country. Decreasing the power of organised crime groups is key for people in certain parts of the world to be able to live securely relying on the states, which they elected to support them and govern society peacefully.

Go Further

- How are organised crime groups like corporations?
- Why does popular culture valorise organised crime groups? And why are entertainment shows about such groups popular?

References

Abadinsky, H. (1997). *Organised Crime* (4th ed.). Chicago: Nelson-Hall.
Abadinsky, H. (2007). *Organised Crime* (8th ed.). Belmont, CA: Thomson/Wadsworth.
Ahmed, A. (2016). How El Chapo was Finally Captured, Again. *The New York Times*. Retrieved July 4, 2018, from https://www.nytimes.com/2016/01/17/world/americas/mexico-el-chapo-sinaloa-sean-penn.html.

Albini, J. (1971). *The American Mafia: Genesis of a Legend.* New York: Appleton-Century-Crofts.

Beith, M. (2011). A Broken Mexico: Allegations of Collusion between the Sinaloa Cartel and Mexican Political Parties. *Small Wars & Insurgencies, 22*(5), 787–806.

Bell, D. (1953). Crime as an American Way of Life. *The Antioch Review, 13*(2), 131–154.

Birrell, I. (2016). Mafia, Toxic Waste and a Deadly Cover Up in an Italian Paradise: 'They've Poisoned Our Land and Stolen Our Children'. *The Telegraph.* Retrieved July 4, 2018, from https://www.telegraph.co.uk/news/0/mafia-toxic-waste-and-a-deadly-cover-up-in-an-italian-paradise-t/.

Bonner, R. (2012). The Cartel Crackdown: Winning the Drug War and Rebuilding Mexico in the Process. *Foreign Affairs, 91,* 12–17.

Calderoni, F. (2014). Mythical Numbers and the Proceeds of Organised Crime: Estimating Mafia Proceeds in Italy. *Global Crime, 15*(1–2), 138–163.

Carter, T. (1999). Ascent of the Corporate Model in Environmental-organized Crime. *Crime, Law and Social Change, 31*(1), 1–30.

Connell, R. (2002). On Hegemonic Masculinity and Violence: Response to Jefferson and Hall. *Theoretical Criminology, 6*(1), 89–99.

Connell, R., & Messerschmidt, J. (2005). Hegemonic Masculinity: Rethinking the Concept. *Gender and Society, 19,* 829–859.

Cressey, D. (1969). *Theft of the Nation: The Structure and Operations of Organized Crime in America.* New York: Harper and Row.

Day, M. (2015). Europe's Largest Illegal Toxic Dumping Site Discovered in Southern Italy. *The Independent.* Retrieved July 4, 2018, from https://www.independent.co.uk/life-style/health-and-families/health-news/europes-largest-illegal-toxic-dumping-site-discovered-in-southern-italy-an-area-with-cancer-rates-80-10327157.html.

Euronews. (2015). Italy Discovers Biggest Waste Dump in Europe. *Euronews.* Retrieved July 4, 2018, from http://www.euronews.com/2015/06/16/italy-discovers-biggest-illegal-waste-dump-in-europe.

Fijnaut, C., Bovenkerk, F., Bruinsma, G., & Bunt, H. van de. (1996). *Survey Investigation Methods. Final report Organized Crime in the Netherlands.* The Hague.

Fijnaut, C., & Paoli, L. (2004). *Organised Crime in Europe: Concepts, Patterns, and Control Policies in the European Union and Beyond.* Dordrecht: Springer.

Hagan, F. (1983). The Organized Crime Continuum: A Further Specification of a New Conceptual Model. *Criminal Justice Review, 8,* 52–57.

Hakkanen-Nyholm, H., & Nyholm, J. (2012). Psychopathy in Economical Crime, Organized Crime, and War Crime. In H. Hakkanen-Nyholm & J. Nyholm (Eds.), *Psychopathy and the Law: A Practitioner's Guide* (pp. 177–199). London: Wiley-Blackwell.

Hatty, S. (2000). *Masculinities, Violence and Culture* (Sage Series on Violence Against Women). London: Sage.

Holmes, L. (2016). *Advanced Introduction to Organised Crime.* London: Edward Elgar.

Kellner, T., & Pipitone, F. (2010). Inside Mexico's Drug War. *World Policy Journal.* Spring, 29–37.

Lyman, M., & Potter, G. (1998). Organized Crime and the Drug Trade. In *Drugs and Society: Causes, Concepts and Control* (pp. 213–227). Cincinnati, OH: Anderson Publishing.

Maltz, M. (1976). On Defining "Organized Grime": The Development of a Definition and a Typology. *Crime & Delinquency, 22*(3), 338–346.

Office of National Statistics (ONS). (2016). Homicide. Retrieved July 13, 2018, from https://www.ons.gov.uk/peoplepopulationandcommunity/crimeandjustice/compendium/focusonviolentcrimeandsexualoffences/yearendingmarch2015/chapter-2homicide.

Passas, N. (2002). Cross-border Crime and the Interface between Legal and Illegal Actors. In P. C. van Duyne, K. von Lampe, & N. Passas (Eds.), *Upperworld and Underworld in Cross-border Crime* (pp. 11–42). Nijmegen: Wolf Legal Publishers.

Reitano, T., Clarke, C., & Adal, L. (2017). *Examining the Nexus Between Organised Crime and Terrorism and Its Implications for EU Programming.* CT Morse Counter-Terrorism Monitoring, Reporting and Support Mechanism.

Rios, V. (2013). Why did Mexico become So Violent? A Self-reinforcing Violent Equilibrium Caused by Competition and Enforcement. *Trends in Organized Crime, 16*(2), 138–155.

Rios, V., & Shirk, D. (2011). Drug Violence in Mexico Data and Analysis through 2010. Special Report for TBI, USD, San Diego.

Schelling, T. (1971). What is the Business of Organized Crime? *Journal of Public Law, 20,* 71–84.

Senior, K., & Mazza, A. (2004). Italian "Triangle of Death" Linked to Waste Crisis. *Lancet Oncology, 5*(9), 525–527.

Siegel, D. (2008). Diamonds and Organized Crime: The Case of Antwerp. In D. Siegel & H. Nelen (Eds.), *Organized Crime. Culture, Markets and Policies.* New York: Springer.

Slaybaugh, J. (2017). Garbage Day: Will Italy Finally Take Out its Trash in the Land of Fires? *Washington International Law Journal, 26*(1), 179–208.

Spapens, T. (2010). Macro Networks, Collectives, and Business Processes: An Integrated Approach to Organized Crime. *European Journal of Crime, Criminal Law and Criminal Justice, 18,* 185–215.

TendersInfo News. (2014, February) United States: Treasury Sanctions Key Sinaloa Cartel Network.

United Nations Office on Drugs and Crime (UNODC). (2000). United Nations Convention Against Transnational Organized Crime and the Protocols Thereto. Retrieved July 15, 2018, from https://www.unodc.org/documents/treaties/UNTOC/Publications/TOC%20Convention/TOCebook-e.pdf.

United Nations Office on Drugs and Crime (UNODC). (2004). United Nations Convention Against Corruption. Retrieved July 15, 2018, from https://www.unodc.org/documents/treaties/UNCAC/Publications/Convention/08-50026_E.pdf.

Valdés, G. (2011). Untitled Presentation. In *Considering New Strategies for Confronting Organized Crime in Mexico.* Conference at the Woodrow Wilson for International Scholars, Washington, DC.

Van Duyne, P. (1996). Organized Crime, Corruption, and Power. *Crime, Law and Social Change, 26*(3), 201–238.

Vulliamy, E. (2015). Joaquín 'El Chapo' Guzmán: The Truth about the Jailbreak of the Millennium. *The Guardian.* Retrieved July 4, 2018, from https://www.theguardian.com/world/2015/jul/13/joachin-el-chapo-guzman-jailbreak-mexican-drug-lord-escape-prison.

The State

11

Introduction

States are responsible for a range of crimes and victimisations. In this chapter, first, we discuss concepts such as what is a state and conceptualisations of universal human rights; the latter uncovers why and how states can be criminogenic. Drawing on Green and Ward's (2004) types of state crimes, this chapter explores, via case study examples, various dimensions of state power. It considers the power expressed in state negligence (particularly in response to natural disasters and public health crises), police crime, criminal collusion with corporations and organised crime, corruption, state terror, war crimes, torture and genocide/ecocide. The two case studies delve into more detail in particular about state terror by investigating Russia's 2013 invasion of Crimea in Ukraine and genocide by exploring the Rohingya people in Myanmar. We detail who the victims of these crimes are and how the international community can respond to and provide redress for such harm. This includes a discussion of the implications for social justice, future prevention and the role of supranational bodies, such as the United Nations, in intervening and alleviating suffering.

© The Author(s) 2021
P. Davies, T. Wyatt, *Crime and Power*,
https://doi.org/10.1007/978-3-030-57314-0_11

What Is a State?

Before it is possible to analyse the various criminal actions of states, it is important to discuss what a state actually comprises. At the core of what defines and makes states is a particular type of power over the citizens that live there. As Green and Ward (2004: 185) propose, states are 'Institutions which exert a monopoly (or near-monopoly) of coercive force and the extraction of revenue in some substantial tract of territory'. Their definition has a twofold element to power that consists of (1) coercive or physical force[1] and (2) taxation. First, a state's use of physical force against citizens and/or people in other countries is allowed within certain situations. These 'states of exception' are when physical force that is usually deemed excessive is utilised (Green and Ward 2009)—for instance, detaining people against their will or killing people. At these moments (i.e. when punishing people (a citizen) or in war (citizens of other countries)), the normal rules limiting state power are suspended or do not apply. Second, states can also force citizens and corporations to pay taxes—a power, again, that is exceptional and unusual and not given to any other entity. It is important to note that legitimacy of the state is critical.

Both elements of power outlined above clearly manifest in different ways depending on the state, on the different state institutions and the citizenry's ability to influence the overall state's actions. There are four types of states proposed—transition capitalist, advanced capitalist, state-capitalist and predatory (Green and Ward 2004). Transition capitalist states (e.g. Bosnia and Herzegovina and former countries of the Soviet Union) or advanced capitalist states (e.g. Norway, the United States and the United Kingdom) will engage with their populations much differently than the other kinds of states. State-capitalist states (e.g. China) or predatory states (e.g. Syria) control the media and the information that is given to the population rather than the freedom of press and speech that is likely found in transition and advanced capitalist states. In these different states, force is expressed at various levels and with various levels of (dis)approval from the public. The same can be said for these states' collection of tax revenue, where in the case of Norway, for example, there are high taxes relative to other states because it is a cultural norm there that tax revenue from the whole population will support everyone in society.

This brings us to the notion of legitimacy in regard to states. As we introduced in Chap. 2, legitimacy, according to Weber (1918), is the acceptance of authority as well as the need to obey that authority. For Beetham (1991: 11), a 'power relations-

---

[1] Weber (1965) is one of the early proponents that state sovereignty, essentially its authority and autonomy, stems from its monopoly on the legitimate use of force.

hip is not legitimate because people believe in its legitimacy, but because it can be justified in terms of their [the public's] beliefs'. As mentioned, in Norway the welfare state is an agreed-upon principle. Green and Ward (2004), like Beetham, suggest that the rules of the state must be justified in shared beliefs for the state to be legitimate. The state then must uphold these rules as well as act within these rules. When the state violates the rules it has established, then the state is seen as illegitimate. A layer of complexity is added in that it may be a part of the state and not the entire state that is seen as illegitimate and/or criminal. The state is after all a collection of institutions and these may or may not share the same values and goals (Jessup 1982). For instance, as we will discuss more below, it could be that it is only the police or only the tax agency who are deviant. Legitimacy then may also depend on other institutions or apparatus of the state's response to the deviance and criminality of other parts of the state.

The process of developing shared beliefs by a population is called hegemony (Gramsci 1971), where beliefs are instilled in the population at large and then appear as consensus (Green and Ward 2004). The process of hegemony is a complex one that is not completely reliant on the state. Civil society and the private sphere are integral to establishing the system of shared of beliefs. Pressure groups, voluntary/charitable organisations, religious organisations, the media and academic institutions as well as family and friends all contribute to the values that make up a society. If civil society is independent, it can label the state as deviant when a state violates the established rules. If there is no civil society or it is repressed, deviance and crime by the state can be difficult to expose and/or challenge. Hegemony then, whether a population shares belief in the legitimacy of the state or trust in the state, may well contribute to a state being repressive and/or criminal.

State Crime

Exposing and challenging state deviance is crucial, as states are the perpetrators of some of the most serious violent crimes (Green and Ward 2004). As analysed in this section, the violence may come in the form of state power, but may also be interpersonal violence committed by individuals working for the state. State power is able to deny people access to fundamental needs, such as freedom from physical restraint and pain, food, clothing and shelter, education and opportunities to participate in cultural life and political processes (Doyal and Gough 1991). It can also be a source of widespread suffering and death. Individual acts of aggression by state agents can also be a source of suffering and death. In our discussion below, we distinguish the types of state crime into two categories. 1. Those crimes perpetrated by individuals, who are a part of the state apparatus. 2. Those crimes perpetrated through organisational deviance. For example, torture of prisoners during war may be violent acts committed by individual people, who are a part of the state, or such violence may take place as part of a systematic approach developed by the state to demoralise the enemy. States, either as an organisation and/or through an individual person, have and are guilty of negligence (particularly in response to natural disasters and public health crises), police crime, criminal collusion with corporations and organised crime, corruption, state terror, war crimes, torture and genocide/ecocide (adapted from Green and Ward 2004, who did not include public health crises or ecocide). Yet as Green and Ward (2004: 1) rightly point out, 'If states define what is criminal, a state can only be criminal on those rare occasions when it denounces itself for breaking its own laws'. As mentioned above, this could mean that one part of the state holds another part accountable for violating the law. In instances where this does not happen or where numerous institutions of the state are deviant, there are international norms of conduct that can be called upon, particularly the United Nations Universal Declaration of Human Rights (see United Nations 2015), to demonstrate and prove the criminality.

Green and Ward (2004) advocate that adopting a human rights-based approach to defining state crime is useful because it does not rely on the state's definition of what is criminal nor does it rely on ambiguous or unsatisfactory laws. Furthermore, a human rights-based approach to state crime means that the standards on which a state's actions are judged are almost universally accepted. This approach also means that the focus is on the health and wellbeing of a state's citizens rather than on violations of international economic regulations related to tariffs and so forth. Human rights are about more though than just physical wellbeing. 'Human beings have certain needs that are fundamental in the sense that without them they cannot be effective purposive agents, able to pursue their chosen goals and participate in society' (Green and Ward 2004: 7). So harder to define rights, like dignity, are integral to a human rights-based approach to addressing state crime. Of particular importance is that human rights cover *everyone*. As we will see in more detail below, particularly in Case Study 2 in Myanmar, all societies have norms, which limit killing and other forms of violence, but these norms do not always apply to everyone. There are times when certain groups are excluded from the universe of obligation (Fein 1990), meaning violence against these groups is permitted and even routinised. Again, the strength of a human rights-based approach to such criminality is that no person, regardless of class, race, gender and so forth, should be subjected to violations of their human rights. However, states commit such crimes repeatedly.

Types of State Crimes

We propose, drawing largely on Green and Ward's (2004) categorisations, that there are eight types of state crimes. All of them can be committed at the instituti-onal/organisational level, but police crime, collusion, corruption, war crime and torture can also be committed by individual agents of the state.

Negligence

Negligence by the state may not be an obvious crime. There are, however, nume-rous contemporary examples where states have failed to respond, which have led to citizens suffering from lack of basic care. Many of the examples of neglect come from the failure to respond adequately or in a timely manner to natural disasters, but this is also the case with response to accidents and public health crises. In the case of natural disasters, the United States' slow and superficial response to Hurricane Katrina and Hurricane Maria provide ample proof of a state's negligence being a crime. In August 2005, Hurricane Katrina resulted in around 1800 deaths immediately in New Orleans, though the figure is uncertain (Walters 2015), and more than a million people were displaced. Tens of thousands of them lived in the Houston Superdome (an American football stadium) in unhygienic and unsafe con-ditions (Walters 2015). Others, who had no way to escape or chose not to leave New Orleans, were left largely unassisted in a devastated city (Walters 2015). Much of the criticism around the US government's slow and/or neglectful response focused on the apparent racism of the George W. Bush Administration, which ap-peared unprepared and, at times, unwilling to help the black residents, which are a majority of the population (Walters 2015). Likewise, and more damaging, in September 2017, Hurricane Maria ravaged the island of Puerto Rico. Official re-ports say 64 people died, but other research indicates it is likely over 4600 (Mercy Corps 2018). For months afterwards, many people had no electricity and very limi-ted clean water, food, medicine and fuel (Mercy Corps 2018). There are still people today with no electricity and tens of thousands of people displaced (Mercy Corps 2018). The Trump Administration faced similar criticism that the response was slow due to racism (Wolffe 2018). Such examples suggest, the United States has failed and continues to fail to provide the basic necessities of life for it its citizens. They have a responsibility to respond and are culpable in the illnesses and deaths that are a result of the state's failure to respond.

Accidents and public health crises have been met with the same response, which some argue is criminal. After the nuclear disaster at Chernobyl on 26 April 1986, in Ukraine, the Soviet government did not immediately tell citizens of the danger or evacuate people until later. The nuclear explosion happened after midnight on that morning (Chernobyl Gallery n.d.). Pripyat, the town where the reactor was, was not evacuated until the afternoon of 27 April, even though officials knew lethal doses of radiation had been released more than 36 hours earlier (Chernobyl Gallery n.d.). Those who were evacuated were told to only bring two to three days' worth of things as they would be coming back—this was clearly never going to be possible considering the radiation. Whilst difficult to prove that this has led directly to illness and/or death of people, the fact remains that many were being exposed to high levels of nuclear radiation, which had the state informed them, and the global community, of the accident, some citizens further from the reactor could have avoided the radiation. In the case of Chernobyl, once people were told of the nuclear meltdown, they had no say as to where they were relocated (Chernobyl Gallery n.d.). This, too, is a crime by the state as it violates people's right to freedom of movement. More than 30 years later, the effects of this disaster and the response to it are still being felt.

In terms of public health crises, at the time of writing, the world is in the six month of a global pandemic caused by the coronavirus—a zoonotic disease that passed from an as yet unidentified species of wildlife to a human in a market in Wuhan, China, in December 2019. In the coming months, inquiries are likely to be had in regard to the Chinese government's possibly slow sharing of information, which might mean that the virus spread more than would have happened otherwise. But the more likely inquiries to take place are in countries, like the United Kingdom, where the state did not provide medical personnel with adequate personal protective equipment, which endangered their lives resulting in hundreds of deaths of National Health Service workers (Marsh 2020).

Police Crime

There is a distinct body of literature emerging from a critical tradition in criminology devoted to police deviancy (see Shearing 1981; Punch 1985; Stinson 2015, among many others). Shearing (1981) and Punch (1985) both found that the rationale behind police deviancy is often the means justify the ends. In other words, since the police are pursuing justice, they can bend and/or break the rules to do so. As part of this rationale, institutional and legal instruments construct a system that hides police deviance (Shearing 1981). Between police deviancy achieving the desired goal and the institutional denial or hiding of the deviancy, it becomes apparent why police officers are rarely held accountable when their criminality is exposed (Punch 1985). Stinson (2015) suggests the research predominantly revolves around misconduct, individual and systemic corruption and crime committed by individual officers and police organisations.

Whereas misconduct may include corrupt and criminal actions, we separate them here to illustrate the range of severity of police deviance. In terms of misconduct, this includes officers being dishonest and not acting with integrity. Corruption can be 'minor' abuses of authority, such as leaking confidential information, cutting through bureaucratic procedures and accepting small gifts and discounts (Punch 1985). On the more serious side of corruption, police officers have been found to give false testimony, sell drugs, intimidate witnesses and extort money (Punch 1985). As we saw in Chap. 5 about power and race, recently, individual police officers have also been guilty of murdering innocent citizens. Police have also committed crimes and abused their power by unlawfully arresting people and excessively using force. As mentioned above, this is a case where an individual is committing a state crime since they are an agent of the state. Police crime also happens at the organisational or institutional level.

There is a case to be made that criminal justice systems in their entirety are guilty of state crimes when they systematically engage in and perpetuate human rights violations. The highly discriminatory incarceration rates of black people in the United States is one example (see Chap. 5). The death penalty is another practice that some argue is a state crime because the state is meant to protect its citizens and not harm them. In addition, the death penalty can be viewed as criminal due to its application. For instance, if we look again at the United States, it is well documented that the death penalty is disproportionately given to black and/or poor people (Lee et al. 2015; Gould and Leon 2017). There are too many extra-legal factors (i.e. politics, location, demographics) influencing the process for it to be administered fairly. Of particular concern are the known cases of miscarriages of justice, where it has been proven later that the person executed was innocent. For instance, Carlos De Luna was executed in Texas in 1989 for the stabbing death of Wanda Lopez (Liebman et al. 2014). De Luna maintained through his trial and to the moments before his execution that he was innocent and that Carlos Hernandez killed Wanda (Liebman et al. 2014). De Luna was found guilty in spite of police mistakes, conflicting witness statements and missing information (Liebman et al. 2014). It was common knowledge throughout the neighbourhood that Hernandez was the murderer (Liebman et al. 2014). In this instance, we see an entire system at fault and an innocent person murdered by the state.

Collusion

In Chap. 9, we saw how states collude with corporations to break laws to maintain power and to try to secure profit. Similarly, in Chap. 10, we saw how states also collude with organised crime groups for the same reasons. As with police crime, this may be individual state actors who are colluding with corporations or organised crime networks. It can also be more systemic, where whole agencies or the entirety of the state collude. For instance, though not widely discussed, collusion between agencies of the state and corporations are evident in both the recent Volkswagen emissions scandal and the 2008 financial crisis. In terms of Volkswagen, while it was revealed that they (and other automobile companies) had used software to cheat emissions testing, what is discussed less often is the continual and high amount of subsidies and tax breaks that have been in given in the United Kingdom and elsewhere to diesel car manufacturers (Tombs 2015). Furthermore, France, Germany and the UK governments behind the scenes have lobbied the European Union to maintain loopholes in the emissions testing (Tombs 2015). So, while Volkswagen appears to be trying to bypass the legal system, that system is being supported and manipulated by states in somewhat similar ways.

The financial industry suffers from collusion as well. In 2008, numerous banks collapsed after the economy collapsed. The collapse happened largely because of price fixing and currency manipulation that these same banks had been involved in (Reich 2015). At the time, the term 'too-big-to-fail' was used when the banks were bailed out by governments because their complete collapse would be too detrimental to the economy and society. In the United States, in 1990, the five largest banks held just 10% of the United States' banking assets; just before the crash in 2008, this amount had risen to around 25% (Reich 2015). In 2015, the amount held by the largest five banks is 44%. Even though it seems after the 2008 collapse that this is exactly what should not be happening (what if the economy crashes again and the collapsing banks have twice as many assets as they did last time), the US government has done nothing to break up these monopolies and protect consumers and the economy (Reich 2015). Critical criminological and social harm analysis suggests that the reason no action is taken is because these corporations finance the campaigns of politicians. Again, we see individual-level deviancy (politicians not voting against their personal interests), but on such a large scale that it becomes institutional.

Corruption

We have seen some examples of corruption already when discussing police crime and collusion. And as we have already seen, corruption is not just a feature of crimes by the state or of officials of the state. Organised crime groups, as we saw in Chap. 10, use corruption as part of their toolkit to commit crimes, and corporations are the target and source of corruption too (Chap. 9). It is important to remember that there is no agreed-upon definition of corruption (Holmes 2006). Corruption by public officials though is typically what is thought of as corruption (though as we discussed in Chap. 9, we propose anyone in a position of power is at risk of becoming corrupt, including in the private and third sectors (Wyatt et al. 2017)). Corruption by the state can be of local authorities around tender processes and issuance of licences and permits. It may also be public sector corruption, where tax inspectors, for instance, abuse their position. Other corruption by the state may be political corruption. This has been seen in the United Kingdom around 2017 during the scandal with the spending of taxpayer money by members of Parliament. Their lavish hospitality (expensive trips, hotels, accommodation and food) is one form. Other forms are taking bribes, granting favours, giving appointed positions and buying influence. Lobbying of politicians where gifts are given and favours granted, particularly in the United States, is a questionable practice that we would argue sits on a very blurry line of potentially corrupt behaviour.

Whilst corruption is a slippery term and there is no widely accepted definition, empirical research about people's perceptions of corruption indicate even where corruption is normalised, there is still a sense by the public that it is wrong (Holmes 2006). Holmes (2006) found this to be the case in many of the former states of the Soviet Union. Even though bribery is widespread and common, citizens of these former communist countries still perceive the bribery to be a corrupt practice (Holmes 2006). Doig (1996: 36) defines bribery as the

> transaction of soliciting or receiving inducements or rewards to local government politicians (but not MPs) and all public officials for decisions or actions—or, conversely, the failure to act or to make a decision—that favours the donor or their organisation.

Another common form of corruption is 'patronage' or 'clientelism', where the corrupt person's family, friends or network are benefiting from the corrupt acts (Klitgaard 1988). Whereas corruption may seem less severe compared to police violence or state terror, which we talk about next, it can fundamentally impede the rule of law and justice in a whole society leading to suffering and harm.

State Terror

Green and Ward (2004) propose that the fifth category of state crime—state terror—has two elements. First, civilians are attacked and injured or killed by agents of the state. The motivation for this is to intimidate the general population through a brutal show of force into obeying the state. In addition, the state may assassinate or have extrajudicial executions carried out in order to eliminate specific opponents or the opposition. This is what is presumed to have happened in Pakistan with the assassination of opposition candidate, former Prime Minister Benazir Bhutto in Pakistan in 2007 (Jones 2017). Whilst the 15-year-old suicide bomber that shot

Bhutto and then detonated the explosives on his body to kill her and those near her was at the time linked to the Pakistani Taliban, former Head of State General Pervez Musharraf has stated he believes that officials in the government have links to the Taliban and this played a role in Bhutto's death (Jones 2017). She was running again for Prime Minister, so it is suspected that the ruling party wanted to eliminate the opposition.

The targets of the assassinations and executions may not only be politicians. They may be carried out against journalists and activists who speak out against the current state. There are numerous examples of this from Russia, where journalists opposing Putin or regional government officials have been found dead (Committee to Protect Journalists No Date). According to the Committee to Protect Journalists (No Date), 38 Russian journalists have been murdered since 1992. These are murders where the motives have been confirmed, which means there may be more murders included in this category if those suspected, but not proven, were to be included. All of the 38 murdered journalists spoke out against problems in the regions they covered—human rights violations in Chechnya, education reform in Dagestan and so forth. Another example is likely murder of journalist, Jamal Khashoggi. Khashoggi, a Saudi journalist, who had left for the United States, where he criticised the new regime in Saudi Arabia, died in the Saudi Embassy in Istanbul (BBC 2019). He had gone there to pick up papers of his divorce but is suspected to have been killed at the orders of the Saudi royal family (BBC 2019). Such a level of violence against people who are trying to advocate for improvements and change seems clearly to be a form of state terror in trying to silence this voice of opposition to the status quo.

Case Study 1:   Crisis in Ukraine and Russia's Invasion (2013–14)
The Russian Federation and Ukraine have a long shared history rife with complications. The eastern portion of Ukraine was part of the Soviet Union (1917–89), but the western portion was not included in the Soviet Union until after World War II (1945). Western Ukraine, having some areas part of the Hapsburg Empire and some areas part of Romania, has always had a tendency to associate with the West and Europe. In 1991, when Ukraine became an independent country, the tensions between the western part of the country, which looks towards Europe and predominantly speaks Ukrainian, and the eastern part of the country, which looks towards Russia and predominantly speaks Russian, were already evident. This is a brief oversimplifi-

(continued)

Case Study 1:   (continued)

cation of a complex situation, but with that backdrop, in 2013 and 2014, these tensions came to a breaking point through a series of events that started with a crisis in Ukraine.

Since Ukraine's independence in the early 1990s, there have been various discussions about the possibility of joining the European Union or at least having closer ties. Under Ukrainian President Viktor Yanukovych, these discussions had been on and off again. At the same time, there were similar discussions taking place with Russia about closer ties to Russia (Trenin 2014). President Vladimir Putin of Russia had been for years developing his Eurasian integration policy (Trenin 2014). In November 2013, Yanukovych ended discussions about EU membership and instead accepted a USD 15 billion bailout from Moscow (Reuters 2014; Trenin 2014). This set off three months of street protests from supporters of EU membership, including the formation of a tent city, mainly in the Ukrainian capital of Kyiv (Trenin 2014), but also in other locations in Ukraine (Reuters 2014). On 30 November 2013, it was estimated that 350,000 people were protesting in Kyiv's central square—Maidan. Yanukovych met with Putin for strategic talks on 6 December 2013, and two days later there were 800,000 people estimated to be involved in the Maidan street protests (Reuters 2014). At this point, Yanukovych speaks to the leaders of the protest, but no progress towards a solution is made. The protest, although quieter and smaller, continues throughout New Year's Day and Christmas.

On 15 January 2014, the Supreme Court of Ukraine banned street protests and President Yanukovych nearly immediately signed the ban into law (Reuters 2014). The protesters were not intimidated and continued with the tent city and street protests; this led to an escalation of conflict between the protesters and the police, who killed three protesters on 22 January 2014. The anti-protest laws were overturned by Parliament in an attempt to restore order (Reuters 2014). Yanukovych agreed to give amnesty to arrested street protesters. It was revealed that Moscow's next aid payment was dependent on repayment of a gas bill that Ukraine owed to Russia (Reuters 2014). Protests continued and the violence between the protesters and the police continued to escalate, resulting in 77 deaths by 20 February 2014. In the background the EU, in particular, and the United States to a lesser extent were trying to broker a peace agreement. Russia was accusing the United States of trying to instigate a coup (Reuters 2014). On 22 February 2014, the

(continued)

Case Study 1:   (continued)

Ukrainian Parliament voted to remove Yanukovych as president and he then fled the country saying that it was a coup. He was indicted in Ukraine for mass murder of the 77 protesters (Reuters 2014).

That brings us to the invasion. On the Russian side of the eastern Ukrainian border, 150,000 troops were mobilised on 26 February 2014 (Reuters 2014). On the day after, armed men seized the Parliament in the autonomous region of Crimea, a peninsula on the Black Sea. The men raised the Russian flag over the building. According to Trenin (2014), Russian special forces isolated the peninsula from mainland Ukraine whilst eliminating the resistance of the Ukrainian military there. The Russian forces then helped pro-Russia Ukrainians to take over the local government, Parliament and law enforcement agencies. President Putin in Russia was given parliamentary approval to invade Crimea on 1 March 2014. Whilst pro-Russia demonstrations took place across southeastern Ukraine (the Russian-speaking part), the leaders in Crimea voted to join Russia. They set the date of 16 March 2014 for a public referendum on the issue (Reuters 2014). Russia encouraged the pro-Russian elements in Ukraine to have such a referendum and campaigned for Crimea's reunification with Russia (Trenin 2014). In what the West claimed was a sham vote, Crimea overwhelmingly voted to join Russia (BBC News 2014; Trenin 2014). A treaty was signed in Moscow two days later incorporating Crimea and the city of Sevastopol into Russia (Trenin 2014).

Since that time, various battles have taken place across the southeast, and Malaysian Airlines flight MH17 was shot down over the area by what Dutch officials determined to be by high velocity projectiles (BBC News 2014). While Russia's aggression seems to have gone no further than invading Crimea, southeastern Ukraine still has pockets of unrest (BBC News 2014) with the cities of Donetsk and Luhansk declaring independence and essentially being run by militants supported, but not openly endorsed by Russia (Trenin 2014).

A Crime of Aggression

The killing of protestors is a combination of both police crime and state terror, since individual agents of the (Ukrainian) state are murdering those in opposition to the ruling party. The acts of Russia may well be state crimes as well, since Russian agents were inflaming the protests taking place in Kyiv and then invading

Crimea. Trenin (2014) suggests that such a show of power, in terms of standing up to the United States and pulling off on an invasion, has increased Russia's status in the Middle East. Furthermore, the power display has also brought Russia closer to China, particularly in regard to trade deals. The meddling in Ukraine and the invasion may also have been motivated by feelings of betrayal (Trenin 2014). As Ukraine developed closer ties to the West, Russia seemed to have felt cornered and reacted to keep a once integral part of its empire within its sphere of influence. By having a permanent presence in Ukraine in Crimea, there will now be a counter voice to Kyiv and Western Ukraine (Trenin 2014). It will also make it impossible for Ukraine to have a closer relationship with the NATO or for a base to ever be in Ukraine (Trenin 2014). Furthermore,

> Russia's unsanctioned and illegal commitment of forces into Ukraine also threatens the very fabric of the Euro-Atlantic Security architecture, which is premised on the primacy of state sovereignty and NATO as the guarantor of that system. No, Ukraine is not a NATO member, but it is unquestionably a part of Europe. (Cecire 2014: no page)

This case study serves to illustrate that an unrebuked invasion of Ukraine by Russia is a significant show of power on the world stage.

Pause for Thought

- How should the national government and the international community have responded when Ukraine's police force killed 77 protestors?
- What responses might have been mobilised by the international community when Ukraine was invaded?

War Crime

In defining what a state is, we mentioned that the monopoly on the use of force is one of the core components. This use of force may well pertain to the police force of a state, but one of the main aspects of use of force by a state is its military and the military's preparation for and engagement in armed conflicts and war. With movements to secure people's human rights and in an effort to not repeat the horrors of wars in the past, there are various conventions and laws governing when war should be initiated and how it should be carried out (see the Geneva and Hague Conventions). The practices of war then are restricted through rules that lay out what is acceptable behaviour by soldiers and armies both towards enemies and civilians (Shultz and

Dew 2006). There should be no indiscriminate carnage (Shultz and Dew 2006) and civilians should not be involved with the fighting (Green and Ward 2004). Furthermore, Green and Ward (2004) propose that soldiers should be able to surrender and any prisoners protected. Those soldiers or states departing from the honourable, noble and manly way of conducting war, such as using un-licenced combatants or un-uniformed soldiers, should be treated harshly (Green and Ward 2004).

Whereas this may appear to be fairly straightforward in terms of an acceptable code of conduct, modern war is challenging the restrictions set. This is in part due to 'non-traditional' conflicts taking place, as we will explore in more detail in the next chapter on insurgencies. In addition, modern conflicts have seen frequent civilian casualties, particularly with bombs. In fact, modern conflicts have a 1:8 military to civilian casualty ratio unlike in the past when it was 8:1 (Kaldor 1999). Furthermore, what are considered to be valid military targets are contestable (Green and Ward 2004). For instance, are industries producing equipment for the war like weapons manufacturers, but which employ a civilian workforce, acceptable targets? In addition, in preparing for war, the military must test their weapons, and this may have devastating consequences for civilians and the environment. In 2013, it was revealed that France had underreported the amount of nuclear radiation resulting from many of its 210 nuclear tests in Algeria and French Polynesian (Chrisafis 2013). One test in Tahiti, in particular, was 500 times the maximum level of acceptable radiation. About 150,000 veterans and civilians worked on these tests and only 11 people had been compensated when this new information was obtained (Chrisafis 2013).

There have been instances in recent conflicts (i.e. Iraq War after the September 11th attacks, the Syrian Civil War starting in 2012) where there are blatant individual and state violations of the rules of war. For example in the early 2000s, the humiliation and torture of Iraqi prisoners in Abu Ghraib prison in Iraq by US soldiers is an individually perpetrated war crime. Such crimes are not simply crimes of obedience (Kelman and Hamilton 1989), where the soldiers are told to engage in these activities, but are potentially a product of the disillusionment and anomie experienced in war (Green and Ward 2004). In this case, and in many war crimes, there is a degree of human agency (Green and Ward 2004), where the (mainly) men choose to commit criminal acts. Green and Ward (2004: 150) label them 'Criminal Soldiers' who are 'Individual combatants [who] have motives for breaking the rules which outweigh the reasons for following them'. In addition to humiliating and torturing prisoners, criminal soldiers may kill prisoners rather than keep them as hostages. This could be because it would be difficult or dangerous to transport the prisoners to base, it could be for revenge, or it could be the violence of the killing is a release of tension (Green and Ward 2004).

Criminal soldiers also rape enemy soldiers and civilians (both women and men) (Brownmiller 1975; Scully 1990). Rape can be seen as an incentive or morale booster for the soldiers, but it also a tactic to terrorise and humiliate the enemy. Rape may also be a result of seeking revenge and/or a form of male bonding through gang rape (Green and Ward 2004). As discussed below, rape of enemy women is also genocidal in that it breaks up families and causes women to have babies from another group (Green and Ward 2004). Rape by soldiers has been explained by the overly masculine nature of the military, which disregards women and non-hegemonic masculinities (Crawford 2014; Robertson 2016).

Green and Ward (2004) propose there are not just the individual-level criminality but also institutional and societal levels. At the institutional level, there are 'Criminal Armies': 'The commanders of an armed force decide to flout the rules as a matter of strategy' (Green and Ward 2004: 150). In these cases, the commanders permit or direct criminal acts. Furthermore, they will adopt policies, and then persist with them, that lead to criminal conduct by the soldiers under their command (Green and Ward 2004). Similar to what we have seen in terms of police crime, the criminal conduct of individual soldiers is justified and presented in such a way to make the crime seem to be legitimate behaviour under the circumstances. At the societal level, there are 'Criminal Wars': 'The nature of the war is such that for one or both sides there is little or no incentive to abide by the conventional rules' (Green and Ward 2004: 150). Again, we will look more closely at this in the next chapter about insurgency where asymmetry in terms of power can lead to the rules of war being abandoned.

Crime in war by individuals or institutions leads to numerous victims. The power of the state, and particularly the power and closed nature of militaries, means that more often than not war crimes are overlooked, hidden and/or unchallenged.

Torture

The seventh category of state crime defined by Green and Ward (2004) is torture. Torture is not isolated to wars and is not isolated to a few brutal regimes (Green and Ward 2004). According to Amnesty International (2017), more than half of the states in the world engage in torture. Torture is

> any act by which severe pain or suffering, whether physical or mental, is intentionally inflicted on a person for such purposes as obtaining from him or a third person information or a confession, punishing him for an act he or a third person has committed or is suspected of having committed, or intimidating or coercing him or a third person, or for any reason based on discrimination of any kind, when such pain or suffering is inflicted by or at the instigation of or with the consent or acquiescence of a public official or other person acting in an official capacity. It does not include pain or suffering arising only from, inherent in or incidental to lawful sanctions. (United Nations Human Rights Office of the High Commissioner 1984)

Stover and Nightingale (1985) add the purpose is to break the will of the victim and destroy their humanity. This might explain why even though political prisoners are the most studied group of people tortured, a majority of victims are criminal suspects from the poorest and marginalised parts of society (Amnesty International 2017). Others argue torture is part of a rational approach to achieve a goal (which is not necessarily information) (Rejali 1994). People are a means to an end. They are opponents to be strategically defeated, in order to create a hostile environment for the opposition (Green and Ward 2004).

The above definitions raise a number of concerns. First, limiting the torturer to someone acting in an official capacity seems to limit who can be held accountable for torture. Second, to not include lawful sanctions seems to mean that if the state makes a particular punishment like water boarding (a technique of pouring water into someone's mouth while they are lying down, which simulates drowning) lawful, then this is not torture. Definitions of state crime cannot be reliant on the very state making the definitions of what is criminal. Otherwise none of a state's actions are likely to be illegal. With that in mind, can some lawful sanctions then be considered torture? Is the use of prison, particularly long stretches in solitary confinement, a form of state torture? There is a case to be made that acts of terror in the domestic sphere could be seen as such. For instance, long-term domestic violence or child abuse where the victim is subjected to the continual threat of and exposure to violence.

Genocide

Genocide is often thought to be the extermination of a group completely. Whereas this may be the end goal, genocides are more complex than this and may also include cultural genocide and ecocide. Cultural genocide is eliminating the uniqueness of a people, in addition to, but sometimes without the killing of the people (Short 2016). Ecocide is a concept gaining momentum in that there is a movement to have it be considered the fifth crime against peace alongside genocide, crimes of aggression, crimes against humanity and war crimes (Higgins 2018). According to Higgins (2018), ecocide is the

> extensive loss or damage or destruction of ecosystem(s) of a given territory, whether by human agency or by other causes, to such an extent that peaceful enjoyment by the inhabitants of that territory has been or will be severely diminished.

This closely links to genocide as the death of the environment will lead to the death of the people there.

Well-known genocides that have been the focus of much scholarly research are the Nazi extermination of the Jews in Europe in the early 1940s and the killing of the Tutsis by the Hutu-led government in Rwanda in 1994. These two examples fit the common perception that a genocide is about the killing of a certain people (Short 2016). The Genocide Convention (1948) also recognises acts short of killing that are intended to destroy, 'in whole or in part, national, ethical, racial or religious group' as acts of genocide. Other acts that can contribute to genocide are the forcible removal of children and rape of women to prevent them having children from the men in their group. Green and Ward (2004: 166) define genocide as the

> systematic, one-sided mass killing of persons selected on the basis of their perceived membership of an ethnic or communal group, with the aim either of eliminating the group in its entirety, or of eliminating whatever threat it is perceived to pose.

Such atrocities are in part made possible because of ideological foundations in the political and social spheres. For instance, the state and ruling class likely have put mechanisms in place to exclude the targeted people from consideration or from the 'universe of obligation' (Green and Ward 2004: 184). The targeted people may pose some economic or political threat or obstacle to the state. Regardless, mechanisms of denial and of neutralising guilt are needed for the exclusion and violence to take place (Green and Ward 2004). These elements are all evident in Case Study 2.

Case Study 2:   The Rohingya People in Myanmar

The Rohingya are a Muslim minority group living in the west of Myanmar, formally Burma. In 1978, the socialist military dictatorship of General Ne Win began a campaign to expel them and then to destroy the Rohingya (see McManus et al. 2015 for a complete timeline). Their systematic destruction, which has continued until the present day, has included four of the five criteria of the 1948 Genocide Convention:

> (a) Killing members of the group; (b) Causing serious bodily or mental harm to members of the group; (c) Deliberately inflicting on the group conditions of life calculated to bring about its physical destruction in whole or in part; (d) Imposing measures intended to prevent births within the group. (Zarni and Crowley 2014: 684)

(continued)

Case Study 2:   (continued)

Furthermore, McManus et al. (2015: 16) argue that of the six stages of genocide proposed by Feierstein (2014), the Rohingya have already experienced the first four stages '1) stigmatisation and dehumanisation; 2) harassment, violence and terror; 3) isolation and segregation; and 4) the systematic weakening of the target group'. The latter two stages—physical extermination and symbolic enactment (Feierstein 2014)—are arguably happening or about to happen.

The actions that make it clear that genocide is taking place are that the organised state operations committed against the Rohingya people have entailed: burning and destroying mosques and carrying out other forms of religious persecution, forced labour, torture, murder and rape (Zawacki n.d.). Tens of thousands of Rohingya have fled into nearby countries (Bangladesh and Thailand), often to be turned away (Zawacki n.d.).

Discrimination against the Rohingya has been embedded in the economic, political and social system through laws and policy (Zawacki n.d.). As a result of legal discrimination, violence by the state and other citizens in Myanmar against the Rohingya is seen as justifiable (Zawacki n.d.). Cheesman (2017) suggests the legal discrimination is made possible by the idea of 'national races' that form the foundation of who can and cannot be a citizen in Myanmar. The Rohingya are not a recognised race and therefore are not able to be citizens. Being stateless means that the Rohingya people have no protection and are subjected to numerous violations of their human rights. The Rohingya remaining in Myanmar are denied healthcare and education, arbitrarily taxed and evicted, and are unable to leave the camps where they live due to fear of violence and arrest as well as lacking the right to move freely (Zawacki n.d.). These are crimes committed against them in addition to being the victims of an ongoing genocide.

Pause for Thought

- How does the destruction of the Rohingya people constitute genocide?
- How has the state and neighbouring countries enabled this genocide?

Summary

This chapter has provided numerous examples of state atrocities and abuses of power. Clearly, from Case Study 1 (the Crisis in Ukraine and Russia's Invasion) and 2 (the Rohingya people in Myanmar), states are guilty of crimes. Ukrainian police killed their own citizens during protests, Russia invaded Ukraine, and Myanmar has committed state crimes in the form of state terror and genocide. The international community though is not without guilt in these situations. As Zawacki (n.d.) argues, according to the United Nations doctrine of 'The Responsibility to Protect' if a state is failing to protect its people, or is actively harming them, the international community needs to step in to protect populations. Some countries and supranational organisations, like the UN, have voiced concerns over the invasion of Crimea and the treatment of the Rohingya, but this has not led to any concerted efforts to stop their suffering (McManus et al. 2015). Accusing a state of invasion or of genocide is a sensitive issue, and in the context of Myanmar that is transitioning away from a repressive dictatorship to a democratic regime, this is particularly true (McManus et al. 2015).

The state is a powerful entity and combatting state crime is a difficult challenge. The complex interplay of power, politics and economics often means that crimes by states are ignored. Other states observing the violence justify their inaction by not wanting to disrupt sovereignty and/or cause more harm by escalating the situation. Unilateral action by states to stop crimes by other states is likely not the way forward. Supranational organisations like the United Nations or the North Atlantic Treaty Organization seem the best response to states abusing their power. These, however, tend to be timid, but hopefully they can be empowered to act and apparatus, like the International Criminal Court, can hold at least individual state criminals to account.

Go Further

- What can the global community do to ensure everyone's human rights are secure?
- What can citizens do when their state violates their human rights?
- Are there further conventions or legislation that can combat when state's abuse their power?

References

Amnesty International. (2017). Amnesty International Report 2017/18: The State of the World's Human Rights. Retrieved June 28, 2018, from https://www.amnesty.org.uk/files/2018-02/annualreport2017.pdf.

BBC News. (2014). Ukraine Crisis: Timeline. Retrieved June 5, 2018, from http://www.bbc.co.uk/news/world-middle-east-26248275.

BBC News. (2019). Jamal Khashoggi: All You Need to Know About Saudi journalist's Death. Retrieved June 2, 2020, from https://www.bbc.co.uk/news/world-europe-45812399.

Beetham, D. (1991). *The Legitimation of Power*. Basingstoke: Palgrave.

Brownmiller, S. (1975). *Against Our Will: Men, Women, and Rape*. New York: Simon & Schuster.

Cecire, M. (2014). The Russian Invasion of Ukraine. The Foreign Policy Research Institute. Retrieved June 5, 2018, from https://www.files.ethz.ch/isn/177541/cecire_crimea.pdf.

Cheesman, N. (2017). How in Myanmar "National Races" Came to Surpass Citizenship and Exclude Rohingya. *Journal of Contemporary Asia, 47*(3). https://doi.org/10.1080/0047 2336.2017.1297476.

Chernobyl Gallery. (n.d.). Timeline. Chernobyl Gallery. Retrieved June 24, 2018, from http://chernobylgallery.com/chernobyl-disaster/timeline/.

Chrisafis, A. (2013). French Nuclear Tests 'Showered Vast Area of Polynesia with Radioactivity. *The Guardian*. Retrieved June 2, 2020, from https://www.theguardian.com/world/2013/jul/03/french-nuclear-tests-polynesia-declassified.

Crawford, M. (2014). A Culture of Hypermasculinity is Driving Sexual Assault in the Military. Retrieved June 28, 2018, from https://www.huffingtonpost.com/michael-t-crawford/a-culture-of-hypermasculi_b_5147191.html?guccounter=1.

Doig, A. (1996). From Lynskey to Nolan: The Corruption of British Politics and Public Service. *Journal of Law and Society, 23*(1), 36–56.

Doyal, L., & Gough, I. (1991). A Theory of Human Needs. In N. Axford (Ed.), *Defining and Classifying Children in Need* (pp. 6–38). London: Routledge.

Feierstein, D. (2014). *Genocide as Social Practice: Reorganising Society under the Nazis and Argentina's Military Juntas*. New Brunswick, NJ: Rutgers University Press.

Fein, H. (1990). *Genocide: A Sociological Perspective*. London: Sage.

Genocide Convention. (1948). United Nations Treaty Series. Retrieved June 25, 2018, from https://treaties.un.org/doc/publication/unts/volume%2078/volume-78-i-1021-english.pdf.

Gould, J., & Leon, K. (2017). A Culture That Is Hard to Defend: Extralegal Factors in Federal Death Penalty Cases. *The Journal of Criminal Law and Criminology, 107*(4), 643–686.

Gramsci, A. (1971). Introduction. In Q. Hoare & G. N. Smith (Eds.), *Selections from the Prison Notebooks* (pp. xvii–xcvi). New York: International Publishers.

Green, P., & Ward, T. (2004). *State Crime: Governments, Violence and Corruption*. London: Pluto Press.

Green, P., & Ward, T. (2009). Violence and the State. In R. Coleman, J. Simms, S. Tombs, & D. Whyte (Eds.), *State Power Crime* (pp. 116–128). London: Sage.

Higgins, P. (2018). Ecocide Crime. Eradicating Ecocide. Retrieved June 27, 2018, from http://eradicatingecocide.com/the-law/the-model-law/.

Holmes, L. (2006). *Rotten States? Corruption, Post-Communism, and Neo-liberalism.* Durham: NC, Duke University Press.

Jessup, B. (1982). *The Capitalist State.* London: Martin Robertson.

Jones, O. (2017). Benazir Bhutto Assassination: How Pakistan Covered Up Killing. *BBC News.* Retrieved June 25, 2018, from https://www.bbc.co.uk/news/world-asia-42409374.

Kaldor, M. (1999). *New and Old Wars: Organized Violence in a Global Era.* London: Polity.

Kelman, H. C., & Hamilton, V. L. (1989). *Crimes of Obedience.* New Haven, CT: Yale University Press.

Klitgaard, R. (1988). *Controlling Corruption.* Berkeley, CA: University of California Press.

Lee, J., Paternoster, R., & Rowan, Z. (2015). Death Penalty and Race. *The Wiley Blackwell Encyclopedia of Race, Ethnicity and Nationalism.* Retrieved June 25, 2018, from https://doi.org/10.1002/9781118663202.wberen013.

Liebman, J., Crowley, S., Markquart, A., Rosenberg, L., Gallo White, L., & Zharkovsky, D. (2014). *The Wrong Carlos: Anatomy of a Wrongful Execution.* New Work: Columbia University Press.

Marsh, S. (2020). Doctors, Nurses, Porters, Volunteers: The UK Health Workers Who have Died from Covid-19. *The Guardian.* Retrieved June 2, 2020, from https://www.theguardian.com/world/2020/apr/16/doctors-nurses-porters-volunteers-the-uk-health-workers-who-have-died-from-covid-19.

McManus, T., Green, P., & de la Cour Venning, A. (2015). *Countdown to Annihilation: Genocide in Myanmar.* International State Crime Initiative. Retrieved June 18, 2018, from https://qmro.qmul.ac.uk/xmlui/bitstream/handle/123456789/25375/Green%20COUNTDOWN%20TO%20ANNIHILATION%3a%20GENOCIDE%20IN%20MYANMAR%202015%20Published.pdf?sequence=1.

Mercy Corps. (2018). Quick Facts: Hurricane Maria's Effect on Puerto Rico. Retrieved June 24, 2018, from https://www.mercycorps.org/articles/united-states/quick-facts-hurricane-marias-effect-puerto-rico.

Punch, M. (1985). *Conduct Unbecoming—The Social Construction of Police Deviance and Control.* New York: Methuen Publishing.

Reich, R. (2015). Corporate Collusion is Rampant and We All Pay the Steep Price. Retrieved June 25, 2018, from https://www.alternet.org/economy/robert-reich-corporate-collusion-rampant-and-we-all-pay-steep-price.

Rejali, D. (1994). *Torture & Modernity: Self, Society, and State in Modern Iran.* Ann Arbor, MI: University of Michigan Press.

Reuters. (2014). Timeline: Political Crisis in Ukraine and Russia's Occupation of Crimea. *Reuters News.* Retrieved June 5, 2018, from https://www.reuters.com/article/us-ukraine-crisis-timeline/timeline-political-crisis-in-ukraine-and-russias-occupation-of-crimea-idUSBREA270PO20140308.

Robertson, A. (2016). *Sexual Assault: The Darkside of Military Hypermasculinity.* Air War College, Air University, United States. Retrieved June 28, 2018, from http://www.dtic.mil/dtic/tr/fulltext/u2/1037607.pdf.

Scully, D. (1990). *Understanding Sexual Violence.* New York: Harper Collins.

Shearing, C. (1981). *Organizational Police Deviance—Its Structure and Control.* Scarborough, Canada: Butterwort Publishers.

Short, D. (2016). *Redefining Genocide: Settler Colonialism, Social Death and Ecocide.* New York: Zed Books.

Shultz, R. H., & Dew, A. J. (2006). *Insurgents, Terrorists and Militias: The Warriors of Contemporary Combat.* New York: Columbia University Press.

Stinson, P. M. (2015). Police Crime: The Criminal Behavior of Sworn Law Enforcement Officers. *Sociology Compass, 9*(1), 1–13.

Stover, E., & Nightingale, E. (1985). *Breaking of Bodies and Minds: Torture, Psychiatric Abuse and the Health Professions.* New York: W. H. Freeman & Co Ltd.

Tombs, S. (2015). Volkswagen: A Routine Case of Corporate-state Harm Production. Centre for Crime and Justice Studies. Retrieved June 25, 2018, from https://www.crimeandjustice.org.uk/resources/volkswagen-routine-case-corporate-state-harm-production.

Trenin, D. (2014). The Ukraine Crisis and the Resumption of Great-Power Rivalry. Carnegie Moscow Center. Retrieved June 5, 2018, from http://carnegieendowment.org/files/ukraine_great_power_rivalry2014.pdf.

United Nations. (2015). Universal Declaration of Human Rights. Retrieved June 11, 2018, from http://www.un.org/en/udhrbook/pdf/udhr_booklet_en_web.pdf.

United Nations Human Rights Office of the High Commissioner. (1984). Convention against Torture and Other Cruel, Inhuman or Degrading Treatment or Punishment. Retrieved June 28, 2018, from https://www.ohchr.org/EN/ProfessionalInterest/Pages/CAT.aspx.

Walter, J. (2015). A Guide to Hurricane Katrina and its Aftermath. *Jacobin.* Retrieved June 24, 2018, from https://www.jacobinmag.com/2015/08/hurricane-katrina-bush-gulf-new-orleans-climate-change-racism-fema/.

Weber, M. (1918). Politics as a Vocation. In H. H. Gerth & C. W. Mills (Eds.), *From Max Weber: Essays in Sociology* (p. 1991). London: Routledge.

Weber, M. (1965). *Politics as a Vocation.* Philadelphia: Fortress Press.

Wolffe, R. (2018). Trump Must Answer for the Deaths of Thousands in Puerto Rico. *The Guardian.* Retrieved June 24, 2018, from https://www.theguardian.com/commentisfree/2018/jun/08/trump-puerto-rico-hurricane-maria-deaths-opinion.

Wyatt, T., Johnson, K., Hunter, L., George, R., & Gunter, R. (2017). Corruption and Wildlife: Three Case Studies involving Asia. *Asian Journal of Criminology.* https://doi.org/10.1007/s11417-017-9255-8.

Zarni, M., & Crowley, A. (2014). The Slow-Burning Genocide of Myanmar's Rohingya. *Pacific Rim Law and Policy Journal, 23*(3), 682–752.

Zawacki, B. (n.d.). Defining Myanmar's 'Rohingya Problem'. Retrieved June 18, 2018, from http://digitalcommons.wcl.american.edu/cgi/viewcontent.cgi?article=1873&context=hrbrief.

Militias and Insurgents

12

Introduction

This chapter focuses on militias and insurgents as powerful actors that are responsible for significant harm and victimisation in different parts of the world. It needs to be noted from the outset that the terminology—militias, insurgents, terrorists—is itself a product of power dynamics and contested. Those labelling groups of violent actors have political motivations for calling them protestors and demonstrators or insurgents and terrorists. Those being labelled similarly have political motivations for calling themselves freedom fighters or liberators. Our analysis of power will explore these tensions in the different examples we use as well. The types of crimes and harms insurgents commit are detailed as well as who has been victimised. We explore their motivations and what enables them to continue offending. Using contemporary examples, such as Al Qaeda and the Lord's Resistance Army, amongst others, we interrogate the relationship between the groups, the state and the victims, which, as with other chapters, links back to the intersectionalities of individual characteristics, such as gender and religion that are linked to victimisation. Our case studies—Boko Haram in Nigeria and the Shining Path (*Sendero Luminoso* in Spanish) in Peru—highlight the connection to gender, religion and political affiliation. Furthermore, we look at the power dynamics of these groups vis-à-vis the global community.

© The Author(s) 2021
P. Davies, T. Wyatt, *Crime and Power*,
https://doi.org/10.1007/978-3-030-57314-0_12

What Are Insurgents?

Unlike the press would have us believe, terrorist, guerrilla or insurgent groups and strategies are not new (Boot 2013). Conflict instigated by non-state actors has been taking place for millennia. What we think of as 'conventional' warfare is actually the latest form of combat. It only came into being in the last few centuries with state formation (Boot 2013). Von Clausewitz's famous *On War*, posthumously published in 1832, proposed that war has a specific purpose and a set of conducts. The state set the purpose and was responsible for the conduct the military was the tool. Armed forces have clear organisation, a chain of command and a set of rules for wartime behaviours (Von Clausewitz [1832] 1976). As mentioned in Chap. 11 on 'states', these codes of conduct are, in modern times, enshrined in the Geneva and Hague conventions, which clearly restrict certain practices and behaviours of soldiers and armies, both towards other militaries and towards civilians (Shultz and Dew 2006).

Such codes of conduct are in contrast to non-state actors, or as Turney-High (1949) called them—warriors not soldiers. Insurgent non-state actors have played and are continuing to play significant roles in political change (Manwaring 2011), such as ousting dictators and/or unpopular politicians and governments as well as fomenting coups. Yet, Turney-High (1949) argued that not all insurgents have political motivations. He proposed that conquest, prestige, ego, honour, glory, revenge, vengeance and vendetta may also spark insurgencies. In addition, he suggested that there might be a time lag from when the initial slight or wrong took place to when the insurgent group responds. Whatever the motivations, the insurgents' goals are centred on challenging the state (Boot 2013; Manwaring 2011) and achieving power (Manwaring 2011).

Sometimes, insurgencies are motivated by understandable concerns. The many insurgent movements in Latin America, for instance, in the 1960s and 1970s arose from historic socio-economic inequality, distrust and lack of confidence in governments and their services (Wickham-Crowley 1992; Manwaring 2011). This was coupled with the rising public consciousness of their lack of human rights (Manwaring 2011). What can be problematic about insurgency movements is to achieve equality and arrest power from nation states, insurgent groups use a range of irregular, non-formal, sometimes violent tactics (Boot 2013). Manwaring (2011) proposes that such groups are possibly as important in dictating political patterns and national and global affairs as traditional nation states. But who exactly are these 'non-state actors'? First, we explore the variations of groups that fall under this umbrella term before detailing the actions they employ to exhibit and capture power.

As Boot (2013) notes, 'guerrilla' is the Spanish word for small war and gained use when the Spanish were fighting in the Napoleonic Wars in the early 1800s. Other terms used to indicate small groups of non-state actors that are challenging the state are rebels, militias, insurgents and sometimes terrorists. We use the term 'insurgents' to refer to guerrillas, rebels and militias. We will, however, make a distinction regarding terrorists, which is discussed below. Insurgents use a mixture of non-violent and violent tactics against political targets (Khalil 2013) (which, as noted above, is different from having political motives). Kilcullen (2010) proposes that the non-violent tactics often take the form of propaganda, which features improved welfare, community justice and recognition for marginalised groups. The non-violent political motives and political targets of insurgencies are what make insurgency distinct from terrorism:

> Thus, insurgency is fundamentally distinct from terrorism, as while the latter is a tactic limited to the sphere of violence, the former is a strategy that also encompasses politics and socioeconomics. Located at these separate 'levels', terrorism may occur in the presence or absence of insurgency, and vice versa. (Khalil 2013: 422)

Al Qaeda is an example of where insurgents also are defined as terrorists. Al Qaeda clearly subscribe to violent tactics as is evident from the 11 September 2001 attacks and the various other violent assaults on public targets that Al Qaeda has taken credit for in the years since. Schmid and Jongman (1988) point out that terrorists are repeatedly violent and that the targets of these violent acts are often random and chosen to create widespread fear. As discussed above, this is different to the specific political targets of insurgents.

From Table 12.1, we can visualise that insurgents may move to be terrorists and vice versa and the use of violence can fall on a spectrum in terms of frequency and who is targeted. This will become more evident as we look at the case study of the insurgency group, the Shining Path—*Sendero Luminoso*—in Case Study 2.

The point of making these distinctions, for our purposes in this book, is to highlight that non-state actors, like terrorists and insurgents, all have power, but this is expressed in different ways. Insurgents gain power more from propaganda, community support, numerical strength and control of territory (Table 12.1). Terrorists, on the other hand, gain power more from instilling fear and using violence (Khalil 2013). What all of these groups have in common is that the reason behind their actions is to control governments (Manwaring 2011). This may or may not require radical change in political, social or economic systems. The varying groups' tactics may differ, as outlined below, but overall their aim is to overthrow the existing political apparatus. Often there are questions of legitimacy (see Chaps. 2 and 11)

Table 12.1 The relationship between terrorists and insurgents

	Terrorists— — — — — — ⟶	⟵ — — — — — —Insurgents
Non-violence	Groups that apply non-violent methods (demonstrations, information operations, welfare and development initiatives, law and order provisions, land reform, empowerment of marginalised subpopulations, etc.) to a limited extent	Groups that apply non-violent methods (demonstrations, information operations, welfare and development initiatives, law and order provisions, land reform, empowerment of marginalised subpopulations, etc.) to a considerable extent
Use of specific forms of violence	Groups disposed to uncompromising forms of violence	Groups less disposed to uncompromising forms of violence
Local support	Groups that gain limited support from local communities	Groups that gain substantial support from local communities
Numerical strength	Groups with limited numerical strength	Groups with considerable numerical strength
Ability to control territory	Groups with limited willingness/ability to control territory	Groups with considerable willingness/ability to control territory

Source: Adapted from Khalil (2013: 427)

related to that political apparatus—the state—as well signs that the state is unstable. This instability may be a sign of diminishing power and thus empower insurgents to try to take control.

Harms and Crimes of Insurgents

Guerrilla, insurgent or terrorist tactics remain pervasive, widespread and (sometimes) deadly (Boot 2013). Whilst states have become far more powerful in the modern era, insurgents are still successful in challenging the state (Boot 2013). Propaganda and psychological warfare are part of the tactics to get sympathy and support from the population and to induce fear in both the population and the state (Boot 2013). For instance, Meyer (1991) notes that conversations, letters, leaflets, posters, newspaper articles and radio and television broadcasts were all employed by insurgent groups in El Salvador, Nicaragua and Peru in the uprisings in the 1960s and 1970s.

This has of course evolved to insurgents utilising the internet and social media to spread their propaganda (Bolt 2012). The content of the propaganda, at least in El Salvador in the late 1970s, focused on raising people's awareness that the government did not have the population's best interests and that the government was responsible for the political and socio-economic problems (Meyer 1991). The propaganda made the case that the insurgent group was the answer to these problems (Meyer 1991). In the modern era, insurgents take advantage of the instantaneousness of communication to spread propaganda. Now though, Bolt (2012) argues insurgents, too like the media, rely on the power of visual images rather than writing to share their message. Insurgent actions, such as bombings and running over civilians with vehicles, become the means to rebel and to bring to the forefront the insurgents' grievances against the state (Bolt 2012). For instance, on 14 July 2016 in Nice, France, a lorry was driven through the crowds of people celebrating Bastille Day (BBC 2016). Eighty-six people were killed and over 300 injured (BBC 2016). The broadcasting of violent images of these actions, or of the insurgents taking credit for these deeds, is meant to spark anger and reaction from the audience (Bolt 2012). It should be noted that propaganda, and to a degree psychological warfare, is not illegal and may, in some instances, not even be harmful. Painting governments in a bad light is an example of this.

As mentioned above, small numbers can sustain insurgent and terrorist organisations, and they often reinvent or resurrect themselves (Boot 2013). As is evident from the list below, such groups have also proven to be highly resilient in the face of state efforts to quash them:

> Islamist groups continue to show considerable strength in Afghanistan and Pakistan, Hamas controls the Gaza Strip, Hezbollah holds sway in Lebanon, al Shabab bids for power in Somalia, Boko Haram advances in Nigeria, and two newer groups, Ansar Dine and the Movement for Unity and Jihad in West Africa, have taken control of northern Mali. Notwithstanding bin Laden's death and other setbacks to al Qaeda central, the war against Islamist terrorism is far from won. (Boot 2013)

Presumably, part of the success of insurgent groups is that they avoid direct confrontation of the nation states' armed forces and police (The Economist 2008). This is possible by adhering to guerrilla war tactics. Nation states face 'an irregular asymmetric (indirect) war' where a minimum of clandestine armed factions blend into the population and are managed by a specialist leadership able to fabricate and manipulate public opinion and action (Manwaring 2011: 877). As discussed above, insurgent groups' use of propaganda is a powerful tool in swaying the public.

In addition to propaganda and psychological tactics, insurgents also destroy physical targets in an attempt to destabilise and disrupt the government. Targeting infrastructure, for instance, is one tactic. This was evident throughout the war in Iraq after the September 11th attacks. Insurgent groups, who were resisting the US invasion, blew up key bridges throughout the country. In 2007, for example, one insurgent group destroyed the main bridge in Baghdad, which linked the capital to the northern cities of Kirkuk and Arbil (Reuters 2007). This is one of many bridges that were destroyed during the US occupation. Destruction of physical targets may not just serve tactical purposes, but may also send symbolic messages to governments and the public. In 2015 and 2016, the Islamic State of Iraq and Syria (ISIS) destroyed ancient Assyrian monuments in Nimrud outside of Baghdad (McKernan 2016). Local people reported ISIS militants using explosives, sledge hammers and bulldozers to destroy the thousands of years-old statues, temples and friezes. This is part of ISIS's war on idolatry (McKernan 2016).

The violence instigated by these non-state actors is not confined to physical inanimate targets. Common crimes committed by insurgent groups are assault, kidnapping, mutilation, slavery, rape and murder of opponents and innocent bystanders (Manwaring 2011). Who the victims of insurgent violence are is one of the main components of the asymmetric nature of the insurgent-state relationship. The fact that the crimes insurgents commit are against prisoners of conflicts and against civilians is in contrast to accepted conventional warfare by states, which (are supposed to) target only combatants. Clearly, as we saw in Chap. 11 on the state, this is not always the case. As an example though, insurgents have been documented torturing, head hunting, scalping and eating both opponents and non-combatants (Turney-High 1949). Such use of violence is unconventional and can be indiscriminate (Shultz et al. 2004) making it difficult to predict and to respond to. The unpredictably is also a factor in the asymmetry of insurgencies. Noteworthy is that this is more than a law enforcement issue; insurgents attacking infrastructure or people is not something that a typical police force could handle. Response to insurgents is a national and even global security issue (Manwaring 2011), which further supports the level of power that these groups are capable of that police officers alone are not able to cope with the crimes that some insurgents perpetrate. There is also difficulty for governments in supporting the victims of crimes committed by insurgents.

Victims of Insurgents

Insurgents are known to assault, kidnap, mutilate, enslave, rape, murder, torture, head hunt, scalp and eat their victims. As stated above, the people subjected to these crimes are both enemies of the insurgent group but also innocent civilians that are not involved in the conflict. The enemies of the insurgents tend to be those people in positions of power in governments. By and large, this is men of the dominate ethnic and/or political group. Subjecting government officials to violence arguably still sits within insurgency as illustrated in Table 12.1. The targets are political and if they are the only victims, the violence is limited. However, when the groups also target civilians and bystanders when committing crimes, we see this as likely moving into the realm of terrorists, who, again as seen in Table 12.1, rely on repeated violence to spread their message and achieve their goals. In the case of these civilian targets, men are still victims, but other people are as well including women and, disturbingly, many of the victims of insurgents/terrorists are children. For example, the Lord's Resistance Army in Central Africa is known for abducting children and forcing them to become sex slaves and soldiers and engage in the atrocities that the Lord's Resistance Army are committing (International Criminal Court 2005). Child victims are the focus of our first case study—Boko Haram in Nigeria. The power dynamics evident in this atrocity highlight the intersectionality of gender, age and religion in the victimisation.

> **Case Study 1:   Boko Haram—the Chibok School Kidnapping, 2014**
> Boko Haram is a militant Islamic insurgent group in Nigeria, who, since 2002, has been fighting to overthrow the government and set up an Islamic state (Chothia 2012). Their full name is Jama'at Ahl as-Sunnah lid-da'wa wal-Jihad, but they have become known as Boko Haram, as it translates to 'Western education is forbidden' (Nti 2014). The version of Islam that the insurgents subscribe to portends that Muslims are forbidden from having part in any political or social activity that involves Western society (Chothia 2012). Whilst this includes such things as voting and wearing Western clothing like jeans and T-shirts (Chothia 2012), the Western activity under focus in this case is receiving a secular education. Part of Boko Haram's vision of an Islamic state includes forbidding Western education, especially of women and girls (Giroux and Gilpin 2014). The founder of Boko Haram, Mohammed Yusuf, was a Muslim cleric, who established a Mosque and an Islamic

(continued)

Case Study 1:   (continued)
school in northern Nigeria (Chothia 2012). Poor families from around the country sent their children to the school, which became a recruiting ground for jihadists (insurgents) to join Boko Haram. After a series of attacks on police stations and government buildings, in 2009, the Nigerian security forces took over Boko Haram's headquarters. During the fight, the Cleric Yusuf was killed (Chothia 2012), though there is some debate that he died in questionable circumstances in police custody (Nti 2014).

Although the Nigerian security services thought this was the end of Boko Haram, in 2010, they regrouped under a new leader. They have continued to carry out their typical attacks, which include drive by shootings from motorcycles of police, politicians and other opponents, including Christians and Muslims from other sects (Chothia 2012). There was mounting evidence that their activities were escalating. For instance, they bombed parts of the city of Abuja in 2011, including the police headquarters and United Nations' offices. Bombings throughout north-eastern Nigeria became weekly and 12 arsons of schools forced 10,000 children out of education (Walker 2012). The targeting of schools, including setting on fire 29 students and 1 teacher in 2013, caused such fear across parts of north-eastern Nigeria that the state of Borno shuttered 85 secondary schools (Maiangwa and Agbiboa 2014). This meant that 120,000 young people no longer received a secondary education. And in 2014, they carried out the Chibok school kidnappings.

On 14 April 2014, Boko Haram kidnapped over 200 school girls, who were all taking their school exams in the town of Chibok (Maiangwa and Agbiboa 2014), although they came from across northern Nigeria. After confusion and misinformation at the time of the abduction, the actual number of girls kidnapped was 276, with 57 girls having managed to escape soon after (Nti 2014). The Nigerian government denied the incident for over two weeks (Nti 2014). Then, there were a series of inaccurate announcements about the number of girls missing (Osasumwen et al. 2017). Finally, probably due to international pressure, the President, Goodluck Jonathan, confirmed the number of school girls that had been taken and that it was perpetrated by Boko Haram (Nti 2014). A video posted online a month after the abduction showed the leader, Abubakar Shekau, threatening to abduct more women and to sell the 'women' off as brides (Nti 2014; Osasumwen et al. 2017). Women referred to any girl aged 12 or more. It was thought then of the 219 girls still in captivity

(continued)

Case Study 1:   (continued)

that some had already been married off and others sold into slavery (Osasumwen et al. 2017). There was also speculation that some girls at least had been smuggled out of Nigeria into Cameroon and Chad (Peters 2014). Even though there was a flood of international concern and numerous offers from the United States and other allies to help the Nigerian government to rescue the girls, no efforts were mounted (Osasumwen et al. 2017)

Since their kidnapping, Boko Haram has been negotiating with the Nigerian state for the release of some, if not all, of the girls (Osasumwen et al. 2017). Twenty-one girls were released in October 2016 (Ogundipe 2016). There were discussions that a further 83 girls would be freed (Ogundipe 2016). The condition for the release of the girls was for some Boko Haram commanders and members to be released from prison (Osasumwen et al. 2017), though media reports highlight that the conditions are not publicly known (Ogundipe 2016). There was speculation, too, that the group was given a large sum of money by the Swiss government and/or the International Red Cross, who were involved in the negotiations (Osasumwen et al. 2017). In addition, there has been a fair amount of cynicism that the gradual release of the girls is a strategy by the current Nigerian president, Buhari, who is suspected of having a relationship with Boko Haram, to look powerful and effective in the time leading up to his re-election campaign in 2019 (Osasumwen et al. 2017).

Pause for Thought

- Are Boko Haram insurgents or terrorists?
- What forms of power do they wield?

Intersectionalities: Gender, Age and Religion

What is evident from the first case study is that power is used against particular groups of people in order to send a specific message and display power in a specific way. In cases like this, terror groups particularly target women victims (Osasumwen et al. 2017). Taking hostages has tactical reasons and taking women, in particular, has possibly several justifications (Osasumwen et al. 2017). It gives terrorist/insurgent groups a negotiating tool and a means of controlling or manipulating the government and the audience (Osita-Njoku and Chikere, 2015; Buba, 2015; Yesevi, 2014; Pratt, 2004). The threat to these girls/women of sexual violence—sexual slavery, rape and forcible marriage—is a tactic that gives these groups a great deal of power. The abduction of women is viewed as an instrumental way to achieve power and a government takeover (Osasumwen et al. 2017).

In addition, it is relevant in this case study that the women targeted are children. This adds a dimension of vulnerability to the victims that enables further manipulation and control by Boko Haram. Attacking children is also a specific way of instilling fear in both the population and the government. This may too be done in order to guarantee a favourable response from the government in regard to the demands of the insurgent groups. The use of children in conflicts is also purposeful to try to sway or even brainwash the children to the insurgent cause as was evident in the Lord's Resistance Army example earlier.

Finally, in the case of the Chibok school girl kidnapping, religion plays a central role. The very foundation of Boko Haram is in opposition to Western education. The Chibok school girls are violating the religious beliefs of Boko Haram by going to a Western school—particularly since they are girls, which shows the clear intersectionality of multiple individual characteristics in relation to power. Similar to religion as a factor in choosing victims and demonstrating power, political affiliation can be the demographic characteristic that influence victimisation as is evident in the second case study.

> **Case Study 2:   The Shining Path in Peru—Sendero Luminoso**
> As mentioned, Latin America was the site of numerous insurgencies throughout the 1960s and lasting through to the current day (i.e. Revolutionary Armed Forces of Colombia (FARC) only recently ceased activities in 2017). In Peru, in particular, it seems that people were upset at the ongoing persistent inequalities (Manwaring 2011), which, according to Guzman (1985) (founder and leader of the movement), can be traced all the way back to the Spanish conquest in the 1500s. All Peruvian governments since then have lacked legitimacy to the population (Guzman 1985). The land reforms taking place across Peru in the 1960s did not improve the lives of many Peruvians, especially those living in the Ayacucho province (Wickham-Crowley 1992). The parcelisation of land and poor trade with the coastal regions of the country did not decrease the Andean subsistence crisis that was taking place in Peru and in other Andean countries (Bolivia, Colombia, Chile, etc.).

(continued)

Case Study 2:   (continued)

Partially as a result of these factors, in the 1970s, a Maoist guerrilla group formed at, and then controlled, the University of San Cristobal de Huamanga in the Ayacucho province (Wickham-Crowley 1992). The University of Huamanga, as it is called, is different to universities in other parts of Peru because the student base was made up of young people from the provinces and local community. The student body was, therefore, not the typical university population of children of the elite and middle- or upper-class Peruvians of Spanish decent. Instead, the young people at Huamanga were the children and grandchildren of indigenous peasants. Most of the students spoke Quechua as their first language (Wickham-Crowley 1992).

The primary objective of this insurgency, throughout the 1970s and 1980s, was power, and the intention, through a highly organised campaign, was gradually to replace the state (Comite Central del Parido Comunista del Peru 1987). The state had been for the centuries since the Spanish conquest dominated by 'foreigners' and the goal of replacing the state was to embed a 'nationalistic', 'Indian', 'popular' democracy (Manwaring 2011). Peruvian socialism, Guzman (1985) claims, is grounded in the Quechua traditions, the pre-Columbian indigenous people. From the beginning then, due to the students, the university make up, and the supporters, *Sendero Luminoso*, had deep indigenous peasant roots (Wickham-Crowley 1992). In 1974, the group lost control of the University of Huamanga and the members dispersed into the countryside as teachers. This meant that *Sendero Luminoso* continued to have high levels of peasant support.

Due to the rural isolated locations and the largely peasant membership, the group did not rely on widespread media campaigns to spread their propaganda (Meyer 1991). Instead, they utilised personal relationships and village networks wherever possible. In particular, they would teach children in the villages to look down upon the government and indoctrinate them to the group. If a village was not somehow linked to members of *Sendero Luminoso*, then members of the group would come into the village, round up all government workers and other people that were seen to be traitors to *Sendero Luminoso* and hold a public trial (Meyer 1991). Often other villagers were cajoled into participating in these public trials, which often ended in execution (Meyer 1991). In addition, to challenge the government *Sendero Luminoso* was responsible for numerous bombings in Lima, which caused

(*continued*)

Case Study 2: **(continued)**

significant electricity blackouts—part of the intended chaos. Verstrynge (2005) argues that *Sendero Luminoso* employed multidimensional tactics to try to change Peru's political arena. This meant using some propaganda and violence but also corruption, subversion and coercion to gain and maintain power and legitimacy. A core part of their tactics was to intimidate the public and the government using brutal force (Manwaring 2011). As mentioned, this brutal force took the form of bombs and assassinations; the assassinations were not only of government officials but also of likeminded, but less extreme opponents to the government (Wickham-Crowley 1992). Other aspects of intimidation employed were the common symbol of their presence in places—a dead dog hanging from a lamppost (Meyer 1991).

In the mid-1980s, it is estimated that they had between 2000 and 7000 members (Wickham-Crowley 1992). This is in spite of *Sendero Luminoso*'s use of extreme violence and ideological rigidity. In the 1980s, the rural support for the group began to wane, but for a time this was replaced by support from the urban poor. In particular, new members were recruited from the slums of the capital, Lima (Meyer 1991). Interestingly, it is believed that nearly half of the members of *Sendero Luminoso* were women (Wickham-Crowley 1992). Other insurgent groups such as EZLN in Mexico, insurgent Kurdish and Tamil forces and several secular Palestinian movements are known to have women members, but probably not to the level of *Sendero Luminoso*. *Sendero Luminoso* never did achieve their aim of replacing the government, due in large part to the election of populist president, Perez, in a democratic election in 1985 (Wickham-Crowley 1992).

Pause for Thought

- Does any of *Sendero Luminoso*'s power come from the seven features of invisibility?
- Which of the spatial typologies are relevant to *Sendero Luminoso*?

Intersectionalities: Class and Race

In the Boko Haram case study, we saw how insurgencies may target victims, at least in part, based upon their intersecting individual characteristics. In this instance, those characteristics are female, young and not practising Islam as interpreted by the powerful—gender, age and religion. In the case of *Sendero Luminoso*, we see that the insurgents' identities also display intersections between individual characteristics. Here, we see class and race combining in such way that contributes to the group's motivations to challenge the government. *Sendero Luminoso* is largely made up of people from lower socio-economic classes and many of the members were from indigenous communities and the manifesto was inspired by indigenous beliefs.

As we discussed in Chap. 5 on "Race and Ethnicity", the experiences of black people in the United States were and are shaped by colonisation and slavery. Similarly, the indigenous people's experiences cannot be uncoupled from European colonisation and invasion. More than 400 years later, the descendants of the Spanish can still be viewed by indigenous communities as outsiders. Gender seems not to have played a role, since nearly half of *Sendero Luminoso* were women. Religion may have played a role (Spanish Catholics versus indigenous beliefs), but this is unclear from the accounts.

The Global Community

How then is the global community impacted by the acts of insurgents in and between nation states? Manwaring (2011) argues that insurgents contribute to the weakening of national stability, security and sovereignty. These in turn affect 'personal and collective insecurity, radical political change and possible state failure" (Manwaring 2011: 861). The tactics of insurgencies have made them very effective as is evident by their resilience and longevity. Insurgent power takes place in such a way to create a very real, rather than abstract, "asymmetric global security challenge' (Manwaring 2011: 861). The asymmetry evident in insurgencies is one of the main challenges in countering insurgent power.

Interestingly, rather than force and violence playing less of role in global affairs after the Cold War as some had hoped and predicted, instead force and violence are prevalent and unanticipated (Shultz and Dew 2006). Insurgent groups can create instability and foment violence over wider and wider areas (that is not to say that states are not capable or responsible for instability and violence as well). The result is the neutralisation, control or replacement of local governments and security forces (Jordan 1999), which furthers the instability and potentially the violence. As stated earlier, this is not a law enforcement problem, nor is it merely a social problem (Manwaring 2011). National security and sovereignty can be threatened by insurgencies and can lead to failed states as well as to the creation of criminal states (Manwaring 2011). Both of these and the concerns they embody can also threaten global security, peace and prosperity (Manwaring 2011). Support and empowerment of local governments may be one way to contribute to reducing insurgencies, but the key approach is to somehow decrease the inequalities that spark the insurgencies in the first place.

In the Boko Haram case study, there is a power dynamic that is worthy of further exploration. Critics worry that negotiating with insurgents and terrorists after commission of crimes like abductions empowers them to continue committing such atrocities. By negotiating and giving in, are governments rewarding the actions of insurgents? Others argue that the dialogues taking place at negotiations are one of the few means in which to find commonground between opposing sides. The dynamic is an interesting one that sets the power of the two factions against each other.

Summary

Insurgents may not be the typical group that is thought of when thinking of crimes of the powerful. When compared to nation states, it may be assumed that these smaller, less organised and less resourced groups are less powerful or even powerless. Clearly though, that is not the case. The combination of propaganda (far-reaching and impactful due to the internet and social media) and guerrilla tactics against physical targets and against enemies and civilians in practice means that these groups are powerful. The human victims of insurgents are targeted because they are vulnerable and less powerful in terms of the individual characteristics of power (i.e. targeting women, young people). New members are recruited because they too may suffer the inequalities that the insurgent groups are lashing out against. This is evident in the *Sendero Luminoso* case study, where indigenous people and others with low socio-economic status are the focus of the group's propaganda. Furthermore, as mentioned, insurgencies are resilient. Many of the groups mentioned here have long histories and have avoided eradication.

For the global community, insurgent groups continue to be a challenge that unexpectedly threatens and harms many parts of the world. We have yet found ways to end these groups, but as Walker (2012) points out extrajudicial executions and meeting brutality with brutality are what helped spawn such groups in the first place. Maybe with further international collaboration and implementation of measures to decrease inequalities, there is hope in the future that fewer insurgent groups will commit crimes against elected governments and innocent people.

Go Further

- Is negotiation a sign of powerlessness on the part of governments?
- How are political targets and political motivations different?

References

BBC. (2016). Nice Attack: What We Know about the Bastille Day killings. *BBC News*. Retrieved June 4, 2018, from http://www.bbc.co.uk/news/world-europe-36801671.

Bolt, N. (2012). *The Violent Image: Insurgent Propaganda and the New Revolutionaries*. London: C. Hurst & Co.

Boot, M. (2013). The Evolution of Irregular War. *Foreign Affairs, 92*(2), 100–114.

Buba, I. A. (2015). Terrorism and Rape in Nigeria: A Cry for Justice. *Arabian Journal of Business and Management Review*. (OMAN Chapter), *4*(11), 1–12.

Chothia, F. (2012). Who are the Boko Haram Islamists? *BBC Africa Service*. Retrieved February 20, 2018, from http://cfec.typepad.com/files/article%2D%2D-boko-haram-background%2D%2D-1-11-12%2D%2D-bbc.pdf.

Comite Central del Partido Comunista del Peru. (1987). Bases de Discusion. Lima, Peru.

Giroux, J., & Gilpin, R. (2014). #NigeriaOnTheEdge. *Policy Perspectives, II*(2), 2.

Guzman, A. (1985). El Discurso del Dr. In R. U. Mercado (Ed.), *Los partidos politicos en el Peru* (pp. 85–90). Lima: Ediciones Latinoamericanas.

International Criminal Court. (2005). Warrant of Arrest Unsealed against Five LRA Commanders. Retrieved February 20, 2018, from https://web.archive.org/web/20110616142249/http://www.icc-cpi.int/menus/icc/situations%20and%20cases/situations/situation%20icc%20 0204/related%20cases/icc%200204%200105/press%20releases/warrant%20of%20ar-rest%20unsealed%20against%20five%20lra%20commanders.

Jordan, D. C. (1999). *Drug Politics: Dirty Money and Democracies*. Norman, OK: University of Oklahoma Press.

Khalil, J. (2013). Know Your Enemy: On the Futility of Distinguishing Between Terrorists and Insurgents. *Studies in Conflict & Terrorism, 36*(5), 491–430.

Kilcullen, D. (2010). *Counter Insurgency*. London: Hurst & Company.

Maiangwa, B., & Agbiboa, D. (2014). Why Boko Haram Kidnaps Women and Young Girls in North-Eastern Nigeria. *Conflict Trends, 3*, 51–56.

Manwaring, M. (2011). Security, Stability and Sovereignty Challenges of Politicized Gangs and Insurgents in the Americas. *Small Wars & Insurgencies, 22*(5), 860–889.

McKernan, B. (2016). Isis 'Destroys Thousands of Years of Culture Almost Overnight' as it Flees Iraqi Army Near Mosul. *The Independent*. Retrieved June 4, 2018, from https://www.independent.co.uk/news/world/middle-east/isis-mosul-iraq-army-terrorists-destroy-demolish-nimrud-temples-artefacts-a7418136.html.

Meyer, C. (1991). *Underground Voices: Insurgent Propaganda in El Salvador, Nicaragua and Peru*. RAND note. Santa Monica, CA: RAND Publications.

Nti, N. B. (2014). Silence on the Lambs: The Abducted Chibok Schoolgirls in Nigeria and the Challenge to UNSCR 1325. Policy Brief 3. Kofi Annan International Peacekeeping Training Centre.

Ogundipe, S. (2016). Nigerian Govt says Boko Haram Ready to Negotiate Release of 83 More Chibok Girls. *Premium Times*. Retrieved February 21, 2018, from http://www.premiumtimesng.com/news/headlines/212893-nigeriangovt-says-boko-haram-ready-to-negotiate-release-of-83-morechibok-girls.html.

Osasumwen, O. F., Adekunle, O., Roland, L. E., & Segun, J. (2017). Implications of the Release of the Chibok Girls on Nigeria's War on Terrorism. *Covenant University Journal of Politics and International Affairs, 5*(1), 40–59.

Osita-Njoku, A., & Chikere, P. (2015). Consequences of Boko Haram Terrorism on Women in Northern Nigeria. *Applied Research Journal, 1*(3), 101–107.

Peter, M. A. (2014). Western Education is Sinful: Boko Haram and the Abduction of Chibok Schoolgirls. *Policy Futures in Education, 12*(2), 186–190.

Pratt, M. (2004). Sexual Terrorism: Rape as a Weapon of War in Eastern Democratic Republic of Congo. USAID/DCHA Assessment Report.

Reuters. (2007). Insurgents Destroy Major Bridge in Northern Iraq. *Reuters*. Retrieved February 20, 2018, from https://uk.reuters.com/article/uk-iraq-bridge/insurgents-destroy-major-bridge-in-northern-iraq-idUKL0237254420070602.

Schmid, A., & Jongman, A. (1988). *Political Terrorism: A New Guide to Actors, Authors, Concepts, Data Bases, Theories, and Literature* (2nd ed.). New Brunswick, NJ: Transaction Books.

Shultz, R., Farah, D., & Lochard, I. (2004). *Armed Groups: A Tier-One Security Priority*. Institute for National Security Studies, INSS Occasional Paper 57. Colorado Springs, CO: US Air Force Academy.

Shultz, R. H., & Dew, A. J. (2006). *Insurgents, Terrorists and Militias: The Warriors of Contemporary Combat*. New York: Columbia University Press.

The Economist. (2008). After Sureshot. Retrieved February 18, 2018, from http://www.economist.com/node/11455759.

Turney-High, H. (1949). *Primitive War*. Columbia, SC: Abe Books.

Verstrynge Rojas, J. (2005). *La Guerra Periferica y el Islam revolucionario*. Madrid, Spain: El Viejo Topo.

Von Clausewitz, C. [1832] (1976). *On War*. Translated and edited by Howard, M. Paret, P. Princeton, NJ: Princeton University Press.

Walker, A. (2012). What is Boko Haram? United States Institute for Peace. Retrieved February 20, 2018, from http://www.institutobrasilisrael.org/cms/assets/uploads/_BIBLIOTECA/_PDF/terrorismo/32b67518d6040e4b1dbde961d7b83472.pdf.

Wickham-Crowley, T. P. (1992). *Guerillas and Revolution in Latin America: A Comparative Study of Insurgents and Regimes since 1956*. Princeton, NJ: Princeton University Press.

Yesevi, C. G. (2014). Female Terrorism. *European Scientific Journal, 10*(14), 579–594.

Crime and Power: Conclusion

13

Introduction

Taken as a whole this book has explored some of the central tenets essential to studying criminology at undergraduate level. It has done so in a rather different way to some of the other texts that are in general circulation and feature on reading lists for students as key reading material. As we implied in the introduction to the book, and will have become evident throughout, 'crime' is used as a shorthand. We include activities that involve behaviour that violates laws (criminal victimisation) and omissions as well as repressive, oppressive and injurious harms that fall within the realms of human rights abuses and atrocities. By doing so, the activities, behaviours, acts and omissions of powerful 'elites' are exposed.

The first three chapters establish the fundamentals about crime and power through an examination of what constitutes power and who the powerful are—individuals and groups. These introductory chapters draw on our useful template for exploring the crimes of the powerful—the seven features of invisibility—no knowledge, no statistics, no theory, no research, no control, no politics, and no panic—and our seven spatial typologies of invisible crimes—the body, the home, the street, the suite, the environment, the state and the virtual. The book has been organised such that it has examined individual characteristics and power dynamics (Part I) and group power (Part II). We have been at pains to stress, however, that these distinctions are not mutually exclusive. The overlaps and blurring together of different levels and constituencies and intersectionalities of power dynamics make our understanding of crime and power an often sophisticated recipe of ingredients.

© The Author(s) 2021
P. Davies, T. Wyatt, *Crime and Power*,
https://doi.org/10.1007/978-3-030-57314-0_13

The impact of colonialism perhaps best illustrates not only the importance of embracing the historical underpinnings and trajectories to harm, victimisation and injustice, but also the ways in which different dimensions to the dynamics of power are braided together. In the preamble to Part I of the book, we elaborate on intersectionalities and how this framework for organising your thinking might help you to appreciate the ways in which micro, meso/mezzo and macro levels of power overlap in mutually constitutive ways. Chapters 4 through to 8 variously explore class, race, religion, gender and age before we explore the crimes of the powerful in Part II in Chaps. 9 through to 12. These chapters variously explore how power is wielded and how power operates when groups of people—corporations, organised crime groups, states and insurgents—who share a common purpose or are part of the same organisation, work together to maintain power and/or make money. Fourteen original case studies have been developed and are embedded throughout the chapters in Parts 1 and 2 of the book. The range and breadth of these case studies illustrate various dimensions of the features of invisibility and spatial typologies, in particular situations and contexts bringing alive the real problems of crime and victimisation, harm, oppression and repression from around the world. In doing so, we have ensured that the rich variety and scope of the discipline of criminology is represented.

Invisibility, Politics and Power

At the turn of the century, in the concluding chapter to *Invisible Crimes: Their Victims and Their Regulation* (Davies et al. 1999), where we reiterated some of the more characteristic features of that particular volume, we also identified a number of recurring themes from the various contributions that, though not new, remained important in discovering numerous acts, events and activities that continued to remain hidden, neglected or 'invisible'. We return to two of these themes here 20 years on. The first theme concerns the methodological and the second theme is that of the nature, form and impact of power and politics. The concern about the methodological pertained to the paucity of conclusive empirical evidence on the value, form and extent of the activities under review and the over-reliance on means of measurement—crime statistics and crime surveys—that are unsuitable to investigations of many crimes, but particularly to crimes of the powerful. The message was as follows:

To explore much crime which is 'invisible' requires in-depth exploration of both the processes and mechanisms associated with it; neither of which is achievable solely through those traditional methods detailed above. (Davies et al. 1999: 241)

The refrain concerning the impact and consequences of power and politics was loud, clear and unanimous from all contributors to that volume. Power and politics

remain key to exploring the invisibility or otherwise of particular acts or events. It is therefore essential that research into hidden and invisible, crime, victimisation and regulation explores these channels and avenues, and investigates their relations to the broader academy.... (Davies et al. 1999: 241)

Methods

This book—*Crime and Power*—has taken up the challenge in respect of both of these thematic observations. First, with regard to methodology, in Chap. 1 we introduce the case study approach as a valuable and necessary approach to studying and uncovering crimes of the powerful. In each of the chapters in Parts I and II of the volume, we have employed the use of case studies to stimulate in-depth exploration of both the processes and mechanisms associated with power and politics. These case studies are used to describe, exemplify, theoretically contextualise and critically analyse the problem of crime, particularly through the lens of power in various forms.

The case study examples cover a variety of different crimes, harms and victimisations ranging from the sexual assault and harassment claims from women working in the film industry against the famous producer Harvey Weinstein (Chap. 4), murder and domestic abuse in the Sauvage family from France, Saudi Arabia's women's driving ban (Chap. 5), Ireland's Magdalen Laundries and the Bon Secours Mother and Baby Home in Tuam (Chap. 6), the struggle for racial equality through Black Lives Matter (Chap. 7), the murder of James Bulger and the exposure of elder abuse in Australia (Chap. 8), Volkswagen's defeat device and the Italian shipping company Carbofin (Chap. 9), the Sinaloa drug cartel in Mexico and the Camorra in Italy (Chap. 10), the crisis in Ukraine and Russia's invasion (2013–14), the Rohingya people in Myanmar (Chap. 11), and in Chap. 12 Boko Haram—the Chibok school kidnapping 2014 and the Shining Path in Peru—Sendero Luminoso.

Many of the case study examples have been partially explored by other scholars. Some have been partially exposed through different news medium and activist activity. Others, like the case study of the murder of toddler James Bulger, which has long and often been used as a signal crime around the world, are widely known. Many of our case study illustrations offer a degree of necessary description as the examples are exploring relatively unchartered territories. Yet, this is accompanied by theoretical contextualisation and often theoretical development with 'pause for thought' moments for the reader to carry the case study further and explore it more deeply with provocation from the study questions. It is not that we abandon the traditional methods or dismiss them as unsuitable. Rather, we propose the use of qualitative case studies as part of a more holistic, mixed methods approach to studying the problems of crime and harm in society. Whilst the sustained use of the case study approach demonstrates how students might go about compiling their own case studies, we hope that those we have featured are of interest for their topicality, variety, reach and continued relevance and significance. Moreover, we have used the case studies to address the second steadfast theme that remains relevant and pertinent in the twenty-first century, that of power and politics.

Power and Politics

Continuing with the research theme, criminological research as a social activity is also a political activity (Davies and Francis 2018). Research and politics connect in differing ways. For example, politics can have an impact on the course which research takes and also on its outcome. The kind of research that is funded and the ways in which research problems and questions are framed are very much influenced by sponsors and/or funders. Sponsors/funders of research include government departments; institutions of criminal justice, such as the police or the legal profession; and pressure groups. Each of these stakeholders has interests to promote and interests to protect. Sponsors mediate relationships between the subjects of research and the investigators. Moreover, they are often interested in policy relevance (in their terms) and insist on contractor relationships in which 'deliverables' are clearly specified. How research activity takes place is also dependent on the willingness of subjects to take part and on whether gatekeepers give access to subjects or other data sources—in the first place.

There are other relevant actors, who have vested interests. The range of stakeholders not only includes sponsors and funders of research but also the aforementioned gatekeepers who control access to sources of data and the various audiences of research findings (e.g. the media, policy-makers and professionals in the criminal justice system, politicians and academics). Gatekeepers may have a formal role and legal powers to restrict access or they may be able to deny access by informal means. In addition, each gatekeeper has differential levels of power with which to promote and protect their interests. The exercise of such power is ingrained in the research process from the formulation of problems through to the gathering of data, interpretation and publication of results.

Another way in which politics and research is connected is in the differing ways in which the activity of research and its outputs contribute to politics. Criminologists who adopt a critical approach see their work not solely as contributing to policy, but, more importantly, as justifying policy. In this sense, they look upon policy-related research as playing a political role in mechanisms of social control and not as benign, value-free contributions to administration and management. The chapters within this volume are all infused with a critical approach to the notion of power and the analysis of ideologies, which underpin social structures (such as law and order ideologies) and the challenging of these ideologies with the aim of replacing them. A criminology that is highly sensitised to the import of power is a political and impactful criminology.

We hope that the wide range of case studies included within the pages of this volume has furthered the understanding of the process by which harms and crimes emerge, occur and are responded to and how power and politics are critical to that process.

Pause for Thought

1. What other case studies would you include in each of the chapters?
2. Can politics and power be separated? If so, how?

Crime and Power

This book has adopted a unique way of providing insights into the dynamic relationship between crime and power. As repeated several times, 'crime' is used as a shorthand. That means we investigate technically legally criminal acts and omissions that violate laws and cause criminal victimisation. But, we also explore legal harms that are repressive, oppressive and injurious that fall within the realms of human rights abuses and atrocities. In order to investigate and explore crimes and harms at the individual level (Part I) and by groups (Part II), we drew upon spatial typologies and invisible crimes (Davies et al. 2014).

Spatial Typologies

The chapters that fall within Part I have illustrated the importance of our spatial typologies and are a reminder for us to go looking for hidden, neglected and relatively invisible forms of crime, harm, oppression and repression in these locations, spaces and places. The case study of the celebrity film producer Harvey Weinstein in Chap. 4, for example, reminds us that the working environment (crimes of the suites taking place behind literal closed doors) can be an insidious and unsafe place to make a living and carve out a career. In Chap. 7, the Sauvage case study illustrates the importance of looking in private and domestic spaces for serious forms of violence, abuse and bodily harm as well as public and state institutions, such as those involved in criminal justice as sites for the furthering of social harm and injustice. The body, the state and the dominant religious and cultural environment feature as sites for the repression and oppression of women, who found themselves in Ireland's Magdalen Laundries and the Bon Secours Mother and Baby Home as featured in Chap. 6. The Black Lives Matter case study in Chap. 5 cuts across several of our spatial typologies showing how black bodies are violently abused in streets, homes and state institutions. The home, state and private institutions feature again in the case study of elder abuse in Chap. 8.

The chapters that fall within the second part of the book feature victimisation and harm on large scales by corporations, organised crime, states and militias and insurgents. These four chapters continue to illustrate the importance of our spatial typologies for knowing about the damage done to homes and streets, bodies and environments. They further exemplify the toxic mix of certain combinations of our seven features of invisibility revealing offences against state bodies, individual consumers and employees and harms inflicted upon the environment (see Chap. 9) and communities by organised crime groups and militias and insurgents (Chaps. 10 and 12), states and state institutions (Chap. 11).

Intersectionalities

Although we write separately of individual characteristics linked to power (Part I) and group power (Part I), the two aspects of power and powerlessness clearly intersect. As power is the ability to achieve a goal (Giddens 1987), whether someone is white, male, Christian and/or middle age and so on may well affect that someone's ability to attain their goal. These individual characteristics are also likely to affect whether or not that someone is accepted into a group and thus accumulate (more)

power through the strength of a collective. Think of, for instance, exclusive societies or groups, such as private social clubs, the Ku Klux Klan or even corporate
boards. Many exclusive groups select members based upon individual characteristics, and those who do not meet these criteria are left on the margins, possibly
powerless in the face of collective power. Who an individual is and their membership or not in a group is inextricably linked.

As we return to several times in Chaps. 4 through 8, the interplay of individual
characteristics also affects a person's power or powerlessness. The combination of
being a black, poor, Muslim woman may well amplify a lack of power often economically, historically, politically and socially inherent to each of the characteristics separately. We focused our discussions on class, race, religion, gender and
age, but there are other features of our identity (e.g. being a non-binary gender or
being from the Global South) that contribute to a person's power and powerlessness.

Pause for Thought

1. Are there other spaces in addition to our spatial typologies, where crime and
   harm are hidden?
2. What other individual characteristics might render someone powerful or powerless?
3. What other forms of collective or group power are there?

The Future

At the heart of power versus powerlessness is inequality. And now and in the near
future, inequality is crucial to prevention and disruption of crimes of the powerful.
We suggest three great inequalities will affect the nature and scope of crime and
harm in the years ahead: income inequality, the Global North versus the Global
South and environmental injustice.

Income Inequality

Since the 2008 financial crisis (see Chap. 9), the phrase the 1%—at least in
English—has entered into common usage. The fact remains a decade after the cri-

sis that 1% of the global population holds a vast majority of the wealth of the planet. These 1% are truly the powerful. Those in the 1% are clearly in the upper class; they are also highly likely to be white men from the Global North (see below for more about this divide). They are most probably religious, certainly not atheists or humanists. We see again the intersections of individual characteristics. Such extreme wealth lends itself to great power and can, but not necessarily always, enable the wealthy person to hide crimes, manipulate people and systems, make the rules to suit himself and undertake many more activities that wealth can buy and the status of being wealthy can enable. With wealth—financial and otherwise—being concentrated in so few hands, it is incredibly difficult to stop harms and exploitation by the 1%. Thus, the other 99% of the global population are subjected to oppressive and repressive working conditions, neglect, lack of social care and a myriad of other social injustices that the 1% keep in place to maintain their wealth, status and power. The Occupy Movements of the late 2000s, involving campaigning, protests and demonstrations in cities around the world, for a time at least, helped to shine light on inequality and social and economic injustice that must be addressed if the lives of billions of people, other beings and the environment are to improve.

The Global North Versus the Global South

As mentioned in relation to income inequality, the Global North has long been privileged over the Global South. This stems for a long complicated history of imperialism, colonialism and conquest that continues to underpin many global relationships. The inequality is visible on the global stage when it comes to power and influence at important international meetings of the United Nations, the World Economic Forum and so forth. The Global North, or the West, often dominates decisions and thus the direction of international collaborations. The Intergovernmental Panel on Climate Change (IPCC) is a case in point, where the Global South countries (e.g. the Maldives a small poor non-white island nation—intersectionalities again!) are largely ignored due to the power of multinational Western corporations protecting their interests to continue finding, using and profiting from fossil fuels. The consequence is that the Global South, in this case, will in many places bear the brunt of climate change, but have been powerless to improve the global response to this crisis.

Environmental Injustice

And climate injustice may be the biggest, most important and most impactful inequality of the future. Not only will the poorest largely powerless countries be hit the hardest by climate chaos (Bangladesh, one of the poorest countries in the world, is likely to suffer extensively from rising sea levels), but the poorest largely powerless individuals will as well. In places already experiencing climate disruption, even in the Global North, such as Texas in the United States with Hurricane Harvey, this inequality and injustice is evident. In August of 2017, the US southern coast—Texas and Louisiana—received more rainfall from a single storm than ever recorded before (CNN 2019). Fifty-one inches of rain fell within one day and winds reached 130 miles per hour. Damage and loss were estimated to be worth US$75 billion and 30,000 people were in need of temporary (though likely for months) housing (CNN 2019). It is not the 1% of Houston (the fourth largest US city) and the greater area, who needed temporary housing or who struggled to escape the coming destruction from the biggest storm in US history. Poor ethnic minorities already in precarious positions are those who are unable to adapt or respond to climate chaos.

Solutions?

All three inequalities and the unjust power structures that underpin them need to be addressed. As will be evident from working your way through the entirety of crimes of the powerful outlined in this book, this is no easy task. Radical changes need to be made to the historic structures of the world economy as well as legal and social systems. For instance, reconfiguring regional, national and (the) global economies to not focus on continual growth, but remain with the limits of the planet and its resources, while meeting the needs of everyone on the planet (Raworth 2018). In her book *Doughnut Economics: Seven Ways to Think Like a 21st Century Economist*, Kate Raworth (2018) proposes a new vision for this reconfiguration. Combining the planetary boundaries that set out the limitations of nine aspects for a global healthy environment (Steffen et al. 2015), with several reinvented relationships to core economic principles, Raworth (2018) proposes doughnut economics:

> The essence of the Doughnut: a social foundation of well-being that no one should fall below, and an ecological ceiling of planetary pressure that we should not go beyond. Between the two lies a safe and just space for all. (Raworth 2018: 11)

The doughnut encompasses:

- Change the Goal. The goal is to get into the doughnut.
- See the Big Picture. Do not rely on self-contained markets, but an embedded economy.
- Nurture Human Nature. There is no rational economic man. We are social, fallible, adaptable humans.
- Get Savvy with Systems. Ditch equilibrium thinking and embrace dynamic complexity.
- Design to Distribute. To be equitable, economies must be distributive by design. Growth will not even things out.
- Create to Regenerate. To be sustainable, economies must be regenerative by design. Growth will not clean up the environment.
- Mature economies must become agnostic about growth (Raworth 2018: 26–27).

The move away from growth and thus away from, or at least towards a different form of, capitalism would have huge (positive) repercussions. Yet, it would be incredibly difficult to realise such changes because it completely challenges and removes power from individuals, corporations and states, who are likely to protect their power through various measures.

As mentioned, the radical changes needed to restructure society are not just to the economy but to legal systems as well. Current Western legislative systems maintain the control of the powerful and protect from the criminal justice system (Pearce 1976). The economic vested interests of the powerful are enshrined in the criminal, civil and administrative codes. Yet, there are alternatives. One suggestion is Earth Jurisprudence—a radical approach to legal systems that remove humans from the centre of concern (Table 13.1).

A non-human-centred approach to legislation results in more equality amongst people by disrupting power structures, which have solidified around wealth, class, race and patriarchy. By recognising a whole Earth system, the economic and social structures for people also become just and fair.

Final Pause for Thought

1. What other inequalities and injustices stem from power?
2. What can be done to solve income inequality? The unequal power between the Global North and the Global South? Environmental injustices like climate injustice?

Table 13.1 Principles of Earth Jurisprudence

Principles of Earth Jurisprudence	Description
Principle One	'The Universe is the primary law-giver, not human legal systems' (Cullinan 2011: 13).
Principle Two	'The Earth community and all the beings that constitute it have fundamental "rights", including the right to exist, to habitat or a place to be, and to participate in the evolution of the Earth community' (Cullinan 2011: 13).
Principle Three	'The rights of each being are limited by the rights of other beings to the extent necessary to maintain the integrity, balance and health of the communities within which it exists' (Cullinan 2011: 13).
Principle Four	'Human acts or laws that infringe these fundamental rights violate the fundamental relationships and principles that constitute the Earth community ("the Great Jurisprudence") and are consequently illegitimate and "unlawful"' (Cullinan 2011: 13).
Principle Five	'Humans must adapt their legal systems, political, economic and social systems to be consistent with the Great Jurisprudence and to guide humans to live in accordance with it, which means that human governance systems at all times take account of the interests of the whole Earth community and must: – determine the lawfulness of human conduct by whether or not it strengthens or weakens the relationships that constitute the Earth community; – maintain a dynamic balance between the rights of humans and those of other members of the Earth community on the basis of what is best for earth as a whole; – promote restorative justice (which focuses on restoring damaged relationships) rather than punishment (retribution); – recognise all members of the Earth community as subjects before the law, with the right to the protection of the law and to an effective remedy for human acts that violate their fundamental rights' (Cullinan 2011: 13).

Source: Adapted from Cullinan (2011: 13)

3. What would be different about societies built around doughnut economics? Around Earth Jurisprudence? And how do these changes in society link to power and powerlessness? And thus to crime and harm?

Closing

For our closing words, we take the opportunity to say we hope that your criminological imagination has been stimulated through exploring crime and power through our features of invisibility, spatial typologies and unique case studies. We hope you have gained a critical eye for the role power plays in your everyday life and everywhere in the world around you. Most of all we hope that, even in a small way, you have been inspired to challenge crimes of the powerful and work for justice and the end to suffering and injury.

References

CNN. (2019). Hurricane Harvey Aftermath. Retrieved from December 4, 2019, from https://edition.cnn.com/specials/us/hurricane-harvey.

Cullinan, C. (2011). A History of Wild Law. In P. Burdon (Ed.), *Exploring Wild Law: The Philosophy of Earth Jurisprudence*. Mile End: Wakefield Press.

Davies, P., & Francis, P. (Eds.). (2018). *Doing Criminological Research* (3rd ed.). London: Sage.

Davies, P., Francis, P., & Jupp, V. (Eds.). (1999). *Invisible Crimes: Their Victims and their Regulation*. Basingstoke: Macmillan.

Davies, P., Francis, P., & Wyatt, T. (2014). Taking Invisible Crimes and Social Harms Seriously. In P. Davies, P. Francis, & T. Wyatt (Eds.), *Invisible Crimes and Social Harms* (pp. 1–25). London: Palgrave Macmillan.

Giddens, A. (1987). *The Nation-State and Violence, Volume Two of A Contemporary Critique of Historical Materialism*. Basingstoke: Palgrave Macmillan.

Pearce, F. (1976). *Crimes of the Powerful*. London: Pluto Press.

Raworth, K. (2018). *Doughnut Economics: Seven Ways to Think Like a 21st Century Economist*. New York: Random House Publishers.

Steffen, W., Richardson, K., Rockström, J., Cornell, S., Fetzer, I., Bennett, E., Biggs, R., Carpenter, S., de Vries, W., de Wit, C., Folke, C., Gerten, D., Heinke, J., Mace, G., Persson, L., Ramanathan, V., Reyers, B., & Sörlin, S. (2015). Planetary Boundaries: Guiding Human Development on a Changing Planet. *Science., 347*(6223), 1259855. https://doi.org/10.1126/science.1259855.